MUSEUM OF FINE ARTS, CENTRAL PARK.

FRONTISPIECE.—New York, Vol. Three, p. 389.

THE

# AMERICAN METROPOLIS

From Knickerbocker Days
to the Present Time

# NEW YORK CITY LIFE

IN ALL ITS VARIOUS PHASES

BY

**FRANK MOSS, LL.D.**

*of the New York Bar, Counsel to the Society for the Prevention of Crime, Trustee of the City Vigilance League, President of the New York Board of Police, etc.*

WITH AN INTRODUCTION BY

REV. CHARLES H. PARKHURST, D.D.

*AN HISTORIGRAPH OF NEW YORK*

PROFUSELY ILLUSTRATED

In Three Volumes—Volume Three

NEW YORK
PETER FENELON COLLIER, PUBLISHER
1897

# CONTENTS

*VOLUME THREE*

---

## CHAPTER SEVEN
(*Continued*)

*THE FIVE POINTS: A WANING CRIMINAL CENTER*



---

## CHAPTER EIGHT

*THE BLOODY FOURTH: RELICS OF PIRACY*

## CHAPTER NINE

*NEW ISRAEL: A MODERN SCHOOL OF CRIME*



## CHAPTER TEN

*THE NINTH WARD: GREENWICH VILLAGE*

CONTENTS

# LIST OF ILLUSTRATIONS

---

*VOLUME THREE*

# LIST OF ILLUSTRATIONS

# THE AMERICAN METROPOLIS

FROM KNICKERBOCKER DAYS
TO THE PRESENT TIME

# NEW YORK CITY LIFE

## IN ALL ITS VARIOUS PHASES

---

## CHAPTER SEVEN

*(Continued)*

### *THE FIVE POINTS: A WANING CRIMINAL CENTER*

Upper Mott Street—Cathedral—Police Headquarters, and the old Criminal Resorts that Surrounded it—Reminiscences of the good old Days of Rampant Crime—"The nearer the Church, the closer to God"—Crossing the Ocean to Italy—High Life in Mulberry Street—New York's Bunker Hill—Center Market—Fun of the simple old Days—The Butchers' Ball of 1839—Italian Vendettas—Perils of Childhood—Voyage to Judea—Baxter Street—The old Colored Population and the present Irreligious Jewish Inhabitants—Veritable Tales of the old Clo'shops—Center Street—Criminal Trials—The original Struggle to reclaim the Five Points—Saint Pease

In the house still standing at Number 100 Mott Street the notorious bank burglar Johnny Dobbs kept a place. There he took the proceeds of the Kensington Bank robbery, and there it was divided. For two days a great package of money was secreted in the wall behind a mirror. This great criminal, who handled at least two million dollars of stolen money, was found dead in a street gutter several years ago.

Further up Mott Street, hemmed in by squalid tenements, are St. Patrick's Cathedral and Police Headquarters, each of which would furnish interesting material for a chapter. One feature of the church we will mention—that is, its catacombs, in which are entombed about five hundred bodies, many of which were the tenements of famous men of earlier days.

There lie the remains of Francis Delmonico, John McKeon, some of the Paulist Fathers, Monseigneur Preston, Vicar-general Starr, Bishop Connelly, the second resident Catholic Bishop of New York, and Dubois, the third; John Kelly; the lawyers, Brady and O'Connor, and the old bankers, Hargous and Donnelly. The oldest tomb contains the body of Valentine Sherry, who died in 1805, eighty years of age, and who rests alongside of his wife, who died one year after her husband, at the age of twenty-six years. The coffins are visible through a break in the cover of one of the sepulchers.

Police Headquarters, at 300 Mott Street, has a history so familiar that it is hardly necessary to take the space to recount the men who have managed things there these last thirty years, and what has happened to them. Here was the headquarters of the department when Commissioner Acton and Superintendent Kennedy and Inspector Carpenter immortalized themselves in managing the defense of the City during the draft riots. Then came Matsell, Jourdan, Kelso, Walling, Murray and Byrnes as superintendents, and such commissioners as Smith, Charlick, Gardner, French and McClave. A volume would not contain the thrilling stories connected with this building. Let one incident from the riots of 1863 suffice at this time. Superintendent Kennedy having been seriously injured by the rioters, Commissioner Acton had taken active charge of the police force. The police were on the defensive in all parts of the City, and in some places they were besieged in their station-houses. The body in reserve for emergencies at headquarters numbered only two hundred men, having been depleted through the day by demands from various sections. Inspector Carpenter was in command of this reserve force. The mobs had confined their depredations to the upper part of the City, and had not ventured into the business quarters far downtown; but, being emboldened by their great successes, a vast number of the rioters, led by several of the determined organizers of the revolt, started down Broadway, bent upon invading Wall Street and wrecking its financial institutions. Some faithful person succeeded in getting information to Police Headquarters; and when it came, for a moment there was a feeling of despair in the hearts of the brave men who had been performing superhuman deeds and were almost worn out with fighting and loss of rest. It was plain that if the mob should accomplish its purpose the results would be disastrous beyond calculation, and there were only two hundred tired policemen to oppose several thousand desperate rioters, emboldened by their successes and frenzied by the free use of stimulants. In a few moments a plan of action was determined upon.

The head of the mob was rapidly nearing Houston Street, when the policemen, led by Carpenter, rushed out of headquarters in a double column, and hurried through Houston Street to Broadway. Their orders were to strike hard and quick and take no prisoners. The mob did not expect to meet any opposition, and its leaders were astonished when they saw the thin lines of policemen rush across Broadway as though they were going through Houston Street to the west side of the City. In a moment the mob was at Houston Street, and Carpenter gave the command right face. Then there was such a battle as outdid all other fighting in that three days' horror. The rioters were not given a moment to recover from their surprise. The heavy clubs broke their heads and stretched them by scores on the pavements. After ten minutes of hard work the multitude melted and rushed wildly away before the mighty police battering-ram. Inspector Carpenter and his little battalion saved Wall Street and the banks and the business houses.

Close to Police Headquarters is a rear tenement house (308 to 316 Mott Street), containing about one hundred and fifty Italians, who are blissfully ignorant of the name which the property acquired half a century ago. Then the neighborhood was well kept and beautiful; there were no Italians and there was no Police Headquarters. Some of the houses still standing in Houston and Bleecker Streets prove the former thrift and respectability of the neighborhood. In time the comfortable old houses of Mott Street overflowed with squalid tenants, and this great rear barracks was built in the garden, with a space of only six feet between it and the front buildings. Among the tenants in the front house was Mary Disbrow, who moved into two rooms of the rear house when it was finished. She was old, mysterious, miserly, and had no companion but a great black cat. She was regarded as a witch. A year after the completion of the rear tenement the old woman was found dead in her room, fiercely guarded by the cat. She had taken poison. Over seven thousand dollars was found in her apartments. By her bed there was a piece of crumpled paper, on which she had scribbled: "My curse upon this house and all within it." When the finding of this "curse" became known by the tenants they were seized with a panic and they stampeded from the house. Then the Italian wave flowed over the property, and the name, "The Miser's Curse," was forgotten. Occasionally something has happened to bring it back to memory. Handsome, wicked Blanche Douglass, the last person seen with Jenny Cramer, who was found murdered at Savin Rock near New Haven, Connecticut, in 1881, was one of the dirty little children who played in the yard of "The Miser's Curse," and some of the old tenants of the house remembered the curse when they read of Blanche's shame and her apparent connection with the famous tragedy.

We have considered the shocking condition of

New York thirty or forty years ago, with special reference to violent criminal centers in the Bowery districts. While we are thinking of Police Headquarters, a surprising situation comes to our minds —a situation which was perfectly apparent until quite recently. Police Headquarters, the very heart of the system devised for the repression of crime and the protection of the people, was the physical center of an array of criminals and criminal institutions that could not be matched in any settled community in this country. On the same block with the headquarters building was a place where policemen gambled, and a block away, at the corner of Houston and Crosby Streets, were the "House of Lords" and the "Bunch of Grapes," two famous resorts for a large, valiant and successful colony of thieves and burglars. Near by was Harry Hill's, which, though managed in an orderly way, brought together an immense congregation of criminals of both sexes. The "Florence," a saloon at Broadway and Houston Street, was a resort for thieves. The Allen's "American Mabille" was on Bleecker Street near Broadway. The "Black and Tan" was at 153 Bleecker Street. Big and little gambling-houses were numerous on Broadway and throughout the neighborhood. The game at Number 818 Broadway had a national reputation and was backed by notable citizens. Broadway was filled with basement dives, like the "Dew Drop Inn," and the Bowery was lined with dangerous bagnios. Long before Dr. Parkhurst's day, Dr. Howard Crosby made a tour of these places, and he and Mayor Hewitt worked hard to close them.

At 22 Thompson Street was "Tom" Bray's, a resort for crooks for forty years. Several men were killed there and a number were badly cut and shot. Bray died worth $350,000. The house is still standing. The house Number 12½ Thompson Street was once kept by Mrs. Gadsby, who maintained a

Tom Hyer.

"fence," and entertained crooks. The "St. Bernard Hotel," at the northwest corner of Prince and Mercer Streets, was one of The Allen's resorts, and was patronized by bounty jumpers and other crooked people. The "Liberty House," kept by John Casey, occupied the building still standing at the northeast corner of Greene and Houston Streets. It was a thieves' headquarters. There Dan Lucy killed a bartender and mortally wounded two other men. At "Patsey" Egan's, on the corner of Broadway and Houston Street, a hot-bed of crime, "Reddy" the Blacksmith killed the Philadelphia rowdy Jimmy Haggerty. Peter Mitchell kept the house at the southeast corner of Wooster and Prince Streets (still standing), and accommodated high-class thieves.

"Yankee" Sullivan.

He made $300,000 there in two years, and ended his career by hanging himself to a whisky tap. The house at the southwest corner of Wooster and Houston Streets was "Bunker's," a resort for crooks of all kinds and both sexes. Bunker got into a row one night in this house with a man who is still alive, who retaliated with a cheese knife, and chopped off four of Bunker's fingers and stabbed him six times in the stomach. Bunker had the remarkable "nerve" to pick up his fingers and carry them to the station house, so that he could have them sewed on, but he died in the hospital. There were several murders in this house.

A nasty little place was that of Johnny "Camphene" at 19 Houston Street (corner of Mercer

BILL POOLE.

Street). He pretended to sell liquor, out when he ran short on several occasions he served camphene, and collected his price for it too — hence his sobriquet. At 12 Houston Street, Harry Lazarus, an English thief, was killed by Barney Friery. A thief was asked why the crooks flocked into the neighborhood of police headquarters. He said, "The nearer the Church the closer to God," and the god was in 300 Mulberry Street. In those days the

Fifteenth Precinct was full of panel-houses and other dangerous places, and while it was under the command of Captains Byrnes and Brogan and other famous police officers, Wooster and Greene Streets contained continuous exhibitions of vice, which made the precinct one of the great sights of the world,

WILLIAM J. SHARKEY.

and which demoralized the youth of the City to a frightful extent. The front platforms of the cars which passed through these streets were crowded with boys and young men, who were watching the painted women that boldly "solicited" from stoops and windows in broad daylight. In 1894 there were places "running" that had maintained a continuous existence for over twenty years. East of "Police Headquarters," Elizabeth Street was a famous thoroughfare of vice. Gamblers and bullies thronged the most noble avenue of the City, and with them was a choice sprinkling of expert thieves, who touched elbows with honest pedestrians. "Tom Hyer," "Yankee Sullivan," "Bill Poole," "Lew Baker," "Shang Draper," "Sharkey," "Paudeen McLaughlin," "Tom Dunlap"—these ruffians and criminals, and many others of whom they were types in their day, were so secure from interfer-

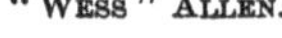

"WESS" ALLEN.

PETER EMERSON.

ence that they had their brawls and wrangles in public, and shot and murdered each other in the hotels and saloons.

Among the burglars who were constantly in sight were "Red Leary," "Billy Connors," "James Burns," "George Howard"—otherwise known as "George Leonidas Leslie"—"Tom Dunlap," and "Scott," who were associated with "Shang Draper" in the Northampton bank robbery; "Four Finger Jack" and "Peppermint Joe"; "Worcester Sam,"

"Johnny Dobbs," "Jimmy Hope," and "Abe Coakley," who, with "Howard," robbed the Dexter Savings Bank and killed its faithful cashier, Mr. Barron; "Canada Mack" and "Mark Shinburn," who, with "Sharkey" and "Charles King," an imported English thief, managed the Ocean Bank robbery; "Wess Allen," the all-around thief and desperado; "Dan Noble," alias "Dyson," who robbed the Royal Insurance Company, and who, with "Knapp," "Baker" and "Doctor Cramer," were concerned in

FRANK McCOY.

JOHN IRVING.

the "Lord bond" robbery; "Jim Brady," "Coakley," "Sam Perris," who, with "Leslie," "Hope," "Red Leary," "Shang Draper," and "Johnny Dobbs," managed the Manhattan Bank robbery; "Big Frank McCoy," "Billy Porter," "Johnny Irving," and "Old Billy Vosburg." "Dan Noble" is living quietly on his money now, and occasionally may be seen on the streets. Now he is a "Colonel," and a well-known apartment house bears a part of his family name. Frequently he may be seen at an Eighth Avenue saloon, where such old-timers as Andrew Roberts, Steve Ramon, Bill Bartlett and George Bidwell (now out of business) meet to chat over old times.

Spence Pettis and Chauncey Johnson, Tim Sullivan and George Standley, were often seen near police headquarters and the array of lesser thieves, such as pickpockets and shop-lifters, was most formidable. Country people learned to have a

William Vosburg.

Michael Kerrigan.

dread of New York that has not yet disappeared. An associate of these men has given me many reminiscences of their lives and their conduct. There was one thief called "Big Pickles," a man of phenomenal strength, who, on failing to open a five hundred pound safe at which he was working, picked it up and carried it downstairs on his back. They played rough pranks on each other. On Center Street near Grand Street there still remains a collection of ramshackle buildings that were dives and the resorts of thieves in the fierce days of the Five Points. South of Grand Street a building remains which was called the "Ruins," in which the thief and all-around criminal, "Oyster Malloy," kept his place. "Tommy Taylor," a similar character, an English pickpocket, was next door to him, and below him was "Mush Riley's" place (221 and 223 Center Street). All of these people were brought together in a rough practical joke,

Ike Vail.

William O'Brien.

about which the old thieves laugh to this day. The "mob" of this neighborhood had been very successful and had lived so high that ordinary luxuries palled on their appetites. They craved for something new. "Mush Riley" gave it to them. He invited the whole company to a dinner which he praised in advance, and about which he maintained a mysterious secrecy. The principal dish was a savory stew of unique flavor. When all had partaken, the skin of the animal which had been served was shown to the guests, and then they discovered that they had eaten Riley's Newfoundland dog. Among those who participated in this feast were "Bill Knapp," "George Knapp," "George Ingalls," "Mike Byrnes," alias "Old Dublin"; "Dan Noble," "Doctor Cramer" and "Dutch Heinrichs." This "Mike Byrnes" was a quiet old rascal. He purchased a tumble-down building on 26th Street between Eleventh and Twelfth Avenues, where all was rough and unlighted at night, and there he quietly set up an illicit still. When the fires were lighted and the scouts were out, no chances of discovery were run, and any inquisitive mortal who essayed to investigate suspicious circumstances was thrown into the river. Several revenue officers were killed before this place was stamped out. There was a large number of English thieves who operated successfully and resorted to the "House of Lords," such as "Chelsea George," "Cockney Ward," "Dan Dougherty," "Charley Gleason" and "Izzy Lazarus." One night an acquaintance of mine was present at "Bill Dunn's," which was next door to the "House of Lords," and he saw one of these precious gentlemen come in with a new hat, pressed tight on his head. He was evidently in luck, for he insisted upon treating everybody to champagne in bumpers—a bottle for each man; then he took off his hat, laid it on a table, and it was full of diamond jewelry. This same interesting character tells of bales of counterfeit money that arrived at one of the rendezvous, and of the liberality with which it was dealt out to the friends. There is an amusing story of the advent of "Gentleman John," an imported English thief, who for fun was set on the house of Police Commissioner "Hank" Smith. Smith was a well-known character about town, and there was no real intention of causing him any loss, but it was not believed that the new thief could accomplish anything. To the surprise of his associates he got into the house, went through it, and made a large haul. It is said that "Dan Noble" had as many as twenty or thirty men placed on the police force. Mrs. Mandelbaum, the notorious "fence," elsewhere referred to, was a member of these thieves' organizations, and divided the honors with "Old Snow" in disposing of the plunder. The communications between the thieves and the noted receivers of stolen goods were perfectly obvious, and there was no interference with them until earnest District-attorney Olney started in with Pinkerton detectives and broke up the combination. The corner of Houston Street and Broadway was a regular meeting point for thieves. They became so bold that they transported their plunder through the streets in daylight. The gang known as the "Hartley Mob" frequently used a hearse and carriages, which would proceed like a funeral, the plunder being concealed behind the black drapings of the hearse and on the floors of the carriages. An interesting case was that of "George King," otherwise known as "Curly George." He was a remarkably handsome man, with black eyes and curly hair. He was no thief at first, but a man who made the rounds of fast life. He became interested in a girl named Millie Clegg, whose brother was a physician. The doctor, whose sobriquet was "Two-to-One," had discovered that stealing was easier than physicking and more profitable, and he was a confirmed thief. It so happened that the next door neighbor of King frequently had large sums of money in his safe. The doctor laid a plan to rob the safe, and he found his opportunity by cultivating the acquaintance of King. One night the safe was robbed of twenty-one thousand dollars. King's safe was also rifled, but nothing valuable was taken from it. The purpose of this maneuver was to divert suspicion from him. Then King drifted into criminal business with the doctor, and became quite a noted thief; but after several years of stealing he reformed, bought a race track, and settled down to a fairly honest life.

There are many thieves, including Western sandbaggers and lead-pipe men, hanging about our "Raines Hotels," but they are rather quiet in New York, evidently devoting themselves to the country.

Resuming our journey, a walk of three blocks from Mott Street brings us to Canal, through which we may slip into Mulberry Street, and work our way back through its crowd of coprophagous lazzaroni. We are less than two hundred and fifty feet from Chinatown, and our route through Mulberry Street is parallel to our trip through Chinatown; but in traveling two hundred and fifty feet we have gone thousands of miles. The rear windows of the Italian quarters on Mulberry Street look upon the rear windows of the Chinese dens on Mott Street, but the front windows of the same houses have an ocean between them. The poison in Chinatown is perfectly manifest, but it is to a large degree insoluble. That which is so manifest in Mulberry Street is noxious and dangerous, and it mixes in all the currents of life. As the mass grows larger by immigration it more completely permeates the life of our City, and tends the more to lower the general tone of the population; it seems even to poison the air. Mulberry Street, bad as it is, has lost its chief sight, "Mulberry Bend," the unequaled squalor and viciousness of which have given way to a pretty park and a public bath that will accomplish much for the regeneration of the Five Points; but those Italians who have been dispossessed and driven out of that foul nest of crime and villainy have gone into other localities, and many of them are found in "Little Italy" in east Harlem, which is fast approaching the character of old "Mulberry Bend," and is threatening the peace, the health and the prosperity of upper New York. We can well afford to travel these few blocks back and forth, first looking at the men, then at the women, then at the children, then at the shops. The articles of food which are exposed for sale, and around which the purchasers crowd like swarms of flies, are unwholesome and nauseous in appearance, and make us wonder at the stomachs that can endure them. Curious institutions are the bakeries. The bread is baked in immense circular loaves like life preservers, which are exposed for sale on the steps of the cellars in which they are baked and on the contiguous sidewalks. The proximity of mud and other dirt does not touch the appetites of the ravenous eaters. We saw such a pile of bread on a stone sidewalk just above a cellar stairway, watched over by an ancient dame, who was not at all discomposed by the operations of another woman who sat fifteen inches from the left hand rampart of the bread fort, relieving a squalling child from a heavy burden of live stock which were browsing among its glorious black curls. Just above the bread vender's position was a little meat shop, in which a lazy storekeeper was gossiping with a number of his cronies while he made sausage. On the chopping block in front of him were some collapsed entrails and a little pile of derelict meat which he had chopped. Without looking at his job, he stuffed the expressive meat into the expressionless casing, ramming it down with a raw thumb, which at least imparted a living flavor to it. That part of the sausage which he had finished looked like an enlarged water-logged earthworm. Soaked beans, parched peas, painted cakes, cracked eggs, black cheeses, mouldy sausages, specked fruit, broken fish, limp vegetables—these are the stock in trade of many stores. Colonel Waring's men frequently turn the water from the fire plugs onto the asphalt pavements and sweep the detritus into the sewers. The rush of the cleansing streams is grand and inspiring. If a few of the people should be swept—accidentally—into the sewers, they would not fall into uncongenial situations. They would be set in appropriate frames.

In the saloons are crowds of men engaged in card playing.

Italian Stabbing Affray over a Game of Cards.

Here are the vermin-laden beggars and banditti of southern Italy, incrusted with dirt, crawling with vermin, given to hard drinking, idling, gaming and fighting, and presenting the most stubborn front to all efforts to civilize and Americanize them. The great American institution, the free school, is right here on Mulberry Street, and it is doing a noble work with the Italian and Jewish children. Those Italians living in this neighborhood who are thrifty, industrious and orderly, are entitled to the greatest credit, for they live distinctly above the tone and influence of their community. All other foreign colonies give way to the Italians. They have pushed up through Mulberry Street, and have invaded the French quarter, a large part of which they seem bound to colonize; they have forced the Jews of Baxter Street and Bayard Street to give them room; they have crossed the Bowery and have captured much ground from the Greeks about Roosevelt Street; and they have made the toughs of Cherry Street feel very sick, for they cannot endure the "Dagos." The colony in Harlem, recruited directly from Mulberry Street, has pushed the Germans, Irish and Americans out of the district bounded by 105th and 115th Streets, Second Avenue and the East River. Many of the fifteen thousand Italians in Harlem's Little Italy are industrious and frugal people. There are several missions among them, which, with great effort and under great discouragement, do succeed in uplifting many of the people. There is an American church on 118th Street which welcomes the Italians, and gives its support to a little mission which works among them. Many of these humble people are on the church's roll of membership, and at the monthly communion service a large number of them attend and receive the emblems of the Christian faith at the altar. They have visibly improved from month to month in cleanliness, respectability and thriftiness of appearance. They respond heartily to the cordial Christian sympathy that is extended to them. At a prayer meeting recently one of the Italians arose to give his "testimony." He began by singing in Italian "The Sweet By-and-By." The large congregation caught the man's enthusiasm, and sang the chorus with him. When he had finished the song, with deep religious feeling showing in his face, extending his hand toward the people, he said: "Thisa vera good countra—vera good!" then raising both hands he said: "Thata countra our home—home for all us—we all go there!" The man's simple, rude earnestness and enthusiasm, and the pathos of his home-longing in a foreign land, were thrilling; they were natural oratory. These people can be lifted up and largely redeemed from their baseness by rigorous enforcement of health regulations, by close attention to the schooling and training of the children, and by the sympathetic approach of kind people. At present they are a reproach and a menace to our City.

A walk of two or three blocks up Mulberry Street keeps us still in the midst of Italy's cast-off legions, but brings us to Bunker Hill, the place which General Knox was so defiantly holding on the morning, in 1776, when General Howe threw his troops across New York Island at Kip's Bay. This spot, which was about one hundred feet above the present level of Grand Street, was the destination of the "Great Federal Procession," detailed in the appendix to chapter two, and the place where the feast of five thousand was held on that day.

The present occupants of Bunker Hill could not be made to understand the meaning of those events. After the Revolution this hill was the scene of duels, meetings of the people, and bull-baitings, and in more recent times it was a battle-ground for the Five Points' Boys (or Dead Rabbits) and tho Bowery Boys. The hill was on the Bayard property, and on its southeasterly side was the burying vault. When the work of digging down the hill was begun, the bodies of the Bayard family were removed from this vault and a hermit took possession of it and lived there for some time, a mystery and a terror to the children, until one day he was found dead there. The bull-baiting was managed by one of the Fly Market butchers, Mr. Winship, who built a fence inside of the old fortification and made an arena which would seat two thousand persons. The bull was chained to a swivel ring in the middle of the ground and was tormented by dogs. Shabby old Center Market is not far from this spot. It was the first large market in New York. Many resorted there for gossip and recreation. Among them was a retired carpenter, known as Lozier, who was famous for his humor and his practical jokes. One day in 1823 this old carpenter and some of the butchers were talking about things in general, when he said:

"I have had a long conversation with some friends about New York Island, and we have come to the conclusion that the island is getting too heavy on the Battery end, where it is altogether too much built upon, and we therefore consider it dangerous; so our intention is to have it sawed off at Kingsbridge; and turn that end down where the Battery is now located. But the question is, how shall it be done, as Long Island appears in the way? Some think it can be done without moving Long Island at all; that the bay and harbor are large enough for the Island of New York to turn around in; while others say, Long Island must be detached and floated to sea far enough, then anchored, until this *grand turn* is made, and then brought back to its former place. 'Lozier,' took hold of this enormous job, and daily he held consultations with many visitors, before strangers, who, overhearing the talk, believed, and ofttimes suggested opinions on difficult points.

"'Sawing the island off' was the question of the day, and 'Lozier,' having the job, was waited upon by numerous persons, and among them were several mechanics. Some were engaged to build barracks, which were to accommodate the hundreds of workmen; others to make the large sweeps, about twenty-four in number, of two hundred and fifty feet in length, which were to be used on the opposite sides of the extreme ends of the Island, to sweep it around after it was *sawed* off. The iron-work on these sweeps was to be made in a peculiar but substantial manner, and an excellent neighboring blacksmith was very anxious to do the work. He said: 'There is no work in my line that I cannot do'; and although his wife had no faith in the job, he presented himself daily to 'Lozier' to receive the dimensions of each part. Laborers and others who were seeking work were sent by the butchers to 'Lozier,' who questioned them particularly as to their being long-winded, as he wanted a good many 'pitmen,' who could go *below* to *saw*.

"In this manner a great many were engaged, who soon became anxious to be set at work; but 'Lozier' said that he had not engaged a sufficient number, and that he could not think of going on with this large job until he had all the men he needed. This led those who were engaged to seek others, and at last the numbers were so great that it became too warm for 'Lozier,' and he was forced to set a day to begin work. He thought it best to divide his dupes, and one party was directed to be at the 'forks of the Broadway and Bowery' (near the present Union Square), and the other to be at the *corner of Spring Street* and the Bowery, where it was expected a large number of live hogs would be ready to be driven up to Kingsbridge. Provisions and tools were to be transported in wagons and carts, and a few wagons were to carry up the wives of several of the workmen, who were to do the cooking and washing.

"The day came, and great numbers gathered at the two points, but 'Lozier' could not be found. Some of the more knowing ones soon discovered that they had been 'sold,' but they desired to appear as if they had not been engaged, so they cast ridicule upon the excited and angry ones, and soon there were but few who would confess that they had been engaged 'to saw the Island off.' 'Lozier' lay quietly housed up for several weeks, not daring to venture forth even to the 'rendezvous'; and when he did so, he was disguised into the general appearance of a different person, and resumed his proper name. Some of the most excited men threatened that if they ever got hold of 'Lozier' they would 'saw *him* off.' "

This story would seem apocryphal, but for the authentic source (Devoe) from which the information was obtained. In those days (seventy-five years ago) our people were much more simple and credulous than they are now. Another instance of simplicity is seen in the story of "George Ship's Ghost." Ship was a butcher in the Oswego Market, on lower Broadway, who had come to America with the Hessian troops but had deserted and become an American soldier. He owned a swift horse and used him in frequent visits to a friend who lived near the Manhattan Well (Spring Street), galloping home at break-neck speed in the early hours of the morning. Occasionally the flying horse and rider were observed by watchmen and belated travelers, and it was noticed that the ghost, for such he seemed, disappeared in the neighborhood of the Bull's Head yards (Bowery). Ship increased the excitement by wrapping himself in a white sheet when he rode at night. Some of the butchers who saw the apparition suspected that the horse was their comrade's steed, and they questioned him about it; but he pretended ignorance of the "ghost," and proposed that they stop it by building a barricade across the street. The butchers did this, and Ship helped. He noted a place in the obstruction which his old cavalry charger could clear. That night the "ghost" came flying down the road as usual, and it seemed to go through the barricade without trouble. Then all the people believed that they had a real ghost among them, and the City went wild with excitement. Some of the butchers decided to build another barrier, and this time they made it too high for the gallant steed; but the butcher-ghost was quick when he reached the obstruction, and making a sudden turn crossed lots into the Bowery Lane and from thence rode into Bayard Street where he lived. Unfortunately for the hoax, two or three of Ship's associates were in his stable, and when he jumped off of his horse he was seized, and then the secret was out. For many years "George Ship's Ghost" was a standing joke.

The butchers were so proud of Center Market that they determined to commemorate its opening with a grand ball and supper, which was announced in glowing letters as follows:

"A Butcher Ball and Supper,

"In commemoration of the opening of the new Center Market, will take place on the 17th of January, in the spacious rooms over said market.

Tickets, $5, to admit a gentleman and two ladies, can be had on application to either of the following Committee, at the market or their residences:

"James B. Dominick, 93 Mercer St.
James Whinney, 184 Ludlow St.
William H. Mook, 3d Ave., near 24th St.
T. H. Mook, 3d Ave., near 24th St.
H. J. Ryer, 145 Center St.
Moses E. Arment, 171 Rivington St.
Frederick Johnson, 28 Second St.
Frederick Clinch, 56 First St.
Joseph W. Clinch, 56 First Street.
William T. Ryer, 145 Center St.

"The New York Brass Band is engaged. Leader of the Cotillon, Mr. Brown. Leader of the Brass Band, Mr. Lothian."

The "Evening Star," January 18, 1839, gave this account of the function:

"The ball in honor of the opening of the new Center Market was quite a brilliant affair last night, and all the ceremonies of reception, ladies' saloons, gentlemen's retiring-rooms, etc., etc., were arranged with as much taste and fashion as they could have been at Almack's. It should be known that this market, after the design of Mr. Thomas, the architect, *is the first in this country which may be deemed a complete building.* Faneuil Hall, Boston, is something like it, but the London markets of the first class come nearer to it. The saloon fronting Grand Street was fitted up with much taste with banners, portraits, and various decorations. Not having time to introduce the coal-gas, the saloon was lit up with *spirit-gas*, which burned but dimly, owing to the heat of the rooms.

"The dancing to a splendid band, which played all the fashionable airs and waltzes, was kept up with great spirit; the ladies, who were numerous, and splendidly dressed, entered fully into the spirit of the scene; but the supper, or banqueting-rooms, created surprise and admiration. The long corridors over the market, from Center to Broome Streets, were thrown open and brilliantly illuminated; each saloon had four tables, covered with all the delicacies of the season, in the very best style, by Mr. and Mrs. Niblo, who, with an army of waiters, were in attendance; and, when a thousand persons were seated at the tables, with all the brilliancy of dress and joyous hilarity, the *coup d'œil* was really beautiful. His Honor the Mayor, and the members of the Corporation, were of course all present, with a number of invited guests; and when it is recollected that giving a grand ball by a Committee of the Butchers is not an every-day affair, they deserve great credit for the manner in which it was carried through.

"There were very many handsome ladies present, and the greatest order and decorum were observed. They are a class of rich, substantial citizens, and all have received good educations, with the usual accomplishments.

"On each plate was the following, printed on vellum paper:

"'BUTCHER'S BALL, JANUARY 17, 1839.

"'IN COMMEMORATION OF THE OPENING OF CENTER MARKET.

"'Music and Mirth, and beaming eyes
Of peerless Beauty, here unite,
To gild each hour as it flies,
And every joyous heart delight;
While fitly, 'neath this festive dome,
Circe and Plenty shall provide,
To dedicate her chosen home,
Our City's ornament and pride.'

"The spirit-gas made the ballroom very hot, and the frames of the windows being so swollen that they could not be opened, the glass was knocked out by the president's orders. At midnight, while there were many persons dancing, it was discovered that the floor was settling. The committee of arrangements did not alarm any one, but went down into the market-room and braced the sinking floor with some timbers that were there, and they managed to get through with the evening's festivities without alarm or accident."

It does not take long in New York to pass from one distinct phase of life into another, and so it happened that in strolling up through Mulberry Street we got into Center Market and into reminiscences of old times. Our main business was with the Italians of Mulberry Street and its neighborhood, and before passing from them to the Jews of Baxter Street we should give some attention to the "Blood Oath," as it is called, which has caused many crimes in the Italian colony. When an Italian has stabbed or shot another, it is almost impossible for the officers of the law to get any information from the Italian witnesses of the act, but the friends and the relatives of the murdered man take it upon themselves to avenge him by killing his assailant, and the feud goes on apparently without ending. This awful custom has been imported from the continent of Europe, and resides among a hot-blooded people, now numbering many thousands in our City. This low, fierce life is mainly confined to the slum colonies of the Five Points, East Harlem and North New York, and does not in any way reflect upon the numerous respectable, responsible and courteous Italians engaged in business in the many marts of the City. Here is a list of Italian stabbing affrays in the City of New York that occurred in less than a year. The unwillingness of the victims and witnesses to testify is apparent from the large proportion of acquittals and dismissals:

Antonio Avocella, stabbed Antonio Russe, convicted; sentenced to two years' imprisonment.

Tony Allranio, stabbed John McKelly, acquitted.

Carlo Bassoni, stabbed Marino Botesta, acquitted.

Tony Chigarelli, stabbed Tony Barnica, dismissed.

Frank Branico, stabbed Emmenual Di Conto, dismissed.

Guiseppe Bruno, stabbed Antonio Tazio, dismissed.

Tony Bonelli, stabbed Eugenio Tremanu, acquitted.

Savato Bourto, stabbed Michael Bruennello, dismissed.

Francesco Borgiani, stabbed Joseph Ostellio, acquitted.

Michael Boscia, stabbed Mitteo Copaliano, acquitted.

Baptiste Barviari, stabbed Louis Considine, acquitted.

Vincenzo Bosta, stabbed Vincenzo Guito, dismissed.

Michael Bertano, stabbed Frank Alliso, acquitted.

Michael Borcia, stabbed Matteo Capobranco, acquitted.

Nicola Bertolius, stabbed Michael Derpino, dismissed.

Louis Benony, stabbed A. Cuzzani, dismissed.

P. Bartoleme, stabbed Alfonso Briano, dismissed.

L. Bunsania, stabbed R. Muli, dismissed.

Francisca Cianco, stabbed Pasquale Lombasso, convicted; sentenced to four years' imprisonment.

Notis and Vincenzo Charada, stabbed John Sullivan, acquitted.

Senania Chano, stabbed Frank Cauprato, dismissed.

Lorenzo Cappricia, stabbed Michael Unziatti, convicted; sentenced to one year's imprisonment.

Antonio Cator, stabbed Joseph Prius, dismissed.

Vincenzo Coccoli, stabbed Martin Lemarri, acquitted.

Vincent Chicari, stabbed Tony Carrara, convicted.

Joseph Cinti, stabbed Pasquale Carrara, dismissed.

Camilio Cumhire, stabbed Calvin Gurtain, dismissed.

Giuseppe Di Benedetti, stabbed Pasquale Papfonto, dismissed.

Francesco Damota, stabbed Antonio Dumati, dismissed.

Pasquale Etoslina, stabbed John Tanquina, dismissed.

Dominico Esperito, stabbed Pasquale Esperito, dismissed.

Celoslinia Farrada, stabbed Marc Forsola, dismissed.

Fabias Farri, stabbod Dominco Farri, dismissed.

Antonio Fughetti, stabbed Nicola Vilaco, acquitted.

Rosania Fabri, stabbed Natali Tasconia, acquitted.

Domenica Farrar, stabbed Martin Ferari, dismissed.

Annuncio Fuler, stabbed Vincenzo Amigimia, dismissed.

Gordon Rafali, stabbed Aubrian Stenkan, dismissed.

Grassi Enquerio, stabbed Michael Levenin, dismissed.

Alfonso Guida, stabbed Joseph Bergeous, dismissed.

Antonio Geross, stabbed Angelo Lombard, acquitted.

Nicola Luen, stabbed A. Ranelli, dismissed.

Giovanni Saparolli, stabbed Nicola Peprique, dismissed.

Charles Morochi, stabbed Charles Morenette, convicted; sentenced to one year's imprisonment.

Frank Morano, stabbed Michael Boracio, dismissed.

Braisi Muriascolis, stabbed Donati Achet, dismissed.

Tony Mori, stabbed Vincent Curtie, acquitted.

Antonio Manando, stabbed Vincenzo, convicted; sentenced to three months' imprisonment.

Antonio Maroldo, stabbed Michael Petri, dismissed.

John Nicolini, stabbed Michael Bufuno, dismissed.

Peter Perdius, stabbed John J. Unlong, dismissed.

Letteno Petrolia, stabbed Philip Nedebehr, dismissed.

Frank Pasquale, stabbed Ben Diocloti, convicted; sentenced to one month's imprisonment.

Nicola Parravella, stabbed Leonardo Lesnoti, acquitted.

David Petioni, stabbed Ross Conquo, convicted; sentenced to one year and eight months' imprisonment.

Viti Pederal, stabbed James Lawrence, dismissed.

Joseph Perroni, stabbed Antonio Sanquerra, convicted; sentenced to two years and six months' imprisonment.

Pasquale Papparesta, stabbed Giuseppe de Benedetta, dismissed.

Giuseppe Pomilla, stabbed Nicola Berg, acquitted.

Salvini Parrisi, stabbed Louis Vegara, convicted; sentenced to one month's imprisonment.

Jackonia Polenser, stabbed Pasquale Delcorriti, dismissed.

Pietro Pisilomia, stabbed Salvator Broes, dismissed.

Pollemedo Petro, stabbed Joseph Bergano, dismissed.

Felice Peronta, stabbed Nuncio Frotto, convicted; sentenced to one year's imprisonment.

Anthony Pape, stabbed Beletrius Romano, dismissed.

John Pironti, stabbed Luciano Lande, dismissed.

Louis Russo, stabbed Joseph Perezzo, convicted; sentenced to three years' imprisonment.

Giovanni Roquis, stabbed Antonio Senisne, acquitted.

Michael Ruffrio, stabbed Lorenzo Ferrasan, dismissed.

Gio Ranallio, stabbed John Vievi, dismissed.

Pasquale Denderri, stabbed Victor Hutti, dismissed.

Salvini Romulo, stabbed Michael Simuento, dismissed.

Nicoli Savino, stabbed Ferd Trafogia, dismissed.

Bartolomus Stefiano, stabbed G. Raphael, dismissed.

Antonio Celertuio, stabbed John Crowley, dismissed.

Frank Verninoza, stabbed Vincenzo Guille, acquitted.

Vincenzo Sileo, stabbed Rocco Damania, acquitted.

Michael Sulli, stabbed Emanuel Chudwair, acquitted.

Joseph Soliski, stabbed Joseph Brunka, acquitted.

Joseph Scevino, stabbed Joseph J. Antonio, dismissed.

Nicoll Stranoli, stabbed Pasquale Charlotti, convicted; sentenced to one year's imprisonment.

Angelo Sorri, stabbed August Marquati, dismissed.

Felice Stornio, stabbed Thomas Merrari, dismissed.

Valemio Benjarrino, stabbed Frank Fuff, dismissed.

Frank Sandon, stabbed Rafael Bertal, acquitted.

Frank Saraceno, stabbed Nicola Bendimori, acquitted.

Michael Sunvietti, stabbed Sabrini Rivuols, dismissed.

John Scarli, stabbed Domenico Piciela, acquitted.

Vincenzo Tangeiro, stabbed Charles Zumence, convicted; sentenced to one year's imprisonment.

This story of a typical stabbing is extracted from a newspaper account of the occurrence:

"Polazzi, a Sicilian, employed as a buyer by Lord & Taylor, brought upon himself the vengeance of the disreputable elements for identifying the murderous bandit Espossito, and for giving evidence that broke up a Roosevelt Street gang of counterfeiters. He was marked as a victim of the vendetta by a knife thrust, which missed the jugular vein, but laid open one side of his face. Knowing what this meant, he vowed that he would forswear cards with his Italian brothers, for it is over the card table that these ruffians get the opportunity for insulting a man whose removal has been fixed upon. The knife having done its work, the murder is then made out as a case of self-defense. Polazzi, with others, was at the Italian restaurant in St. Mark's Place on the evening of October 14. Flaccomio, his friend, was with him. There were also Carlo and Vincenzo Quarterero, brothers, who had served in the Italian cavalry, and who were well-to-do. Their father was a fruit merchant and exporter at Palermo. He was idolized by Sicilians, many of whom he has succored when the officers of the law got too close on their heels. The attempt to get at Polazzi began very early in the evening. He was insulted because he refused to join in a game of cards, and Flaccomio, who knew the signs, signaled to him to procure weapons, as trouble was brewing. Polazzi went out to arm himself, and the Sicilians thereupon turned upon Flaccomio, upbraiding him for espousing the cause of an informer and betrayer. After a time Vincenzo Quarterero's father-in-law and another man led Flaccomio out of the place, apparently for the purpose of avoiding trouble. As they reached the northeast corner of the Cooper Institute the Quarterero brothers ran up, and Carlo, striking from behind, sent his stiletto straight through Flaccomio's heart. The poor fellow died on the spot. The two brothers made straight for Hoboken, where Vincenzo lived. Here Carlo was disguised in the garb of a priest and smuggled on board of a schooner that was about to sail. No trace was obtainable. Vincenzo calmly surrendered himself to the police. He was tried. The jury disagreed. He brought a mass of evidence among his fellows to establish an alibi."

The story in all the killings and stabbings is much the same. A quarrel is started, then come the knife's quick, sure strokes, and afterward there is wholesale perjury.

Notice also this account of a similar occurrence at Number 47 Baxter Street (now obliterated by the new park):

"It was there that Vincenzo Rioerito was murdered by Leonardo Larubbio on November 16, 1891. It was a murder prompted by a woman's jealousy and a desire for revenge. Vincenzo was a good-looking Neapolitan. He led the life of a renegade in his native town, giving his wife and children but little assistance in their struggle for bread. He concluded that America was the place for him, and so, without mentioning the matter to his family, caring little whether they lived or starved, he bade Italy good-by. He settled in the Bend, and it was not a great while before he found a genial companion in Rosa. Lubini. They took quarters in a tenement overlooking Battle Alley, and lived together in apparent happiness, without the ceremony of a marriage, for several years.

"Vincenzo's wife and children in far-away Italy had almost faded from his memory, when one of his townsmen in Naples drifted into New York. The townsman told Vincenzo of his wife and children; how the woman he had so cruelly deserted had battled to keep herself and her little ones alive, and how the latter had grown into bright, manly fellows, who had come bravely to their mother's support.

"Whether this news awakened the old love he had for his wife, whether he suddenly decided to reform, or whether he had grown weary of Rosa, no one ever knew. But it was only a few weeks after he had talked with his old Naples acquaintance that he packed his bag and took a steamer for Italy. He deserted Rosa with as little ceremony as he had left his wife years before. But Rosa was a different sort of a woman from Vincenzo's patient wife. She was heart-broken at first, but in time she found another lover and went on, to all appearance, living the same old life. All of the love, however, that she had showered upon the man who had thrown her over turned to hate. She lived only for one purpose—that of securing revenge.

Her chance came much sooner than she expected. After the lapse of a year or so Vincenzo suddenly reappeared in the Bend with his wife and children. He had reformed to some extent and tried honestly to support his family. Vincenzo was a little nervous as to how Rosa would receive him. She met him with crafty, but smiling eyes, and bade him welcome. Vincenzo then felt at ease. Not very long after, there was a christening in Rosa's house. A child had come to her and her lover, Leonardo Larubbio. She took pains to see that Vincenzo was among the invited guests. She had chosen that day of all days for satisfying her grudge, and by threats and cajoling had driven her lover to do her bidding. Vincenzo and his wife were among the first to arrive. Rosa received them both with smiles and gentle words. Perhaps Vincenzo had brought his wife with misgivings, but if so his fears were set at rest. Rosa was all politeness to the lover who had discarded her. Vincenzo was the merriest of all the merry throng. He was boisterously happy. He drank to the health of the child and its parents, and Rosa looked on and smiled.

"Rosa herself was the picture of joy. Her hands were hidden under her apron, as if folded in the contentment of the hour. Unseen by Vincenzo, she kept nudging her unwilling lover in the crowd, shooting withering glances at him out of the depths of her smiling eyes. He hung back, but she followed whenever he went near Vincenzo, never taking her eyes off him. Finally her hour had come. Unseen by any of the merry guests, she drew from under her apron a revolver, loaded and cocked, and handed it to Leonardo.

"When the merrymaking was at its highest and the laughter loudest, a shot was fired. There was a shriek and a scattering of the guests. There, stretched dead at the feet of his discarded mistress, lay Vincenzo. Leonardo had taken his cue. Rosa was avenged."

The beautiful little park now filling the place once called the "Bend," in its day of slum occupation, literally "ran with blood" and been "steeped in vice." No spot in New York has been cursed with more murders and crimes of violence.

This paragraph from the New York "Mirror," the famous old weekly published by N. P. Willis, G. P. Morris and T. S. Fay, taken from the issue of May 18, 1833, sixty-three years ago, is full of interest now:

"The decent inhabitants in the vicinity of the Five Points ought to give 'nine cheers' at the breaking up of that loathsome den of murderers, thieves, abandoned women, ruined children, filth, misery, drunkenness, and broils. Our country subscribers are, perhaps, not all aware that our goodly City has already commenced rivaling London in its haunts of beggary and crime. It is curious, too, that in our metropolis this scene should be situated almost in the center of the town(!), and within a

NORTH SIDE OF FIVE POINTS, TO-DAY.

New York, Vol. Three. p. 50.

minute's walk of the most elegant and fashionable section. Three streets—viz., Cross, Anthony, and Orange—converging, furnish this precious place with an appellation now so universally among our citizens associated with everything bad and vulgar that the mention of it requires as much of an apology as of another region apparently neither widely different nor very far off.

"The whole place is now to be cleared, the

Five Points.

wretched rookeries torn down, the miscellaneous inhabitants turned out (as one of them expressed, it, 'right off smack!'), and the lots thrown open for the erection of proper buildings."

This was in 1833!

Thirty years after Mr. Willis' golden prophecy, a friend of mine was walking down Broadway, and looking down Leonard Street he saw a great commotion, and the indications of a fierce street battle between large contending factions. A squad of one hundred policemen valiantly marched down Leonard Street, and in a few minutes came flying out again, hatless, coatless and bloody. It was only the Bowery Boys "doing up" the Five Points Boys—the "Chichesters" against the "Forty Thieves" —and when the police appeared both gangs threw them out of the Five Points, and then turned again to their own difficulties. It is said that the Bowery Boys thoroughly whipped their Five Points rivals, and put a stop to their boasting.

Number 7 Mulberry Street was kept by Tom Walsh, alias Fatty Walsh, one of our important politicians. It was a great resort for low politicians, prize-fighters, bounty-jumpers and tough men. Walsh became an Alderman and Assemblyman; and his brother was County Clerk.

Number 112 Mulberry Street (house still there) was "The little Mac Shades," kept by "Skid Gallagher." There "Scotty the Munger," a desperado, "was shot full of holes" (in the expressive language of my informant) by Tommy McAndrews and Pat McDermott, in a dispute about a dog-fight. Scotty was sitting in a chair in the doorway when the shooting began.

Amid the mass of debased humanity that swarms in Mulberry Street there flash the forms of many rollicking, active and beautiful children, with voices as sweet and smiles as pure as may be found anywhere in the world. We are surprised, shocked and puzzled to see the inappropriate placing of these children, with their lustrous black eyes, fresh blooming cheeks and beautiful white teeth, among their shriveled, blear-eyed, vicious and decrepit elders. Just when the bloom leaves the face, the velvet wears off of the skin, and the sweetness passes out of the countenance, may not easily be told. With the boys, hard work roughens the hands, bends the back, and stoops the shoulders, and the effects of dirt and vicious surroundings rapidly destroy the charm of innocence. With the girls, very soon indeed the weight of infamous treatment, family cares and maternal duties fall upon them. Probably there is no class of women who slave harder, suffer more, and live in such bondage to their lords and masters than do these Italian women.

"Little Lucy," the City's Youngest Drunkard.

The children learn the debaucheries of the slums at very tender ages. It is not so long ago that little Lucie Zucherichi, a five year old child, was taken from a Mulberry Street tenement to the Presbyterian Hospital, dying of cirrhosis of the liver, produced by hard and continuous drinking. The little girl had the physical symptoms and sufferings of an advanced drunkard. Her body was wasted, her abdomen bloated with dropsy so that she had to be "tapped," her eyes bloodshot, her breath foul. She pleaded for whisky. "Give me whisky—little drop whisky—give me whisky and I'll give you a kiss," she lisped. The habit was formed in running for liquor for her miserable parents, and drinking with them in their own home. The physician attending the child said: "No drunkard lies in the alcoholic wards of this city with a worse case of cirrhosis of the liver than this five year old Italian girl."

While this child was lying in the hospital, a boy of eight years, Romelt Vekonski, was committed in a Police Court for being a drunkard, a tobacco fiend, and a hardened criminal.

The last haunt of the persecuted "Whyo Gang" is in the Italian basement saloon at the corner of Mulberry and Worth Streets.

We turn the corner of Mulberry Street at Park Row, and enter the next street—Baxter—the home of degenerate Jews, filled with old-clothes shops, sweat-shops and second-hand shoe-shops; but deficient in "synagogues" and "congregations." Baxter Street was the famous Orange Street of the Five Points; Anthony Street of those days is the present Worth Street, and Collect Street is the present Center Street. (This was once called Rynders Street, in honor of the old "boss of the district.") Two hundred and fifty feet from Chinatown is Italy; and two hundred and fifty feet from that is Jewry, with a class of people and a system of manners and customs entirely distinct from those of the other quarters. Judaism here is distinct in type from that which we will notice in the district called, for convenience, New Israel; for the colony had its origin in a willingness to pander to vice and crime, and to use the strong racial traits not for godly, moral or humanitarian purposes, but for the making of money out of wicked practices. The Jews of Baxter Street, represented mainly by the keepers of cheap clothing-stores and their families and assistants, are not only a brawling and noisy lot, but they know how to use their fists on each other and on the outside public, an accomplishment unusual among Hebrews. The colored people who once lived in Baxter Street were a decent population and were zealous in church going and other religious duties. They moved away, and the people who took their places were of such abandoned character that Baxter Street became the vilest and most dangerous of all the streets in the Five Points. Looking up this street from Park Row we can see much to remind us of the old days, and many houses still remain whose walls witnessed their horrors.

Baxter Street is now but a mean survival of the features of that old life, for its fierce rioters and wildly lawless elements have been extirpated or mowed to the ground. At this day the most obvious of its offensive characters are the pullers-in of the shops, the hungry lecherous-faced men, the women destitute of good and noble features, and the dirty Italians with their stale beer dives, and their bad smells, who seem destined to drive even the Jews out of Baxter Street. Baxter Street abounds in humorous sights and suggestions, if one can find a stomach for humor in such a place. I remember an occasion when I saw a great crowd assembled in Baxter Street a little distance beyond Chatham Street. Making my way through the crowd I found its occasion to be a hot but wordy dispute between the Jewish occupants of two adjoining clothing stores. The sign-boards showed that each proprietor was named Cohen, and they showed that each Cohen was the original Cohen. One of the shopkeepers had put his sign in such a position as to obscure partly the sign of his rival. A demand for the removal of the obnoxious sign and a curt refusal had brought the forces of the two establishments into opposing lines of battle. The stones of the sidewalk had been so laid that there was a straight line between the two positions, and on one side of that line were four men and three women, the army of one original Cohen, and on the other side of the line were four women and three men, the army of the other original Cohen. They were armed with broomsticks and various household weapons, which they shook threateningly at each other while they howled fiercely. The crowd, made up of the choicest representatives of the Baxter Street aristocracy, surged about the contestants and shouted out its feelings on the subject of dispute. This war of words went on for five minutes, ten minutes, fifteen minutes, and yet neither side had advanced into the other's territory, nor had a blow been struck. At the end of this time I noticed that a feeble old Irishman, a relic of stronger days in the Five Points, whose eye had wonderfully brightened under the inspiring sight, began to show signs of disgust; finally he spat on the ground, turned abruptly around, and, as he marched off, he shook his clinched fists and said, "Arrah, why can't yez fight like Irishmen?" I sympathized with his feelings and left the Jews still talking it over.

The great Cohen, the original Cohen, the monumental Cohen, was neither of these two unworthy aspirants; his palatial establishment is now on Park Row, his sumptuous residence is on Henry Street; he has sons, daughters, sons-in-law, daughters-in-law, houses, stocks, and a whole quart of diamonds.

What is left of Donovan's Lane, otherwise known as "Murderer's Alley," is in the yard of Number 14 Baxter Street. This has ever been a breeding place for criminals. George Appo was "kicked up," as he expresses it, right here. At this writing a brave policeman lies in the hospital with a bullet in his head which he received in the hallway of Angelo Macori's "Raines Hotel" in front of this bloody old alley. At four o'clock in the morning, the officer found a man beating a woman in the hallway. He rushed in and separated the combatants and seized the man; then the woman, after the perverse manner of her sex, shot and beat her rescuer, who, wounded as he was, clung to the man whom he was trying to arrest.

A portion of the "Old Brewery" still remains

A Woman Shoots a Policeman.

standing on the west side of the street, south of Worth Street.

The first name that is especially noticeable in going up Baxter Street is Bennett, then comes Isaacs, then Gossett, then as we near Canal Street Moe Levy's great establishment with the blue front appears; next to him is Cohen, and across the street is a powerful rival enterprise, Levy & Cohen. These various groups of stores are noted in the annals and traditions of the Jewish clothing fraternity of lower New York. The combination of a Levy and a Cohen, as shown on the corner of Canal Street, was a great event among the clothiers. The Cohens are direct descendants of the priests, and the Levys are the Levites of old who aided the priests and sang the psalms in the temple service to the accompaniment of the "Neginoth" and the "Nehiloth," the "Gittith" and the "Muthlabben," the "Sheminith," the "Aijeleth Shaher," and other musical instruments, under the leadership of Jeduthun and Maschil the chief musicians. The Levys and the Cohens often have been divided by the sharp strife of Baxter Street business, and a combination between them is looked upon as a sweet and holy arrangement. In those peculiar religious rites where a Cohen has to stand at the altar attended by a Levy—an ancient picture—the partnership may still be united. The sign of this union is blue, so the holy emporium is covered with blue signs. A base and covetous rival in business, "Stark," whose name gives him no holy standing, mocks at the love-feast partners, by a liberal display of alleged white signs. Some of the marriages between the children of rival clothiers have been managed with as much diplomatic tact and have been celebrated with as much royal splendor as the unions in rival kingly families of the olden times. To this day the displays of plush furniture, plated silver, necks and noses, hired dress suits, diamond jewelry borrowed from pawn-shop shelves, imported bolognas and other wedding delicacies, are discussed with sparkling eyes and bated breaths. I have endeavored to collect a few of the most veracious accounts of actual occurrences in some of these stores. Were I to give the numbers and the names of the places I would be sued for damages by those not mentioned; so I will speak of the events as having occurred in the first, third, fifth or seventh store from the end of the street, but you will not expect me, reader, to say which end.

One summer afternoon a sailor entered the second store from one end of the street and bought a suit of clothes which were strongly guaranteed by the store-keeper. When the sailor got out of port he found that he had been badly cheated, and he made a vow that if he ever returned to New York he would get satisfaction from that store-keeper. Three years afterward, the good ship arrived in the harbor, and as soon as our sailor could obtain shore leave he made his way to the shop, where he found the identical person who had served him before, telling the same old fables about his goods. This time he was very hard to suit, and was not satisfied until he had incased himself in the finest suit of clothes in the establishment. While trying on the clothes he industriously masticated a huge quid of tobacco, and while walking about the uncovered floor he made it seem as though he was navigating

56 AND 58 CENTER STREET.

New York, Vol. Three, p. 66.

his natural element. He stood proudly before the little looking-glass and expressed his satisfaction with the suit—then suddenly he was taken with a fit and dropped onto the floor, where he rolled all over the aforesaid natural element. The poor old Jew was frightened almost to death. He did not want to have a dead Christian on his hands, so he pulled off the bedraggled suit, hurried on the sailor's old togs, and rolled him out onto the doorstep, when to his great surprise the wily tar arose, made a peculiar gesture with his thumb and fingers, and started for the Bowery.

In the second clothing-store above that was a man who had the champion "puller-in" of the street. He had the ability to force the most unwilling man into the store and to compel him to buy whether he wanted to or not. One day a man whose right leg had been amputated ambled through the street with the help of a pair of crutches. He was promptly seized by the "barker," who demanded that he should buy a "bair of bants." This took our abbreviated friend by surprise. He said: "Why! Don't you see I have lost one leg. You have no pants for me!" By that time the proprietor had rushed out on the sidewalk to assist his scout, and he chimed in, saying: "Vhy, yes, ve make a specialty uf bants fur von-legged men. Yust come here on de doorstep und I show you some." Then he leaned over to his lieutenant and whispered: "Run in quick to de back room und cut off von leg uf a bair uf bants und pring dem here." While this operation was being performed behind the scenes, he kept his victim engaged in gay conversation until Moses proudly appeared, holding the garment upraised between his hands. A gleam of joy and pride was in the old man's eye as he pointed triumphantly to the sample of one-legged pants that he kept in stock for abridged humanity, but in an instant the smile went out, a look of despair succeeded, and he said, "Mine gracious! Moses! You've ruined me! You've cut de wrong leg off dose bants!"

Three stores beyond this one was another in which a thief attempted a characteristic trick. He tried on a coat, edged to the door while so doing, then suddenly broke away and sped down the street with the new coat on his back. The clerk of the store was quick, while the old man was slow. He grabbed a pistol from a shelf under the counter and leaped through the doorway after the thief with his pistol leveled for a good shot. The old man stumbled to the doorway, saw the vanishing procession, and then recovered himself sufficiently to bawl out, "Jakey! Jakey! Shoot him in de leg, don't spoil de coat!"

The proprietor of the next store once was short of funds and applied to a friend across the street for a loan, with which he was accommodated. In due time he called upon his creditor prepared to pay his obligation, and then found that interest had been reckoned at nine per cent. He said: "Vhy, Israel, dat is usury. You vould not ask usury from von uf your own beoples!" Israel insisted upon his nine per cent. The debtor pleaded but could secure no abatement of the rate. Then a bright thought struck him, he said: "Israel, Fader Abraham vill look down from Heaven und he vill see dat nine per cent, und vhat do you tink he vill say!" Israel quickly responded, "He vill say nuddings. Vhen he looks down on dat nine it vill be upside down, und he vill see only a six." Israel got nine per cent for his money that time.

The usurer was a thrifty man. He had a son who begged for a holiday on his birthday. It was reluctantly granted, and the boy explored the marvelous region of Central Park. On arriving home he saw a regretful expression in his parent's eye, and in order to avert the calamitous utterance that seemed imminent, he began to elaborate his experiences of the day. He said: "An' fader, vat you tink, up dere among de peutiful drees, an' skipping troo de grass, vas lufly liddle birds" (English sparrows or "chippies," no doubt), "an' dey sang so sweet; dey sang Cheep! Cheep! Cheep!" "Shtob! Shtob!" said the stern but excited parent, "Is dot vot dey did sing? Cheap! Cheap! Cheap! Go you right dere de morning up, an' catch me a pasketful of dose birds. Ve vill pud dem in de vindow und dey vill sing aboud de goods! Cheap, Cheap! Cheap, Cheap!"

Some reader may imagine that this story was invented, but what would he say to this sign in a window:

LOOK HOW
CHEEP
THE GOODS.

This little Hebrew story, told by an Irishman, applies to the ancient Jewish Cemetery now so nearly obliterated. In the days when the Irish loved Mott Street, a poor old man found himself in the hour and article of death. The kind priest was with him, the sacrament had been administered, and everything had been done to make him peaceful in his last moments. He turned to his comforter and said: "Father! There is one thing more I want. I want you to promise me that I shall be buried in the Jews' cemetery." Said the priest, "That can't be done, my poor man. Surely, you do not want to be buried in unconsecrated ground?" "Ah, father," he said, "I must be buried there; and you will not deny the last wish of a dying man." "Well! well!" said the good priest, thinking that he would ease the man's mind, "tell me why you want it, and maybe we can arrange it for you." "Father," said the poor fellow, "good father! you see I've been a pretty wild Irish lad in the ould Five Points, and I'm thinking that the devil would never be looking for an Irishman in a Jews' cemetery." He spoke with grim earnestness and looked straight in the priest's eyes, and when he saw in those windows of the soul a faint smile and no anger, he closed his own eyes and peacefully passed away.

The little son of one of these Hebrew merchants attended the public school on Mulberry Street. His teacher asked him, "How much is twice two? His thrifty answer was five. "Wrong," she said, "try it again." "Six," he said, and when he saw from her looks that he had failed again he said "seven." Then she said: "Go home and ask your father to tell you how much twice two is." On his way downstairs he met a late scholar and asked him the important question; the answer was four. Poor little Ikey almost fell down in his earnestness as he grasped his comrade by the shoulder and said: "Dond you go in! De teacher vill ask you how much is tvice two, und if you say four she vill send you home. I offered her five, six and seven, und she vouldn't take it. Dond you go in!"

A friendly historian sends me this veracious statement, for which he vouches:

"Them pants is too short," said a huckster, who was bargaining for a pair of trousers in Baxter Street.—"But dey vill stretch, my frent; dey vill stretch. Yust hang veights on de legs and stretch dem efery night; dot keeps de pags out of de knees." —"They are too dark," continued the customer.—"Dark," said the dealer. "Vat matter ish dot? De color is not fast, und dey vill fade three shades in two days."—"They are too wide in the legs," objected the customer, and the accommodating dealer in accommodating garments said:—"Vell, ven you stretch dem de long vay ton't dey get shmaller sideways? De more you vears dem de better dey fits you."—"Look at that big grease spot," said the particular buyer.—"Oh, dot's notings," said the dealer. "You vill have dem all ofer vaggon crease in less as von veek. I drow off den cents for dot spot. You take dem for a tollar forty."

He took them.

We turn out of Baxter Street at Canal Street and return on our course through Center Street. It will be remembered that this was Collect Street, that it once ended at the Collect Pond, then was carried around it, and then, when the pond was filled up, it went over the ancient springs on dry ground. It was once a thoroughfare of vice and was lined with brothels and dance houses. A few of the old rookeries remain, like Numbers 52, 54 and 56. The changing of the name to Center Street was part of the effort to purify it that was made a long time ago. Most of the buildings that were conspicuous as bawdy houses have given way to business establishments.

The original cheap grocery of the Five Points was kept by Rosanna Peers, and was on the east side of Center Street a little south of Worth Street. Rosanna furnished a few groceries, lots of whisky, and the kind of allurement that was enjoyed by the rough characters that began to flow into Center Street. Soon the street was filled with similar resorts, dance houses were started, and they spread into Anthony (or Worth) Street, and ran into Orange (or Baxter) and Cross (or Park) Streets. Con Donoho's grocery was on the spot now occupied by Paradise Park.

Many recruits for Billy Wilson's Fire Zouaves were gathered from this neighborhood, but they made poor soldiers. Their bravado wilted under fire.

The special points of interest on Center Street are the Criminal Courts, the Tombs, the corner of Duane Street which at one point shows us the remains of "Dooley's Long-room," and the Manhattan Reservoir at Number 25 Center Street. From that spot, looking due south, we can see into City Hall Place where the negroes were burned.

This is the reservoir that sustains the charter of the Manhattan Company, organized by Aaron Burr, and it is in sight of his office in the little building on Reade Street, now occupied as a barber shop.

The reservoir building appears to be an ordinary business house, but two-thirds of its interior is occupied by the tank, which is always kept filled by pumping machinery that draws on the underground streams that once fed the Collect Pond. The water goes to no use whatever,—indeed, it must be unwholesome; but the pumping, on which the charter depends, continues daily, and the overflow is carried off in the sewer. There was a time when the water of this reservoir was conveyed through the lower part of the City by hollow logs, and it used to be a common occurrence in street excavations to turn up those old pipes.

We have referred to the Tombs so frequently that extended remarks about it now are hardly needed. The building will always be hideous in memory, because of the executions that have occurred in its narrow courtyard. The first hanging occurred on January 12, 1839, when Edward Coleman was executed for murdering his wife, who was known generally as the "pretty hot-corn girl." In 1841, Patrick Russel was hanged; then in 1845 Thomas Eager and in 1846 Charles Thomas were executed. In 1849 Matthew Ward was hanged; and in 1851 Edward F. Douglass, Thomas Benson and Aaron B. Stookey were hanged; and so the dreary list was continued until electrocution at the State Prisons was substituted for hanging in the Tombs. The worst mischief of this awful place is that so many innocent persons are confined in it while awaiting trial, and are compelled to endure associations with criminals and with criminal surroundings that must tend to their moral degradation, and to the utmost torture of mind and spirit. At the Tombs the army of persons who spend some time awaiting their ordeal, receive criminals' food, endure criminals' treatment, and achieve criminals' reputations. In a City with such pretensions to civilization as New York, and where the loudest professions of allegiance to all the beautiful doctrines of the rights of man are sounded forth, the torture and the injury of innocent persons that goes on daily at the Tombs is a shameful commentary. The matter is made worse by the ignoble ambition of some assistant district-attorneys to roll up imposing aggregates of sentences through their work in the courts. They imagine that their efficiency is judged by the number of years of sentences that they can show for their work. In an administration where there is little or no management, and the assistants engage in all sorts of scramblings and wire-pullings to get "star cases," many an unfortunate prisoner in the Tombs whose case is weak for the prosecution, and who has no strong friends to pry his papers out of the pigeonholes, lays there for weeks and sometimes for months, until perhaps some missionary, noticing his plight, brings the case to the attention of one of the judges. We have seen cases of unfortunate persons who have been taken back and forth between the court-room and the Tombs a score of times, only to be dismissed without trial. One young man we remember, who had been used by the police of an uptown precinct to get evidence against liquor dealers. One of the liquor dealers stopped his career by making a complaint of attempted extortion against him, on which he was arrested and lodged in the Tombs to await trial. He was a poor, friendless fellow, and the police dropped him at once; so he laid in the Tombs for several months, until some one advised him to address a letter to a judge. The judge assigned counsel to him, who found that the charge was flimsy and defective. One of the district-attorneys took the case up, saying, "I know that the gentlemen in our office do not like to handle weak cases, and consequently unfortunate people rot in the Tombs. When the case against a prisoner is so weak that there can be no conviction, I think that is a controlling reason for attending to him at once." The case was brought up quickly and the prisoner was discharged.

Snuffy Joe (Bernard) and Andrew Morrison, two thieves, were the first prisoners in the Tombs. The "Bridge of Sighs," running from the Tombs to the Criminal Court building, is used by the inmates of the prison when going to the court-rooms for pleading and for trial. Some of the attaches of the two buildings have such a superstitious dread of the structure that they will not pass under it. Frequently, a humorously pathetic spectacle may be seen in the mornings when the prisoners are passing through this bridge, and their wives, children and friends are down in the street straining their eyes to catch glimpses of them, and sometimes making motions to the unfortunates when they see them. The number of women and children who throng the steps, the corridors and the stairways of the Criminal Court building surprises and saddens the observer. A startling feature of the work of the courts is the youthfulness of the majority of the offenders. Trials of burglars ranging from thirteen to sixteen years of age are very common, while grayhaired criminals are seldom arraigned. It does not require much observation in this place, where we are brought face to face with the criminal side of New York, to see that much of our crime could be prevented, that many of our criminals are the victims of circumstances beyond their control, and that our civilization is defective in its failure to deal effectively with the criminal environment of the youth in many sections of the City. We have seen lads and young men convicted on criminal charges when it seemed perfectly clear that in taking the step which led to the crime there was no serious criminal conception or intent. The burden of a single conviction is never shaken off. Juries seldom have compassion upon a defendant who has previously been convicted, and seldom do they pay much attention to his explanations of criminal appearances. The grind of the wheels of justice in this court-house is ruthless and relentless, and there are few cases indeed where the court, the prosecutor or the jury are moved by sympathy. A very large proportion of the defendants are poor and unable to employ counsel, and they have to put up with the perfunctory exertions of the regular criminal practitioners whom the Court assigns to the task. Opportunities for consultation and for careful examination of facts and evidence are very meager, and often the disposition to such labor is lacking in the assigned counsel. The assistant district-attorney seldom has any strong and effective opposition in these cases, and he goes on merrily piling up years of sentences to swell his record for successful prosecution. In the County of New York the prosecution has immense advantages over the defense, and, except in the most unusual cases, if the State officers start in with a determination to convict, they have three or more chances to the defendant's two. If the defendant happens to have a weak spot in his character, though it be unconnected with the offense charged, the chances of his escape are greatly minimized. The cases of Carlyle Harris and Dr. Buchanan are in point. In the case of Dr. Buchanan, all of the resources of the County of New York were used in the procuring of an able body of prosecutors, an effective detective force, and an expensive array of medical experts. These were all arrayed against one man, deprived of his liberty, unable to move about and to direct the preparation of his defense, and restricted by his poverty in the employment of counsel and medical experts. At the trial the court-room was filled with the atmosphere of conviction. One of the first requirements of a successful prosecuting attorney is the ability to manufacture a convicting atmosphere. The defendants in these and other star cases were tried with drums beating and banners waving. From the opening address of the prosecutor to the closing words of the judge's charge there was one recurring rhythmic word-beat, "Convict! Convict! Convict!" It may not be possible or advisable to change the order of things, but the quiet and thoughtful onlooker must be full of sympathy and sadness and anxious reflections when he sees the imperfections of our boasted judicial machinery, the great wrongs to individuals and families that are done in the name of justice and for the needs of society, and the ap-

TEARING DOWN OF THE TOMBS PRISON.

New York, Vol. Three, p. 68.

palling sum of human misery rolled up in the proceedings of these courts, so much of which is due to human imperfection, inaptness, and coldness of heart.

Sentences are imposed in each of the parts of the Court of General Sessions at half-past ten, and there is always something to try the sympathies of the spectator. Here is a hard-faced defiant young man who has been convicted of robbery. The judge says to him, "Did you not say on your trial that you had never before been convicted?" "Yes," says the culprit defiantly. "Was that true?" the judge asks, while he looks ominously at a paper. "Well! I meant that I never did time for a State offense." "Putting it that way," says the judge, "is that true?" The prisoner sulks and makes no answer. Says the judge, "The Chief of Police of Hartford seems to know you pretty well, and he says—" and then there is read a list of offenses charged against the defendant. The judge says, "I have no sympathy with you; the jury recommended you to mercy, but they did not know your career. The extreme penalty for your crime is five years in State Prison. I will consider the recommendation of mercy and give you three years and two months."

The next prisoner has been accused of grand larceny in the second degree. He is a man of respectable appearance, and looks terribly dejected and humiliated as he stands there at the bar. There is a whispered consultation between him and the district-attorney, who then talks quietly with the judge, and we see that the prisoner is about to withdraw his plea of "not guilty" to plead "guilty" to a lesser offense than the one charged. After the formalities are observed his plea is entered "guilty of *an attempt* at grand larceny in the second degree." We wonder at the man's appearance and the course adopted by the district-attorney, until we hear the question, "Do you use liquor immoderately?" answered "Yes." While his case has been proceeding a woman has been waiting her turn. She is not over thirty years of age, and she, too, has the appearance of respectability. She is making a desperate effort to be brave and not to break down in front of the crowd of people that witnesses her humiliation. She pleads "guilty" to a charge of grand larceny, and then, on being asked to give reason why she should not be sentenced, her attorney, who has been assigned to the case, without pay, says: "This unfortunate woman is guilty, but there are circumstances which should be considered by the Court in mitigation of her offense. She is respectable; she has never before committed a crime or been accused of a crime. She has had great trouble. Her husband has deserted her and she has been reduced to great want. She is in a state of extreme nervousness and took the money to meet absolute necessities while in a condition of frenzy." No one denies the statement of the lawyer. She has resolutely composed her features, but now she sways and totters and is about to fall to the floor when an officer catches her and supports her until she can be seated. In this case the Court is moved with pity and defers the imposition of sentence until some further inquiry can be made into the circumstances. These three little cases were observed in one visit to a court-room.

This quotation from Havelock Ellis is apropos: "Most people who can recollect their own childhood—an ability which does not, however, appear to be very common—can remember how they have sometimes yielded to overmastering impulses which, although of a trivial character, were distinctly criminal. The trifling or even normal character of such acts in childhood is too often forgotten by those who have to deal with children. Mayhew, writing in 1862, remarks: 'On our return from Tothill Fields we consulted with some of our friends as to the various peccadilloes of their youth, and though each we asked had grown to be a man of some little mark in the world, both for intellect and honor, they, one and all, confessed to having committed in their younger days many of the very "crimes" for which the boys of Tothill Fields were incarcerated. For ourselves we will frankly confess that at Westminster School, where we passed some seven years of our boyhood, such acts were daily perpetrated; and yet, if the scholars had been sent to the House of Correction instead of Oxford or Cambridge, to complete their education, the country would now have seen many of our playmates working among the convicts in the dockyards, rather than lending dignity to the senate or honor to the bench.' "

In the recent trials of "firebugs" the court-rooms were crowded with Hebrews from New Israel, who sometimes congregated in the corridors and held prayer-meetings — such they seemed to be. When their friends were convicted their grief was uncontrollable. They threw themselves on the floor, beat their heads against the wall, cried and howled, cursed the witnesses, the prosecutors, the jury and the judge, called on Moses, Isaac and Abraham, and had to be thrown bodily out of the building.

The public receives an erroneous impression of the Criminal Courts and their procedure, from the lurid and sensational accounts and illustrations of murder trials published in newspapers of immense circulation. These publications are works of art, as they go, but more than poetic license is taken in order to produce startling sensations and beat other newspapers in the mad rush for the biggest circulation and the most startling effects. The crimes of lust and vice are so frankly and brutally exhibited as to shock the sensibilities of men of the world, and to smirch the innocency of our youth. At the time of this writing, the trial of Marie Barberi for killing her recreant lover with a razor is progressing, and the evening papers are filled with quaint and humorous, and sometimes with indecent, illustrations of this shocking case, full of lust, blood and perfidy. The craze for crude and bizarre joking must be fed even on this horrible case, in which shame for humanity, pity for an unfortunate girl, and horror for bloody circumstances, should shut out indecent humor. I have before me a group of graphic pictures printed in a great newspaper. The title of the pictorial sketch is:

"THE TRAGIC STORY OF MARIE BARBERI FROM THE TIME SHE MET DOMENICO CATALDO TO THE PRESENT DAY."

Picture 1 is entitled, "Domenico Cataldo sees Marie Barberi for the first time."

Picture 2 is entitled, "Two months later he speaks to her and she repulses him."

Picture 3 is entitled, "They become acquainted in a few months and she says he drugged her in a saloon."

Picture 4 is entitled, "Her downfall follows and she begs him to make her his wife."

Picture 5 is entitled, "Her mother pleads with Cataldo in vain. Marie weeps on her knees."

Picture 6 is entitled, "Driven to desperation, she follows him to a saloon with a razor."

Picture 7 is entitled, "She beseeches him for the last time to marry her. 'Only hogs marry' was his brutal relpy."

Picture 8 is entitled, "Then she says all was a blank to her. She 'saw red,' and declares that she knew nothing of the murder until she saw blood on her hands."

Picture 9 is entitled, "She calmly washed the blood from her hands while her false lover bled to death."

Picture 10 is entitled, "Now she is on trial for her life for the second time."

The Tragedy of Marie Barberi, as Produced at the Thalia (Bowery) Theater.

The illustrations are unique, graphic, startling; they cannot be excelled. They were meant to picture the awful drama in its entirety, and they do. This doleful and demoralizing exhibit went into thousands of homes, and was examined by many thousands of children and youth.

These highly-wrought pen-and-word pictures give little idea of the continuous tragedy that is played

An Interpreter in the Barberi Trial.

in these criminal court-rooms; a tragedy all real, but with which the actors are so familiar that even they do not realize its awful import, and go on daily with their round of occupation, enjoying their pleasures, and feeling none the worse for the great sum of human misery in which daily they cast up the figures. The most faithful performers in this continuous drama are the interpreters. Their self-importance and their self-consciousness are conspicuous. When a foreigner's life and liberty are at stake, and when he is unable to provide his own interpreter as a check on the official translator, he is in great danger; for the false rendering of a word, or even the literal statement of an idiom, may be of serious consequence to him. Many complaints are made on this score. Interpreter Morossini has a florid manner about him which, while it shows his earnestness, sometimes puts a depth of meaning into his words that the witness never intended. No matter how stolid, phlegmatic, cool or calculating a witness may be, the interpreter renders his words with oratorical force and much waving of the hands and shaking of the head.

The Five Points district, bad as it is, is steadily improving and gives now but a faint picture of its former desperate viciousness. The cutting of Worth Street (old Anthony Street) through to the Bowery let in a stream of travel that has scoured out much of its foulness. Horse car lines through Mulberry and Baxter Streets would work such an improvement as would justify the City in establishing them. The careful attention of the board of health as well as the police is lessening the grossness and the quantity of crime and dirt, and the improvement of the pavements and the regular invasions of the street-cleaners are tending in the same direction. Paradise Park helped to lift the neighborhood, and the new park will accomplish a great work. Chief among the agencies of reform are the Five Points Mission and the House of Industry. When all the harsh hands of the law failed to make an impression upon the dense ignorance and criminality of the Five Points, the gentleness of missionaries and kind women broke into the impregnable fortress of vicious ignorance, and gentleness and sympathy began to accomplish that which rigor and severity had failed to do. When Christian ladies obtained possession of the "Old Brewery," the very citadel of crime, and began to teach the lesson of Christian love, their task seemed to be more hopeless than that of the self-sacrificing missionaries in heathen lands. It is to the credit of the liberal religion and charity of New York that that pioneer institution and the House of Industry (which occupies infamous old "Cow Bay") have been so well supported. Their work should be enlarged and should be extended to every one of the numerous dark regions in our City. The first superintendent of the Five Points Mission, Mr. Pease, was a man of rare gentleness, firmness and perseverance. He was scorned by those he came to save; he and his mission were hated with all the bitter hatred which the evil mind oft feels for the good, made still more bitter by the sectarian venom of ignorant Catholics toward "heretic Protestants." Every annoyance that low cunning could invent was thrown in his way. He determined to change the ordinary methods of mission work and to invite the people to employ themselves in sewing and other occupations in the mission building, and to enjoy society and recreation there as well as to listen to preaching and exhortation. His first effort was to organize a sewing-school for girls. Daily the operations of that school were interrupted by a wild child of the slums, who swung open the door and cursed the missionary and his work. She called him names and exposed the vicious history of various girls and their parents. It was impossible to chase her away or to catch her, for she was as wild as a hare and as fleet as a fawn. At that time Anthony (Worth) Street was lined with infamous houses, whose inmates and frequenters swarmed about loud and bold, and the children understood them and their ways almost as well as the grown people. The missionary followed her to her home. She herself eluded him, but when he saw the place in which she lived, and considered the brightness and the natural genius of the child, he determined in his heart that he would capture her. He says:

"I was busy one morning in the workshop, laying out work, when I cast my eye toward the open door, and there saw Wild Maggie waiting for a word upon which she might retort. Without seeming to notice her, I said, loud enough for her to hear, 'Oh, how I wish I had some one to help me lay out this work.' There was a look of intelligence spreading over her face, which seemed to say as plainly as looks could say, 'I could do that.'

"'Will you?' I said; she started as though I was mentally replying to her passing thoughts.

"She did not say 'Yes,' but she thought it. I had touched a chord.

"'Maggie,' said I, with all the tone and looks of kindness I could command, 'Maggie, my girl, come in; you can help me; I know you are smart. Come, I will give you sixpence if you will help me a little while.' She stepped into the door, looked behind it suspiciously, and started back. She remembered the trap. 'No, I won't. You want to catch me and send me to the Island. I know you, you old Protestant. Old Kate told me yesterday that you had sent off Liz Smith, Nance Hastings, and humpbacked Lize, and a lot of girls.'

"'So I have, but not to the Island. They have all got good places where they are contented and happy. But I don't send anybody away that don't want to go. I won't send you away, nor won't keep you if you don't want to stay.'

"'Will you let me come out again, if I come in, when I am a mind to?'

"'Yes, certainly, my dear child.'

"'My dear child.' Where has she ever heard those words? In former days, before her father and mother had sunk so low as they now are, when she used to go to school, to church, and Sabbath-school, and wear clothes such as she was not ashamed of? Want of clothing will sink the highest to the lowest state of rags, and dirt, and misery.

"'Will you swear that you will let me come out, and you won't beat me. Limping Bill and one-eyed Luce, his woman, says you licked little Sappy till she died.'

"'They are great liars.'

"'So they say you are; that you preach nothing but lies.'

"'Well, I won't lie to you, Maggie, and I won't whip you, but I won't swear. Did you ever know any good man swear?'

"She thought a moment, and replied, 'Well, I don't know—I know them that swear the most will lie. Will you let the door stand open? If you will I will come in?'

"'Yes,' and in she came.

"'Now, what do you want I should do?'

"' There, do you look at me. I am laying out shirts for the women to sew. That pile, there, that is the body; this, the sleeves; that, the collar; these, the wristbands; these, the gussets; here are six buttons, and here is the thread to make it, and then it will be a shirt when made. Now, we roll it up and tie a string around it; now it is ready to give out. Now, you can do that just as well as I can, and you don't know how much it will help me.'

"'Yes, I can, and I can beat you.'

"So she could. She was just as quick at work as she was at play and mischief, and the piles disappeared under her nimble fingers much more rapidly than they did under mine, and so I told her. Who had ever praised her work before, though all had 'her deviltry'?

"The spirit of reformation had already commenced its glorious work.

"When that job was finished, she turned her sweet blue eyes upon me, with an expression which said as plain as eyes can speak, 'I am sorry that job is done. I like that. Can't you give me another?'

"There was no other which she could do just then, but she said, 'What shall I do now?'

"'Well, Maggie, I have no more work for you to-day; but here is your sixpence, I promised you, and here are some cakes. Come again to-morrow; you can help me every day. I like your help.'

"She did not want to go. She had tasted of a fruit which had opened her eyes, and she would fain clothe herself in fig leaves, so they hid the deformity of dirt, and rags, and sin. Wild as the fawn, as easily as the fawn subdued. At the approach of man, that timid animal bounds into the thickest brake and hides away; but once in the hands of man, it turns and follows him to his home, licking his hand as though it were with its own dam. So was Wild Maggie tamed.

"'What shall I do now?'

"What should she do? A score of little girls were huddling around the door, for the news was out that Maggie, Wild Maggie, had been caught and caged, and they wanted to see 'what would come of it.'

"A thought struck me. I asked her if she could read. Yes, and write. Had she been to school? Yes. 'Then you shall play school. You shall have these benches, and you shall call in those children, and you shall be the teacher, and so you may play school.'

"Was there ever a happier thought engendered? Maggie was delighted, the children came rushing in, ready for 'a play never before enacted in this theater.'

"For an hour or more she plied her task diligently, and it was astonishing with what effect. How she reduced her unruly materials to order. How she made them say, Yes, ma'am, and No, ma'am, to their school mistress. How she made them sit and 'look like somebody.' Taught this one his A B C's, and that one to spell B-a-k-e-r. How she told this one to wash his face next time he came to school, and that one, if she had any better clothes, to wear them. Poor Maggie, she never thought of the poverty of her own.

"'Now,' said she, 'every one of you sit still; not a word of noise, and no running out while I am gone, or I shall punish you worse than shutting you up in a dark closet. Mr. Pease, will you look to my school a moment?'

"Away she bounded. Oh, what a step! Step! it was more like flying. A moment, hardly time for a few pleasant words to her school, and she bounds in again, with a little paper parcel in her hand. What could it mean? It means that,

"Many a flower in wilds unseen,
 The sweetest fragrance grows;
From many a deep and hidden spring
 The coolest water flows.

"She first inquires, 'Have they all been good?' 'Yes, all.' Then she unwraps her parcel. How they look and wonder 'what is it?'

"What is it? Simply this—

"She has been out and spent her sixpence to do unto others just as she had been done unto. Did ever cakes taste sweeter. Did ever benevolence bet-

Five Points Mission House (Successor of Old Brewery).

ter enjoy herself than Maggie did, while thus distributing her rewards? What a lesson of self-sacrifice! The first sixpence, the whole treasure of this world's goods, spent to promote the happiness of others. This was a hint. It were a dull intellect that could not improve it. The children were further fed and bid to come again to-morrow. 'And this was the beginning of our ragged beggar children school, that has proved such a blessing to this neighborhood.'

"'Maggie,' said I, taking her by the hand and

"Hot corn! Here's your nice hot corn!"

looking her in the eye. 'Maggie, you have helped me a great deal to-day; will you come again to-morrow?'

"The string was touched, and tears flowed.

When had tears, except tears of anger, filled those eyes before? What had touched that string? Kind Words!

"'If you will let me stay, I won't go away. I can learn to sew. I can make these shirts.'

"'Yes, yes; and if you are here, these children will come, and we will have a school every day.'

"And so Wild Maggie was Wild Maggie no more. She was tamed. Her life had taken on a new phase. To the questions, what would her father say? what would her mother say? she replied, 'What do they care? what have they ever cared? Though they were not always so bad as they now are.'"

Through Maggie her parents were reached and the good work spread into many of the desolate homes of the Five Points. The work done through her is but a sample of what has been going on for many years among the people of the Five Points, and accounts more than anything else for the improvement that has taken place. Occasionally Mr. Pease started some erring couple on a new life of honest marriage. He had many encounters with rough characters, and in one of these he nearly lost his life. There was a wretched family in which the mother and her young daughter had been rescued from vicious life. One night a fierce villain whom she had formerly known, but whom she had forsaken for her new life, stole into her apartments as a burglar and attempted to kidnap the child. The mother awoke and struggled with the ruffian, but he struck her down and bore the girl in his arms to the street. There, fortunately,

Mr. Pease's encounter with a villain.

was Mr. Pease, who was out on a night trip. He comprehended the situation, for he had heard the screams in the house and had recognized the child in the man's arms. There were stout muscles and iron determination behind the missionary's gentle

The Twopenny Marriage Couple.

Christianity; he felled the kidnaper with a sudden blow of his cane, tore the child from his arms, pushed her back into the hallway, shut the door and confronted the burglar. In a moment the situation was reversed, for Pease was on the ground, his adversary's fingers clutched his throat, and a knife was raised above his head. Just then the watchman appeared, and a blow of his bludgeon saved the good man's life. He was a saint!

# CHAPTER EIGHT

## *THE BLOODY FOURTH: RELICS OF PIRACY*

**Roosevelt Street—Greeks—Into the "Bloody Fourt"—Cherry Hill—Select Society—Famous Criminal Resorts Located—Pirates—Roll-Call of the Harbor Thieves—Patsey Conroy—Exhibitions of Nerve—Gotham Court and the Swamp Angels—Paradise Alley—Sailors' Boarding-houses—George Appo, a Child of the Slums—An Autobiography—The Hardships of Reformation**

CAN it be that this street leading out of Park Row into Cherry Hill was the center of fashion sixty years ago! This is the very street in which was the aristocratic private school where A. T. Stewart as a teacher earned his first money in America. There is nothing that remains to remind us of those good days, except a few old mansions, dilapidated and overflowing with human vermin, that still show their scarred fronts in Roosevelt, James, Oliver and several other adjacent streets. The decayed civilization of a decade ago has yielded to a degenerate ancient civilization that manifests itself in noisy rankness. Roosevelt and Marion Streets are full of Greeks, but the Romans push them as hard as they did in olden times, and seem even now to hold them as vassals. The Greeks, while poor, ignorant and untidy, shine by contrast with their Italian neighbors, and are in every way a better contribution than they to the life of our

City. As a people they are industrious, peaceable, honest and thrifty. We have become familiar with the strange characters of foreign alphabets in our City. For a long time the sign-boards have familiarized us with Jewish letters and Chinese word signs, but it is still a novelty with us to observe the Greek letters in Roosevelt Street, not on the pages of classic literature, as would seem to us more fitting and proper, but upon the grimy fronts of repellant cafes, filled with men in modern and rather frayed and soiled American clothing, instead of the flowing gowns that we expect to see behind those idealic characters. (The scholar of languages finds his Syriac characters traced on sign-boards and window-panes in the same forms as appear in the original manuscripts of the New Testament, on lower Washington Street, and illustrated by living pictures which are all out of harmony with our preconceived notions of Eastern types.) Here is a snap-shot of a Greek restaurant on the north side of Roosevelt Street near Park Row. The artist hurried his work so as to avoid a mobbing which seemed imminent, but was not expeditious enough to prevent a number of the Greek inhabitants of the house from lining up for the picture. Several things should be noticed in this photograph: the broken curbstone; the number of relics of "to let" signs on different portions of the building; the word "cafe," that evidently has done duty before; the home-made lettering underneath that word; and the curtains, torn and stained. Across the street, further down from

GREEK RESTAURANT ON ROOSEVELT STREET

New York, Vol. Three, p. 94.

Park Row, is the Parthenon Cafe; and, as befits its title, it is cleaner and statelier than the other cafes, and seems to be the best of its kind. Next door to the first cafe was the saloon of a Roman, denominated "D. Michael Angelo." Underneath the Parthenon Cafe is the banana emporium of a Roman gentleman; east of it is the laundry of a Celestial gentleman, and east of that is a retail establishment for the sale of Turkish products, while above them all may be seen the important sign-board of Madame ———, Levatrice. This is a little picture of life from the cradle to the grave, the "levatrice" in the upper story attending to one extreme of existence and the banana gentleman in the cellar providing for the other extreme. The levatrices are very important personages among their people. They get all of the births except what the "charity doctors" get. An American doctor has a hard time of it on such an occasion; for he does not appreciate the human interest and sympathy which causes the whole community, men, women and children, to crowd into the little room where the great event is to come off. Ventilation and elbow-room are not thought of. Only a resolute man with a choice stack of swear words can rout the mob.

George Dessaros was a Greek inhabitant of Roosevelt Street. When George was at home in Greece, his constant companion was his cousin Louis Tcholaskas. Seven years ago Louis disappeared. George mourned for him, grew discontented, and started for America as a sailor. In January he became sick with pneumonia and was taken to Bellevue Hospital. He went into delirium and raved about his cousin. His senses returned. He put out his hand and touched his cousin, who lay on the next cot in our little world. In a moment there was a demonstration by two wild men. They recovered speedily.

Those parts of the Cherry Hill district into which the Italians have crowded, while unspeakably dirty and disgusting, are losing the ferocious attributes which formerly distinguished them. Bill Sykes is not so common a type either. The people are not engaged in such lives of crime as make them slink out of sight and avoid the eyes of the public and the police. They have their street gatherings, populous and noisy, and their amusements. As a sample of a grand function, which engrossed the attention of Roosevelt Street society during this year, read this announcement, which we found in the window of a retail grocery store, and which we secured with difficulty for twenty-five cents (see page 97):

There are now about five thousand Greeks in New York, and they take great pride in the fact that no Greeks can be found in the Penitentiary or the State Prison, and that there are no Greeks in the City requiring outside charity. They are engaged principally in the selling of fruits, flowers, confectionery and tobacco, and while most of them are poor, they have an ambition to succeed, and in time many of them will be found among the well-

*A Silk Umbrella will be drawn for by the Ladies present.*

SECOND ANNUAL

## MATINEE RECEPTION

OF THE

# PATSEY MAURO ASSOCIATION,

TO BE HELD

*AT NEW IRVING HALL, 214-220 BROOME STREET*

ON SUNDAY AFTERNOON, MAY 17th, 1896.

Music by PROF. CHAS. SEELIG, Full Orchestra.

**TICKETS, Including Gent's Hat Check, 25 Cents.**

---

OFFICERS.

Joseph J. Ross, *President.*
Ernest L. Palando, *Vice President.*
Tony Spinelli, *1st Vice President.*
Ralf Donzellio, *2d Vice President.*
Andy J. Campbell, *Financial Secretary.*
Jame Serapelli, *Recording Secretary.*
Peppie Ross, *Corresponding Secretary.*
Patrey Blois, *Treasurer.*
Antoney Gorrilla, *Sergeant-at-Arms.*
Michael Farraro, *Assistant Sergeant-at-Arms.*
Charles Moncalieri, *1st Assistant Sergeant-at-Arms.*
Michael Sbizziero, *2d Assistant Sergeant-at-Arms.*

COMMITTEE OF ARRANGEMENTS.

Michael Morello, *Chairman.*
Jolin Cerdola, *Assistant Chairman.*
Frank R. Concellare, *Floor Manager.*
Frank F. Rose, *Assistant Floor Manager.*
Charles F. Decesar, *1st Assistant Floor Manager.*
Joseph S. Rose, *2d Assistant Floor Manager.*
Sullivan D. Sherry, Vito Vignola, Marshall.

---

**Dancing to Commence at 1 P.M., Sharp.**

to-do and influential people of the City. The Greeks who live in Roosevelt, Madison, Oliver, James and Catherine Streets are generally poor, but there are many in fairly good circumstances in 113th, 116th, 124th and 125th Streets.

Nos. 115 and 117 Roosevelt Street, at the corner of Water Street, were wild places in the rougher days of Cherry Hill. Number 115 was Louis Lang's, and Number 117 was "Liverpool Mag's." There sailors were "plucked" daily.

Now we find ourselves in the Cherry Hill district. We are in the midst of a decrepit civilization, built upon the ruins of a departed aristocracy; and yet, bad as it is, its improvement has plainly begun, and there is good reason for hoping for a deliverance from the worst evils during the present generation. One may now walk through Water Street from end to end and find nothing to attract his attention more than the famous and beneficent Water Street Mission underneath the Brooklyn Bridge; but it was only a few years ago that this street was filled with bagnios of the foulest and most dangerous character, and no respectable person could traverse it in decency or safety. Sailors from every clime and nation, and the fiercest and most abandoned ruffians of this and our neighboring cities, here met and caroused with women, equal in degradation and animal characteristics to those of Whitechapel in London.

This news item displays one of these female characters—a hold-over:

### "Jabbed a Cop with her Hatpin.

"IT NEARLY ENTERED HIS EYE—SHE STABBED A SAILOR TWENTY YEARS AGO.

"Policeman Florence J. Driscoll of the Oak Street Station found a drunken woman surrounded by a crowd at James Street and New Bowery last night. As she refused to move on Driscoll arrested her. On the way to the police station the woman turned suddenly and said with an oath:

" 'Oh, you're one of those new cops, are you? I'll teach you a lesson.'

"She drew her hatpin, eight inches long, from her bonnet and thrust it at the policeman's left eye. The point of the pin hit the bone just at the corner of the eye, and bent nearly double, but the policeman's sight was not injured.

"The woman described herself at the station as Nellie Lang, 38 years old. As she stood facing the sergeant she endeavored to shield her face from him, but he recognized her as Mollie Lawler, whom he arrested, when he was a patrolman twenty years ago, for stabbing a sailor in O'Donovan Rossa's hotel at Mott Street and Chatham Square. The sailor nearly died, and Mollie Lawler, then a girl of 18 years, was sent to the State Prison by Recorder Hackett for ten years."

At the twenty-fourth anniversary of the Water Street Mission in 1896, the head usher was "Bowery Ike." During the service he gave his testimony to the saving power of God's love. He said he had been converted a year, and that it had taken a long time for the "jimmy" of salvation to find a way into his soul. "I was brought up among thieves," he said. "I stole for my profession. I traveled from one end of the country to the other. I came in here one night and my heart and soul were touched. The religion of Jesus Christ satisfies me." Another said, "I met Christ on a railroad train. I had been cracking a safe. I got to thinking of my life and a light came into my heart. I came here. The desire to steal went out of me. Thank God I can stand here to-night with a clear conscience." A man who had come in a carriage reached over and shook the hand of the reformed thief. The superintendent, Mr. Hadley, invited visitors to begin a new life. One man, who said he was in great temptation, asked for sympathy and prayer. A lady prayed with him; then he prayed for himself, saying, "Lord! Lord! Help me to do right!" A man in broadcloth knelt by him and offered the sympathetic prayer of a brother. There are indeed rescue agencies at work in this sin-cursed region, and they succeed because they are full of genuine sympathy, and they lead sinful men and women out of their old criminal environments into the new atmosphere of fraternity and God's love. Among those who earnestly work in these godly enterprises are William T. Wardwell, Phineas C. Lounsbury (ex-governor of Connecticut), and John S. Huyler, the confectioner.

On Water Street near Dover were Pearsall's and

Fox's, where robberies, assaults and murders were constantly committed. In these houses sailors were "shanghaied," and men were drugged, robbed, and dropped through trap-doors. An informant saw a well-dressed man walking through Water Street in this neighborhood; a woman in one of the houses dropped a bucket of ashes on his head; while in this predicament a gang of thugs rushed upon him, tumbled him down a cellar, stripped him of his clothing, and threw him up on the sidewalk, naked.

At 273 Water Street (building altered) was Kit Burns' rat pit and dance house.

At 279 Water Street (building altered) was Tom Norton's, a bagnio filled up with river pirates and Water Street hags. Norton was mate on a "Black Ball" packet ship, and he made a fortune with his dance house.

The house at 340 Water Street (still standing) was Mother McBride's dance house.

The house Number 316 Water Street (altered) was John Allen's. Thirty years ago he was called the "wickedest man in New York."

The famous "Flag of our Union" (where Scotchy Lavelle was bouncer) was on James Street between Cherry and Batavia Streets. The house still stands. It is of brick and has three stores in it now.

The house Number 310 Water Street was the Saranac, kept by Jim Davis as a tough sailors' boarding-house and resort of crooks.

Number 337½ Water Street, "The Pipe," kept by Butch Haley, Number 11 Peck Slip, "The

Band Box," kept by Mike Haley and Johnny Bull, Number 71 Oliver Street, kept by Patsey Manley the prize-fighter and Hen. Van Winkle, and Number 18 Catherine Slip, "The Glass House," kept by Martin Bowe, were all famous resorts for the thieves and cut-throats of the Fourth Ward, and the old buildings are still standing.

The Bowe family was one of the most noted in the Ward. It consisted of Martin, Jack, Will and Jim, all fighters, shooters and cutters; and only the hardest characters frequented the saloon. The bartender, Jack Madill, killed his wife there and was sent to Sing Sing prison for life.

The Fourth Ward Hotel, at the corner of Catherine and Water Streets, is an old time assignation house of the lowest type, and has been the scene of many murderous affrays. There poor old "Shakespeare" was murdered in the style of "Jack the Ripper."

Among the notorious sailors' resorts of Cherry Street were Tommy Hadden's at Number 110, Dan Kerrigan's at Number 110½, and Mrs. Tighe's at Number 61. The buildings are still in existence.

Hadden was a noted "shanghaier" of sailors, and served two terms in States' prisons for that offense. Kerrigan was a plucky prize-fighter; he fought the longest fight on record, three and a half hours, with Australian Kelly—it was a draw. At Mrs. Tighe's, Jack McDonald, a "runner," killed officer Thompson with a knife, and received the light sentence for it of four and a half years in

Sing Sing prison, because the officer had hounded him and clubbed him without cause. Mrs. Tighe's house was arranged with bunks, like a ship.

Tim Murphy had a saloon in Catherine Market at Cherry Street, and his customers were the fierce and brutal men of that neighborhood. He was a big courageous man, and held his position by sheer force—often jumping over the bar and "wiping up the floor" with obstreperous drinkers. The cutting and shooting matches that occurred there are too numerous to be mentioned.

In the Five Points vice was the reigning quality, crime was its attendant; in the Fourth Ward crime was the dominant quality, vice was its servitor. Even the "Forty Thieves" of the old Five Points and the "Whyo Gang" of more modern times were plebeian criminals when compared with the fierce law-breakers of the Fourth Ward, its murderous highwaymen, its pirates and harbor scourges. The life of the policeman in the Five Points was always hard and uncomfortable; in the Fourth Ward, if he were a faithful and honest officer, every moment of duty put his life in jeopardy. It was an easy matter for the criminals of both districts to communicate by way of Bayard Street. Generally the desperate characters of the Fourth Ward disdained association with their neighbors of the Sixth Ward. The first earnest efforts of the police to cope with the pirates of the Fourth Ward were made in 1852. In that year Superintendent Walling says that three thieves, Nicholas

Howlett, William Saul and William Johnson, pulled out from James Slip and boarded the ship "William Watson," which was lying at anchor. They stole what they could from the deck, and on being discovered by the watchman, Charles Baxter, shot him to death. Mr. Walling was put at the head of a party of detectives to ferret out the crime, and it was done so successfully that Saul and Howlett were hanged in 1853. From that time the police operated systematically against the various gangs of thieves, and for many years there was a fierce warfare. There is no doubt that there were times when the thieves of this locality bought safety from police interference; nevertheless, the good work has gone on until the district is comparatively safe. Saul and Howlett belonged to the gang called the "Daybreak Boys." In one year twelve of that gang were shot. It was this warfare that brought about the use of the police patrol boats. Some of the famous criminals in the Slaughter House and Hook Gangs were Ned Perry, Joseph Gayles, alias "Socco the Bracer," "Bum" Mahoney, Bill Lowrie, Sam McCarthy (Cow-legged Sam), Billy Woods, Denny Brady, Larry Griffen, Patsey Conroy, Louis Engleman, Martin Broderick, Blindy Winslow, "Paddy the Boy," Will Dugan, John Allen, Jim Brady, Abe Coakley, Mary Varley, "Blacksmith Dave," "Scotchy Lavelle," Bill Cummings, "Slobbery Jim," Charley Morrell (One-arm Charley), Bill Murray, George Williams, John Watson, George Madden (Low Madden), Michael Noles (Piggy),

John Kane (Beeny), James Wallace (Nigger), Jack Perry, Tommy Shay, Edward Sullivan, Tom the Mick, Larry Nevins, Merricks, James Coffee, Preslin, Le Strange, Lewis, McCracken, Riley, Whalen, Bob Taylor, Old Tom Flaherty, James Smith, Gallagher and Bonner. The hanging of Saul and Howlett at the Tombs was the first hard blow that the pirates received. Among the friends who attended their taking off and offered their consolations were Tom Hyer and Bill Poole, the noted pugilists, who have been mentioned before. Johnson, their associate (who saved his life by turning State's evidence), disappeared, and it is believed that he was killed by other members of the gang for his perfidy. The principal resorts of these pirates were "Slaughter-house Point," a saloon at the southeast corner of James and Water Streets, which was kept by Pete Williams (and which was closed up by Captain Thorne after seven murders had been committed in it). The building is still standing; it is Number 11 James Slip. Saul and Howlett were among its frequenters. The "Rising States," opened by Bill Lowrie and his consort Moll Maher, on Water Street near Oliver; the "Hole in the Wall," kept by "One-arm Charley," with the assistance of Kate Flannery and "Gallus Mag" (there "Slobbery Jim" killed "Patsey the Barber"); Jack Perry's on Water Street; George Christopher and "Long Mary's" saloon, at 275 Water Street; "Ann Sourk's" dance-house, Kate Carroll's "Flag of our Union," "Liverpool Mary Ann's," and Mary Varley's home at 56

James Street, were other rallying points for the pirates. In 1858, officers Blair, Spratt and Gilbert shot a dozen of the pirates. The thieves took great risks. On one occasion Patsey Conroy, a fearless and remorseless man, Bill Cummings and two other thieves clambered onto a brigantine which lay at the foot of Jefferson Street. They seized, bound and gagged the watchman, and then rushed into the cabin and overwhelmed the crew of sixteen men, and cleaned out all of the portable articles that were worth stealing.

Conroy kept a "dive" in the basement of Number 90 Bowery. There was a mock pretense of its being a restaurant, but no food was sold there. It was simply a headquarters for the gang. The police shunned it, and only one officer dared to make an arrest there, detective Holly Lyons. The place was an arsenal and was always garrisoned, and when an inmate was wanted, the officer waited for him to come out.

On one night four wounded thieves met in a saloon on the Bowery at Hester Street, which is still in existence. There were Patsey Conroy, who had a bullet in his arm; Bill Cummings, who had received a shot in his chest, and "Biled Oysters" and Charley Mosher, who were slightly hurt. They were in hard luck, and Cummings was in great pain, though holding up bravely. Jim McGuire, another thief, came in with a big "swag" that he had just captured, and he ordered a round of whisky. Cummings, who spoke with difficulty, complained about the whisky and said they ought to have champagne. McGuire good-naturedly changed the order. Then Conroy demanded a share up of the plunder. McGuire offered ten dollars to each man. Cummings ridiculed it as "chicken feed" and unworthy to be offered to companions in distress. McGuire walked out, but before he could get away he received a blow in the stomach such as Lavelle and Flaherty used to administer so scientifically, and his "swag" was quickly taken. When a policeman appeared, Conroy coolly said: "Officer, there's a man who has fallen off a car; better take him up," and then the gang walked off. Mosher was the Charley Ross kidnaper, who was shot while trying to rob Judge Van Brunt's house at Bay Ridge. "Biled Oysters" was a wild Irishman, who, when his mother commented on his diamonds and fine clothes, said: "Arrah, mother, I've struck it. I'm living on biled iysters."

After "Slobbery Jim" committed the murder at the "Hole in the Wall," he disappeared from New York, but was heard of again as a captain in the Rebel army. "Ned Perry" killed a private detective in the Harbeck Stores in Brooklyn and received a life sentence for the murder. "Socco the Bracer" was shot and killed by police officer Musgrave, while trying to escape capture, after robbing the brig "Margaret" at Pier 27. His companions threw his body into the water, and several days afterward it floated into the slip at the foot of Stanton Street. "Dugan" and "Carroll" were sentenced to twenty years in the State prison for robbing the brig "Mattano" and severely beating the captain and his wife. This pirates' record might be continued at great length, but the purposes of this work do not require it.

Recently we have heard of "Beeny" and "Nigger," who are doing a little small and pitiful stealing uptown. The ferocious gangs have "petered out" very small.

Captain McCullagh (now Acting-Inspector of Police) earned his fame by breaking up the gangs of the Five Points, which included such all-around criminals as Danny Driscoll, Danny Lyons, Owen Bruen and "Hoggy" Walsh. Detectives O'Brien (now Chief of the Detective Bureau) and McCauley did their best work in fighting with the gangs of the Fourth Ward, such as the "Border Gang" and the "Short Tails."

The most picturesque features of the Fourth Ward are to be found in Cherry Street, which we have noticed slightly in a previous chapter; and the alleys of Cherry Street have been unfailing sources of startling news items, thrilling pictures and interesting accounts of low life in New York. There is Gotham Court at Numbers 36 and 38 Cherry Street, once the rendezvous of the "Swamp Angels," who used the great sewer running under the alleys to the river, for hiding plunder and for dodging the police. Away back in 1871 this place was declared by health inspectors to be infiltrated with disease and so wretched in construction as to be unfit for human habitation, and yet the buildings stand, and,

until recently, contained nearly a thousand people. There are two rows of tenement houses five stories high, back to back, under one roof and reaching two hundred and thirty feet from Cherry Street toward the Oak Street Police Station, with entrances by two alleys, "Single Alley," on the east side, six feet wide, and "Double Alley," on the west side, nine feet wide. These houses have no back windows, and their front windows open on these narrow alleys, which are the roofs of immense sewers that formerly could be entered by manholes in the alley-ways. The inhabitants of Gotham Court made entrances to these manholes through the cellars of their buildings, which entrances they guarded with jealous care from the police and other officials. During the cholera epidemic the death rate in these buildings was at the rate of one hundred and ninety-five in a thousand, and it has been reported that out of one hundred and thirty-eight children born there in three years sixty-one died. This "court" was the haunt of highway robbers and house-breakers. The sewers are nine feet high and four wide, with side ledges, and they are infested by great rats. The police have found the bodies of murdered men in them. Dr. Stiles, a Health Inspector, once reported upon them as follows:

"The horrible odors from this immense subterranean *cloaca* have no vent except through the small iron gratings in the pavement of the yard of the court overhead, and through the cellars and up the stairways, and thus through the entire house. It must be remembered also that, after it reaches the open air of the yard, the odor rises up between the two piles of building (each five stories high) which are separated by a width of nine feet. The poison thus concentrated is very directly applied to each and every apartment in the building, and there is no escape, because from the peculiar back-to-back construction of the tenements not a single room has any through and through ventilation."

The report also speaks of the lawlessness connected with the sewers in such strong terms as "vice, drunkenness and terror reign rampant. The police will not follow the criminals into these dark cellars and recesses, and escape is easy."

The Board of Health acted upon this appeal and filled up the cellars of the buildings and closed the entrances of the sewers. That action broke up the rallying place of the "Swamp Angels." The build-

ings were constructed in 1851 by Silas Wood, a benevolent Quaker, with the intention of rescuing the poor from their miserable homes. Sanitary science was then unknown. The lot next to Gotham Court,

Number 34 Cherry Street, was owned by a brother of Silas Wood, who sold half of it to Alderman Mullins. The alderman built on this purchase a structure fashioned like Gotham Court, and there arose a dispute between him and John Wood concerning the boundary. A quarrel occurred, and Mullins knocked Wood into the middle of the street. The Quaker arose, saying: "Friend Alderman, I will pay thee for that blow," and he built a great tenement in the rear of his lot, with a blank wall against Mullin's building. This narrowed the alley's entrance of Mullin's building to about two feet, and that blank wall still remains. The house is called Mullin's Court. The miserable buildings have been occupied by Italians, who seemed to be perfectly satisfied with their quarters, and lived as though they enjoyed their surroundings. Double Alley is also known as Paradise Alley, and under that name has been made quite famous in street songs.

Recently the Board of Health has removed the tenants from the court and the alleys, and now they are desolate and deserted.

This is the neighborhood described in these famous street-songs.

### The Sunshine of Paradise Alley.

There's a little side street such as often you meet,
Where the boys of a Sunday night rally;
Tho' it's not very wide, and it's dismal beside,
Yet they call the place Paradise Alley.

But a maiden so sweet lives in that little street,
She's the daughter of Widow McNally;
She has bright golden hair, and the boys all declare
She's the sunshine of Paradise Alley.

CHORUS.

Ev'ry Sunday down to her home we go,
All the boys and all the girls they love her so;
Always jolly, heart that is true, I know,
She is the sunshine of Paradise Alley.

When O'Brien's little lad had the fever so bad
That no one would dare to go near him;
Then this dear little girl so brave said I think I can save,
Or, at least, I can comfort and cheer him.
Soon the youngster got well, and the neighbors all tell
How the daughter of Widow McNally
Risked her life for a boy, and they hail her with joy
As the sunshine of Paradise Alley.

She's had offers to wed by the dozen, 'tis said,
Still she always refused them politely;
But of late she's been seen with young Tommy Killeen
Going out for a promenade nightly.
We can all guess the rest, for the boy she loves best
Will soon change her name from McNally;
Tho' he may change her name, she'll be known just the same
As the sunshine of Paradise Alley.

---

## The Sidewalks of New York.

Down in front of Casey's old brown wooden stoop,
On a summer's evening we formed a merry group;
Boys and girls together, we would sing and waltz,
While the "Ginnie" played the organ on the sidewalks of New York.

CHORUS.

East side, west side, all around the town,
The tots sang "Ring-a-rosie," "London Bridge is falling down";
Boys and girls together, me and Mamie Rorke
Tripped the light fantastic on the sidewalks of New York.

That's where Johnny Casey and little Jimmy Crowe,
With Jakey Krause, the baker, who always had the dough;
Pretty Nellie Shannon, with a dude as light as cork,
First picked up the waltz step on the sidewalks of New York.

Things have changed since those times, some are up in G,
Others they are on the hog, but they all feel just like me;
They would part with all they've got could they but once more walk
With their best girl and have a twirl on the sidewalks of New York.

Will Mr. Krehbiel add these to his repertoire of "folk songs"?

Once Paradise Alley was filled with the Irish. Not far from it such notable merry-makers as William J. Scanlon and Ed. Harrigan were born. Now the last rallying place of the Irish on Cherry Street is "Murphy's Alley," or "Dan's Alley," which is the first alley from Franklin Square. There is a "Mike's Alley," but it is full of Italians and stilettos.

Further uptown, and beyond the boundaries of Cherry Hill, is another hard river-front locality, which is rapidly improving—"Corlears Hook." The time was when that locality rivaled the Fourth Ward for those kinds of crime peculiar to the river front. The saloons bore such names as "Hell's Kitchen," the "Tub of Blood," "Snug Harbor," "Swain's Castle," "Cat Alley" and the "Lava Beds." Among its famous criminals were "Skinner Meehan," "Dutch Hen," Jack Cody, "Army Smith" and "Army Trainer," Tom Downey, Hen Devine, Jim Sullivan, Sam Moorehead and his brothers Gundy and Ed; "Sweeney the Boy," who slept in the marble-yard for twenty-two years; "Bryan

The Careening Place.

Boru," who was found dead in the same yard half eaten by rats; and "Hop Along Peter." Jack Hussey, the famous life-saver, who formed the Volunteer Life-saving Brigade, lived at Corlears Hook. There is a pretty little summer-house in a park where the gang once had its headquarters. Cherry Street led to the shipyards, which were begun in English times, and which in the early days of the nation were full of life and activity; for in those days New York led the nation in the building of wooden ships. Such fine old ship-builders as Mr. Webb had their yards at this place, and many of the ship-builders lived in the upper part of Cherry Street. The dry-docks in that neighborhood are the successors of the old shipyards. Where we now see vessels in the dry-docks, high above water, there used to be vessels of all kinds, from the sloop to

Sailors' Boarding House, Twenty Years Ago.

the man-of-war, careened over and resting on the surface of the water, so that their bottoms might be scraped and painted. The cherry orchard was south of the two-story gable-roof house on the west side of the street, just above Roosevelt Street, and it extended to the junction of Cherry and Pearl Streets. The house which we have mentioned has walls over two feet thick, and its back yard is paved with cobble-stones. It was built about the year 1700 for General Latham, a British army officer. Where the orchard stood are alleys and courts and rows of tenement houses.

From James Street to Catherine Market, Cherry Street has many sailors' boarding-houses, like Mother Raabe's and Dora Schmidt's. There are Irish, En-

Old Time Sailors' Dance House.

glish, Dutch, Danish and Norwegian houses; in fact, you may find nearly every nation except our own prominently represented in these little hotels. Close to them are liquor stores and places of worse character, and around them are many representatives of the hard population of Cherry Hill. Similar sailors' resorts may be found in contiguous streets. That the outer appearance of these places has been improved we may judge from this illustration of twenty years ago. The sailors' dance houses, which were a repulsive feature of Water Street fifteen years ago, have disappeared. The first sermon preached to seamen in America was delivered by the Rev. Ward Stafford on December 20, 1816, at Number 37 Cherry Street, and four years afterward the Mariner's Church in Roosevelt Street was dedicated. The Colored Sailors' Home was organized in 1842 at Number 190 Cherry Street.

The Fourth Ward has equaled the Sixth Ward in the potency of its influences for making criminals. What could be expected of the children of criminals, growing up in an atmosphere of crime, taught crime by their parents and associates, and compelled to shift for themselves in tender youth? The careers of such notorious characters as Danny Driscoll the murderer, and George Appo the thief and swindler, are striking illustrations of the work that has been going on for years among the unfortunate children of the slums, and is still going on in a very large degree. From a very careful investigation of the case of Appo, and considerable knowledge of his life and character, it seems to me most probable that with the surroundings and educative influences which, theoretically at least, the State should provide for its children, he would not have been a criminal, but an intelligent and estimable person. The downtown army of newsboys is made up largely of children of the Fourth Ward. Many of these will grow up to be criminals, but with good influences they would become good citizens. It is a matter for thanksgiving and hope that there are such influences at work, and one of the best and most practical beneficences in our City is the Newsboys' Lodging-house, through which, in the most sensible way, right principles are established in the lives of many of the street waifs. Theoretically (again we say it) the State is bound to take care of its children who are not properly housed and nurtured; and there ought to be some broad, grand, effective method of caring for the armies of children who are now growing up to recruit the criminal ranks of the future. The knots of young toughs that infest Cherry Hill are composed of restless lads who have imbibed such anti-social ideas that their standing among their fellows will not be assured until they have done a turn in prison, and when that event has taken place they will be criminals for life. A little sketch of George Appo, mostly from his own hand, will be interesting and instructive at this point. When we first met him he was undoubtedly a desperate criminal, quick to use the knife, and a hopeless pickpocket. He has said to me that the good people of society don't understand the thorough pickpocket; that he has an appetite for his work as sharp and resistless as the appetite of the drunkard; that the sight of a watch chain dangling on a vest arouses an insatiable desire to secure the watch at the end of it, especially if there is a locket on the chain. It happened that the approaches to Appo were made in a kindly way, and that the men who served him with a subpœna performed their work with great considerateness. When Appo told his story before the Lexow Committee it at once put a great gap between him and his former thieving associates and their police allies. He was in great personal danger, and in fact frequently suffered violence afterward at the hands of his enraged pals. Much kindness was shown him in finding honest means of livelihood for him. This treatment worked an entire change in the desperado. He said he had

Fingers Distorted by Long Practice in Picking Pockets.

never before received a kind word or act, and a genuine reformation occurred in him. It was not a religious reformation, nor a complete reformation; for he persisted in the use of liquor and opium, to which stimulants he was a slave. The combined influences of those poisons has on several occasions led him to deeds of violence which have brought him again into the clutches of the police; but his old besetting sin—that which he looked upon as his sin—picking pockets—he gave up and never again lapsed into it. He has suffered the pangs of hunger many times, when he might have obtained re-

SAILORS' HOME, 106½ CHERRY STREET.

New York, Vol. Three, p. 117.

SAILORS' HOME ON CHERRY STREET.

New York, Vol. Three, p. 118.

lief by the exercise of deft fingers which were aching for use, but the temptation has been withstood; and that to me is evidence of a reformation which entitles him to kindly thought, and emphasizes the value of sympathy in the treatment of many habitual criminals. The little sketch which follows is taken verbatim from an account of his life which I paid him to write at a time when he was destitute. If you had heard Appo tell this story you

New Style of Picking Pockets.

George Appo.

Old Style of Picking Pockets.

would have been charmed by his gentle and polite manner and by his soft and flexible voice and pleasing enunciation:

"In the year 1858 July 4th, George Appo was born in the city of New Haven, Conn. My father, a Chinaman was born at Ning-po, China, and my mother was born in the city of Dublin, Ireland. Soon after my birth my parents came to New York City to live and took residence at Number

45 Oliver Street. This house was owned by the Fletcher family from whom my father had rented. I was then two months old. One evening my father coming home from work at his Tea Store found no supper ready for him as usual. My mother lie asleep in bed and me in the cradle by her bedside, and as he glanced about the room he noticed three empty wine bottles upon the table and of course suspected mother was drunk, so went out and not caring to disturb her had supper at a near by restaurant. On his return home he awoke her and asked what was the matter. She told him the fact of the matter was that, that very day was Mrs. Fletcher's birthday and they both had been celebrating the event. My mother had no doubt taken a drop too much and as a consequence my father began to scold her. He was overheard doing so by Mrs. Fletcher who came roughly into the room and began to call him very insulting names and finally struck him a blow on the head with a flat iron, and my father stabbed her to death with an ornamental dagger that he had on his mantel-piece. He was tried, found guilty of murder in the first degree and was sentenced to one year and at the expiration of that year to be hung by the neck until he was dead. During the course of the year Governor Hoffman granted my father a commutation of sentence from death to life imprisonment and finally granted him a commutation from life to ten years. I was then but six months old and my mother took my baby sister away with her on

board of a ship, 'Golden-Gate,' bound for California, where she had a brother living. This ship was wrecked off the Pacific Coast and all with my mother and sister aboard was lost. As a result I was left alone and cared for by a poor woman who brought me up as best she could amidst the gloomy and bad surroundings of 'Donavan's lane' a filthy alley located at 14½ Baxter Street and when I reached the age of twelve I learned the profession of a Pick-pocket. I followed this unfortunate mode of living for two years and at the age of fourteen years in the year of 1872 I was arrested and pleaded guilty and was sentenced by Judge Dowling to the School Ship 'Mercury' where I stayed for 14 months and was released by Commissioner Freal for good conduct in saving the life of one named James Harvey from drowning. After my release I went back directly to my old haunts and bad associates in the Fourth and Sixth Wards, and applyed myself more diligently than ever to pocket picking and in April 3rd, 1874 at the age of sixteen I was again arrested for picking the pockets of John H. Bannon, a city contractor, pleaded guilty and was sentence to serve 2 years and 6 months in State Prison at hard labor. I was the smallest prisoner ever admitted; a suit had to be made for me. I was released from there April 2nd, 1876 and immediately on my release I began to pick pockets, and after about one month's freedom I was shot by an unknown person from whom I had abstracted from his pocket $150.00 while on

Fulton Street. He, it seems, discovered his loss about one minute after I got his money and he gave chase for me. I ran down to Pearl Street and as I neared Number 300 a tenement house and a cork store, I turned into the entrance and heard the report of a pistol behind. At once I felt a burning feeling in my stomach and seeing a woman washing clothes in the yard, I called her and begged her to hide me. She took me and put me between the mattress of her bed and told the pursuing crowd that I had gone over the back fence and for nearly an hour I lay bleeding and suffering between that mattress, and the good woman brought me a Doctor and he after being told that I had shot myself accidently, gave me a letter to St. Luke's Hospital, where Prof. Sabine extracted the ball and cured me. It was during the course of this above mentioned term in prison that I was taught how to operate the many systems of stealing. In a word I left there a full fledged crook, and for about 8 months I worked safe and successfully, but being by this time unfortunately too well known to the detectives I was again arrested for picking the pockets of H. Gilbert on Wall Street who was then Secretary of the Custom house on his way to make a deposit at the Bank of America, and as he neared the bank I abstracted from his inside overcoat pocket a large package of greenbacks successfuly, but the ever watchful and dutiful detective McDuggle happening to see me from across the street and I seeing him coming on a run towards me I took to my heels around to William Street, then to Nassau and finally into the rear entrance of the Equitable building followed by a large crowd of people shouting 'Stop Thief!' and when I got into the building, seeing the crowd too close behind me, I took the package of bills, turned and threw and showered them amongst the crowd who in their anxious desire to possess the money fell on top of one another in their greed. Anyway I was captured, pleaded guilty and was sentenced by Judge Gildersleve to 2 years and six months in State Prison at hard labor Jan. 10th, 1877. It was during the course of this term of servitude that I was so brutely and inhumanly treated by the authorities in charge of Clinton Prison. On my arrival at this Prison I was assigned to work in the 'wood chopping Gang' this gang sawed and chopped all the wood for the Prison, as at that time 1877 and 78, they never burned coal because there were no Rail Road running up the mountains then. While at work one day sawing wood my old pistol shot wound broke open again and I was taken to the Hospital and received kind medical treatment from the good Doctor Ferguson who was then in charge. About 3 weeks after my admittance into the Hospital Dr. Ferguson resigned and another Doctor took his place and on the first day of this new Doctor's instalment he came into the ward and every patient who was able to sit up out of bed was discharged as cured whether he was or not.

I had only been out of bed 2 days and was just getting over from the effects of a severe surgical operation performed one week previous by Dr. Ferguson, when this new Doctor came to my bed and asked what was my complaint, I told him, he said, 'Let me see your tongue' and at the same time feeling my pulse he then discharged me and my wound not yet healed. I was then assigned to work on the Hat Contract, 'Sizing Hats.' This work is the hardest work in that business and able-bodied men soon become physical wrecks both in and out of Prison. One had to stand over a large tub full of boiling hot water soluted with acid and in his nakedness jump up and down and rub the hat on a rough board until it has been reduced to the necessary size required. This was the work I was assigned to. I worked most of that day and did the best I could and when I found I could not stand it any longer I went to the keeper Mr. Hagerty, and said to him, 'Keeper, I am not able to do that work. Please put me at some other work that I can do and I will gladly do it.' 'Go back and do that work,' said he. 'I am not able to do it.' Then said he, 'Go get your hat and coat and come with me.' I did so and he brought me to the Deputy Warden (James Moore), and charged me with refusing to work. I did not refuse to work. I am an invalid and not able to do the work and put me at something I can do and I'll gladly do it. He, the Deputy, said that he had a Doctor to decide that. He sent for the Doctor who came to the Guard room and the Deputy said to him, 'Here is a man who says that he is an invalid and not able to do his work.' The Doctor said to me let me see your tongue and as usual my pulse at the same time saying, 'I guess you are able to do your work.' I told him to take me in an adjoining room and I'd prove to him different, and before I knew anything the deputy, (who was drunk, a common thing for him) shouted 'Seize him!' Five keepers then took violently hold of me and through fear I struggled to defend myself, and they broke my arm, knocked out my front teeth and cut my head with their clubs and finally handcuffed my hands behind my back, put me into the 'paddle' and when I came to I found myself lying on the floor and they pouring water on my head in their efforts to revive me from unconsciousness. When I came to, this drunken deputy warden said to me, 'Do you think you can now go and do that work?' No! said I, I'll not do another stroke of work for the balance of my term, and you cannot make me. Put him in the paddle again! No! said the doctor, lock him up in the dark cell. I was then taken without any medical attention to my arm or wounded head and shut up in the dungeon where I remained for 14 days. Woro it not for a kind hearted keeper I would no doubt have been carried out dead as many poor unfortunates have been, and no one in the outside world ever hears of these murders. I myself went before a notary public and will to this day prove that a keeper killed in cold blood a man named James Flarity, who was driven insane by the brutal treatment of a drunken deputy, and when Politicians stop placing ignorant rum shop and political leeches in power to reform their unfortunate fellowmen, then the question will be answered, 'Can a criminal be reformed?' My term of servitude expired on Jan. 9th, 1879 and on my release I went to the press and notified the public of the doings of these brutes in power, and a regular live committee was formed outside of politics and these ignorant brutes were discharged and the paddle stopped. Still I was discharged from that Hell's Kitchen a physical wreck, and permanently injured for life and through dire necessity was compelled to again steal or starve. I left New York, went to Philadelphia where in April 1880 was arrested while working the 'pennyweight' (stealing jewelry by slight of hand from jewelry stores) for this crime I was sentenced to one year's solitary confinement in the Eastern Penitentiary, Pa. and on March 9th, 1881 was released on good conduct and as I could not obtain any work in Philadelphia and being an entire stranger I jumped a train and reached New York City and again tried to obtain honest employment and failed. So I began to steal again and was arrested indicted for grand larceny pleaded guilty and was sentenced to 3 years and six months in State Prison and on December 26th, 1884, I was released on good conduct. During the course of this three years and six months term I used to make good use of every hour of leisure I could call my own to study and try to cultivate my moral and intellectual faculties and at the same time improve my heart; in fact, I had believed that I had found the road towards reformation. So just as I arrived in New York I went direct to the Bible house where at that time the Rev. Dr. Harris who was then the Agent of the 'Prison Aid Association.' I met him there and on meeting him he said to me, 'Well, Sir! What can I do for you?' Doctor, said I, I have just been released from State Prison. I do not come to you, to ask pecuniary aid or sympathy. I am here to ask you to obtain for me if possible, honest employment. I am willing to work at anything. He then asked me what I had ever been employed at. I told him nothing but running a machine in the hat factory at the State Prison, and that I was 'before the mast' for 14 months on board the School Ship 'Mercury' and if I could, would willingly go before the mast at once. He then gave me a letter to Mr. Malory of the Malory Steamship Company, in which he mentioned I had just been released from States Prison, and if he (Mr. Malory) had a vacancy aboard ship to let me fill it as a favor to him (the Doctor). I called at Mr. Malory's office, Pier 20, N. R. and handed Mr. Malory the doctor's letter. He read it, looked at me and said, 'Young man who is this Doctor Harris? I do not know him.' He is, said I, the Agent of the Prison Aid Association and is trying to get me honest employment. Well, I am sorry for you, I do not know this Doctor Harris and as there are hundreds of able-bodied seamen idle about the docks I cannot give you work. I thanked him and went back at once to the doctor, telling him what Mr. Malory said. The doctor laughed and as there was a little snow upon the sidewalks of the city he gave me a shovel and broom and told me to go down to Wall Street and about the business district and demand employment to clean the walks. I did so, and received nothing but 'get out of here!' so I returned to the doctor and gave him back the shovel and broom and he told me that he could do nothing more for me. I did not become discouraged. I started out on my own shape, so to speak, and went direct to Gardener & Co., Hatters, 80 & 82 Greene Street, saw Mr. Gardener and applied to him for employment at his manufactory. He asked me what branch of the hat business I worked at, I told him in the mill department, and that I had learned the business in States Prison and was just released from there and I asked him as a favor not to tell any of my shop mates. When he employed me, which he did and the second week I had been working, the engineer lost his overcoat and of course I was the suspected thief, as Mr. Gardener had told the foreman that I was an ex-convict and the whole shop finally knew it. I then went to work myself to find who had stolen the coat and discovered that it was pawned by one of the employees, and got it back to the owner, and then resigned my position because Mr. Gardener had abused my confidence by telling the whole shop that I was an ex-convict, and for them to keep an eye on me. I then became discouraged through fear that if ever I did get work again and my associates should lose anything I would naturally be suspected and accused, so I again started out to a life of dishonesty. So one night in January 1884, I accidentally became acquainted with a seemingly refined gentleman, Mr. Tom Woods, who was looking for an opium smoking 'joint' and as he was a stranger in New York, and I could see that he was a slave to the Oriental curse, I took him to a joint run by one Mat Grace on Crosby near Houston Street, and we soon became familiarly acquainted, so much so, he told me his line of business and I told him mine. He said that picking pockets was altogether too risky and that I could do better at the flim flam game. So him and I started out on the road and worked this 'graft' very successfully. I would go into a saloon order a drink, and lay down a ten dollar bill in payment, the attendant would give me nine dollars and ninety cents change. I would at once put the five dollar bill he gave in change as well as the ninety cents into my pocket, saying at the same time, 'What did I give you?' 'Why, ten dollars' says attendant. 'I thought I had given you a one; could you let me have a five for this? (Showing him five one dollar bills). He would then hand me a five dollar bill and I would then count slowly, 1-2-3-4 and then put the five dollar bill he just gave me, and then another one dollar bill on top of the five and say, 'If you wish, you can keep it all and let me have my ten dollar bill back again, the small bills will come handy to you. I had intended to give you a one in the first place.' He would then eight times out of ten hand me back my ten dollar bill and I would push the last five dollar bill back that he gave me with the first five ones, and leave the store four dollars and ninety cents the winner. This business proved far better than pocket picking, so I stuck to it and gave up all rough ways of stealing and to use the slang of the profession, I began to study all the '*sure thing grafts*,' such as bunco, dice, short cards, flim flam, fake jewelry and 'green goods.' The latter business has made many men wealthy, especially men who were formerly in power as honorable public servants, until the wool had been pulled from the people's eyes. It was while working the green goods game that I was so unfortunate in getting shot and losing my right eye. The man who shot me came on from Greenville, N. C. to the city of Poughkeepsie, N. Y. to buy counterfeit money, and I went to that city to hand them a letter and conduct them down to New York to meet the gentleman with whom they were to do business, but as they said that they had expected to do business there and that a police officer had warned them, I was about to say good-by to them

GEORGE APPO WHEN A BOY AND AS HE LOOKS AT THE PRESENT DAY.

when one sneaked behind me and shot me through the right eye. For this so called crime, I was tried, found guilty and sentenced to 3 years, 2 months and to pay a fine of $250.00, and through the untiring effort of my counselor Daniel O'Connell, the Court of Appeals decided in my favor and after serving 11 months, I was released and again stood alone with the whole world against me in my determined resolve to reform from the past and lead a better life. I called on my good and noble counselor and thanked him for his untiring efforts in my behalf. I then resolved to call on James McNally the backer of the green goods game for financial aid. I learned that he was living at Bridgeport, Conn. and as I had worked for him for five years steady and proved myself a valuable and honorable man in all things, I believed he would assist me if only on account for being shot and blinded while in the act of service for his gain and profit. I arrived at Bridgeport without a dime and the moment I stepped from the train I was met by his best man (Big Walter Haynes by name), who told me that McNally was not in town and then left me, went and telephoned to him, 'Appo is in town.' I then had to wait for five days and all the time McNally was there in hiding, and when he found out that I was determined to see him he showed himself and said, 'Well, George! I am glad to see you home.' Yes Jim, said I, but no thanks to you, why did you desert me? 'Well, George it has cost me this last summer $40,000.00. The very house I built you own it as much as I do.' Jim, I did not call here to hear about your financial or domestic affairs. I merely called to ask you to pay me a portion of the money, $200.00 that you owe me. That is alright Geo. I will see you to-morrow in New York at 12 P.M. sharp on Roache's Corner 38th Street and 7th Ave., and fix you up alright. He gave me a ticket to New York one dollar and fifteen cents was its cost, and for one week I waited at the appointed place for his coming, but he never came. So one day I was unexpectedly served with a subpœna and conducted before the Lexow investigation committee by Mr. A. F. Dennett. For further details can be found in the Investigation of the Police Department of the City of New York, 1894, Vol. II."

The evidence before the Lexow Committee of which George Appo spoke had special reference to the "green goods business" (in which he was an expert "steerer") and to its official protection. This is an incident that he recited:

"There was a man that had a friend, a victim; it was done about three weeks previous to this man coming on; I went to Philadelphia after him; I brought him on; it was a Sunday morning; I brought him to a certain hotel here in the city; then I took him from the hotel to a saloon where he was to meet the goods; while there, two men came in, the turner and the old gentleman, the so-called old gentleman, and sat down; and he said that he didn't have the key of the safe, but he would take his order; they asked him how big a deal he was going to make; he said '$800'; he would invest $800; they only had $85 in samples to show him; the rest of the bank-roll was locked up in the safe and the banker was downtown attending to some fellow that got arrested in the business and they couldn't get the bank-roll, so we showed him $85 in samples and the result was they says, 'I will take your order; I will give you $15,000 in the goods, but I will have to ship them to you C.O.D., and you will leave $400 deposit; I will give you a receipt for that, and when the goods reach you, I will send them by Adams Express, and remit you through registered letter the receipt, so that you can take this receipt and go to the Adams Express Company and get the goods there, for which you will pay C.O.D., the balance, which will be $400 more;' so, he says, 'I will take these samples here'—the victim did, and he put them in his coat pocket; he says, 'Do you want my money now?' he says to the turner; the turner says, 'Yes, if you please; I will give you a receipt for it'; he goes down in his pocket and he pulls a big 48-caliber and lets go.

"Q. Fired? A. Yes, sir; I got the gun away from him.

"Q. Didn't some one throw a coat in his face, if I remember right? A. No; I grabbed the gun myself; wrenched it out, and the turner and the old gentleman ran out and left me alone there with him; the turner took the gun out of my hand when he ran out and left me alone there with him; I, thinking that he was going to pull another one to give it to me, picked up a spittoon to defend myself with, and he drew a big bowie knife and slashed me across here. (Indicating.)

"Q. Slashed you across the hand? A. Yes, sir.

"Q. Have you got the marks there yet? A. Yes, sir.

"Q. After this man cut you with a bowie knife what took place? A. He ran out into the street, and he saw the turner running down the street, and he ran after him; the turner took his overcoat off and threw it in the fellow's face; he was a Tennessee detective.

"Q. A town marshal? A. He was a Tennessee detective; marshal of some town.

"Q. A town marshal from Tennessee? A. Yes, sir; two officers heard the rumpus; saw them running Sunday morning and a big crowd, and they arrested him; brought him to a station-house and turned out all hands; all hands were turned out; I was not arrested though; I was not brought there; the marshal was arrested there and the turner, and they both got turned out.

"Q. Turned out from the station-house? A. Yes, sir.

"Q. That is, discharged? A. Discharged.

"We all work under police protection, I will swear to that. Because they see me going along with victims, why don't they stop me and arrest me. Every one of them know me. My picture is up in the Rogues' Gallery in the Central office, and they pass me by in the street and I have a victim alongside of me, and they bow and look and all. that sort of thing.

"Q. Is it known through police circles who the backers of these various green goods shops are? A. That has been running for the last twenty odd years; there are men who made fortunes in the business, making from fifty to two hundred thousand dollars."

Here is another little incident:

"Q. Where did you get shot? A. I got shot through the eye in Poughkeepsie.

"Q. Do you carry the ball yet in your head? A. Yes.

"Q. Do you know any arrangements between the police and Hadlick or McNally that no one else will be allowed to work in the precinct with their men? A. As long as I have been working for them I have never seen anybody else around there; I have heard of them being chased away; I have seen this Hadlick put up a job on another fellow to have him shot and the bank-roll taken away from him that was working on the quiet; what is called stealing the guys; he put up a job on a man—I don't want to mention his name, because I might incriminate him; he is a good fellow, and, of course, he has got to make a living; he rigged up a fellow as a guy, and I saved him from losing his bank-roll; that was done at a certain hotel.

"Q. You saved him from losing his bank-roll? A. I saved him from losing his life and losing his bank-roll; they put up a job to murder the man; what they call stealing a guy—for instance, I take a man; I rig him up; I say, 'Do you want to make $5,000 or $10,000?'—'Yes, sir.' Well, you go up to a hotel-room, and I will touch the wires to a party band, bring him there with his bank-roll, and you play guy; when he comes in and shows his goods, take your gun, stick him up and take his money away from him; if he goes to make a kick, shoot him; he cannot do that much; the law will protect you; see how Tony Martin got killed there in Brooklyn; them men got out; it was cold-blooded murder; willful, deliberate, premeditated murder; fixed up; my case was fixed up there in Poughkeepsie; the man sneaked up behind me in cold blood and shot me, and sent me to State prison for three years and two months.

"Q. And got money away from you? A. Yes, sir; every dollar I had in the world, about $365.

"Q. Will you tell the Senators the average amount of business that McNally did while you were with him? A. He has had the cream of the business; he has had on an average to my knowledge about $8,000 worth of game in one day."

This little story is worth reading:

"Q. Was it at that time that you were arrested

with a revolver in your possession? A. Before they were closed up; no; I was laying down there smoking one day; I had just come into the city; I was laying down smoking a pipe and a party came up and handed me a letter in a lady's handwriting; it read, 'Friend George.—Please come down to the corner of Forty-second Street and Seventh Avenue and take me down into the joint; I have got a very bad habit and they will not let me in because I am a stranger. Yours, Mamie.' I knew several girls by the name of Mamie that were addicted to the use of opium; knowing her feeling, I went down to see if I could get her in. I went down to the saloon, thinking that she might be in the private entrance there; the family entrance there; the family entrance; the side-door entrance; I looked in and didn't see anybody; when I came out there were two detectives; they said, 'They want to see you down below;' I said, 'What for?' they said, 'Well, Byrnes wants to see you;' I said, 'What does he want to see me about?' they said, 'We have got your pal down here'; I said, 'I have no pal; I don't travel with anybody; whom do you allude to as my pal?' they said, 'Big Walter.'

"Q. Walter? A. That is another big Walter.

"Q. Not Haines? A. No; says I, 'I left my overcoat over there; was it you signod that letter Mamie sent a decoy in to get me out this way?' he laughed; I said, 'I want to go back to get my overcoat;' I had a revolver on me that I had just purchased that day, and it was not loaded; and thinking that they might sentence me to six months or fine me, I wanted to get rid of the revolver; so he says, 'Never mind; come over to the Rossmore Hotel, and I will send a boy after your coat;' so I went over to the Rossmore and went to the bar, and I treated them to a cigar; I said to the bartender, 'Where is the closet?' he said, 'Right downstairs, sir;' I started to go down and tried to get rid of the revolver; that is all I asked to go down for; on the way down I tried to get rid of it and he caught it, the detective; he said, 'What are you doing with this, George?' 'Oh,' I says, 'I will make you a present of it; I was going to get rid of it; that was all;' he said, 'You know we can do you on that;' I said, 'I know it;' 'Well,' he says, 'you know what it will amount to?' I says, 'Yes; about a month or may be $10 fine;' 'Well,' he says, 'you can fix that all right; you have got plenty of money; I says, 'No, I have not;' 'Oh, yes; you are a regular Jew with money;' 'Well,' I said, 'what is your price?' they said, '$25 apiece;' I said, 'I'll give you $25; that is all I have got;' and I gave it to him; I got turned out the next morning; I was only arrested as a suspicious character."

The bullet in Appo's head was located recently by the use of the "X-rays."

Appo tells of several instances where ministers were caught in the green goods game, and he says that the police finally made it a rule that no persons living in New York City and no ministers should ever be buncoed. One of these ministers was a colored preacher from Florida, who put up one thousand dollars of good money to get ten thousand dollars' worth of fraudulent money. Appo asked him how he, as a minister, could reconcile his conscience to the making of money by cheating the government; and the minister said that he was not doing it for himself, but for the Lord; that his people were trying to build a church, and couldn't raise the money that they wanted, and he thought it was proper enough to take the money that he expected to get for that good cause. What occurred when he arrived at home and found himself short one thousand dollars, with nothing in its place but a brick or a bunch of paper slips, and what the congregation did to him, are matters for imagination; we have no statistics on the subject.

We have in mind another man who is making a desperate effort to redeem the past, although it seems as hopeless as were the struggles of Appo. This man has been successful in keeping out of the hands of the police for some time, and therefore his name will not be mentioned now. He is thoroughly familiar with the dives and the criminals of the Fourth and Sixth Wards. In the Sixth Ward he associated with Driscoll, Oyster Malloy, Buckley Burns, Danny Lyons, Johnny Dolan, John Real, Patsey Conroy (whose dive was at Hester Street and Bowery), Joe Dollard, Dan Noble, Jack Welsh and Sam Perry. In the Fourth Ward his friends were among the hardest cases. He can tell the stories of the frequenters of the New England Hotel at Bayard Street and the Bowery. He can tell the names and the fame of the pirates of the Fourth Ward. Of his forty years of life, twenty-two have been spent in prison. At the breaking out of the war he was a boy in Baltimore. His father enlisted, and, unrestrained, he roamed the streets. A regiment passed through the city on its way to the war, and its martial music and brilliant uniforms aroused the spirit of adventure, and he, with a number of other boys, marched behind the regiment and followed it out to the war. The soldiers would not let the boys starve, and they marched and camped and marched and camped, until they had their fill of soldiering, and this boy slipped off to a near-by city. There he met a man who taught him how to go through hotels and glean small valuables from the rooms left unlocked by careless guests. He never had to work for a living. From the beginning his living was given to him or he seized it by his wit. His first honest money was earned at the age of forty years, when, in a desperate effort to yield to the pleadings of a good sister and be an honest man, he took employment on a farm at eight dollars a month with board and clothing. He did his work honestly and well, and when there was no more to do he came back to New York with a beautiful letter of recommendation, no money, and the world before him. With his letter of recommendation he expected to get work at once, but there was nothing for him in New York City. His hideous past closed every avenue of honest employment, but his old associates made alluring inducements for a return to the way of the sand-bagger and the house-breaker. He is now considering a kind offer to work on a farm for his board and clothes. I mentioned his case to another criminal, who is having a hard struggle in trying to lead an honest life. He said sententiously, "I would advise him to take a little digitalis—a pistol makes too much of a muss."

It is almost impossible for the criminal to reform. The desire for reformation, the wish to escape from a hazardous life and to live in peace and respectability, comes to many criminals, and many honest efforts are made that result in dismal failure and relapse into the old methods of life, which are the only salvation from starvation or suicide. There are many difficulties in the way of finding and knowing the criminals who are honestly anxious to reform, and we believe that those problems are now being considered practically and sympathetically, and that in the near future a method will be devised which will open avenues of hope and honest living to hundreds who would fain break away from their old lives.

While the above matter was being written I noticed several other cases in the daily press which showed graphically the hopeless condition of the convict and the awful obstacles which lie in the way of reformation. On December 1, 1896, an intelligent man with good connections, was arraigned in the Court of Special Sessions charged with larceny. The complainant did not appear, and the Court was about to discharge him, when he pleaded guilty, saying:

"I am one of those unfortunate wretches against whom all mankind seems turned. No one will trust me. No one believes me. I wish I could end this ceaseless struggle now. I am doomed. It will be the electrical chair the next time. The world is against me. Why, only a month ago I was arraigned before Magistrate Cornell. 'This is ——, the ex-convict,' whispered a policeman in the Magistrate's ear. 'Oh, yes,' said the Magistrate, 'I know him. Workhouse!' I have had a fair education, and am by instinct a gentleman. Once I yielded to an overpowering temptation and stole. I was sent to State prison. When I came out I secured employment and tried to reform. I was doing nicely when some one told my employer I was an ex-convict. I was discharged at once. Everywhere I went 'convict' was burned on my forehead. No one would give me work. Want drove me to desperation, and again I stole. Once more I found myself behind prison bars."—"But," interposed Justice Hayes, "there is nothing now to prevent you from leading an honest life. It is never too late to mend, and, to a man who remains honest and desires to work, the opportunity—" — "Opportunity!" interposed the prisoner. "Who is there, pray, to give such as I an opportunity? I will not battle against fate any longer. I insist that my plea of guilty shall stand." —"How many times have you been convicted?" asked Justice Hayes.—"Many times. State prison and the penitentiary are old haunts of mine. There, at least, I am free from the taunts and persecutions of my fellowmen. Now, don't be lenient at this time. Please don't."—"Well," observed Justice Hayes, "your case seems to be an unfortunate one. With your very bad record, and the fact that you stand before this bar a confessed thief, I can only give you a commensurate punishment. The sentence of the Court, therefore, is that you be confined in the penitentiary for a term of eleven months and pay a fine of $250, and stand committed one day for each dollar until paid."

"Thanks, Your Honor," remarked the prisoner. "I was in hopes that the sentence might be even longer," and he was led away.

Ike Vail, a famous crook, has grown to be old, and he, too, says he wants to reform, but he is driven by the resistless winds of crime, even as the hapless multitude were hurried along by infernal blasts in Dante's vision. When released recently from arrest in New Jersey on a charge that failed, he said that he had not done a crooked act for three years; but, said he:

"I am dead flat broke, without a cent to my name. What is a poor devil like I am going to do? Every place I go I am recognized and given ten minutes to leave town. When O'Brien hears I'm in New York he'll send for me. I had a message from him a short time ago. I went to him. He said New York wasn't big enough for him and me, and if I remained, there might be a collision. I knew what that meant. I had been down to the Battery Park, and within a little while it was known to O'Brien. To remain meant that the first time some second-class crank did something in my old line I'd have a job to clear myself. What was I to do? I started for Hoboken. Once here, Detective Jim Gallagher landed on me, and I was given three minutes to get across the ferry, when he took me before the Recorder. I come back and landed in jail. If I go to New York now O'Brien will know it within an hour. If I go over to Brooklyn, I'll get ten seconds in which to reach the Bridge entrance. If I go to any city they run me in, and after a few days in jail I'm told to hustle for the outskirts of that place. If this hounding continues I'll either have to starve, beg, or go back to my old line. If you hear I'm caught dead to rights just make up your mind that the authorities drove me to it."

At about the same time Chauncey Johnson, a famous thief, seventy-five years of age, was arraigned in the Court of General Sessions for a small theft. He used the name of George W. Brown, but his identity became known. He had spent about thirty years in prison. In 1852 he served five years for robbing a silk house; then another five years for robbing a bank in Connecticut of $36,000; then he robbed banks in Philadelphia, and was imprisoned three years; then he robbed the Bank of the State of New York of $15,000, the Adams Express office of a considerable sum, the Marine National Bank of $200,000, and the Central National Bank of $125,000. Now he is a poor, broken, decrepit, toddling old man. Said the judge, "I should think that a man who has spent so much time in prison would hardly demean himself by stealing $25." Johnson answered, "I plead guilty to the essence of your re marks. I had determined never to imperil my liberty again. I strove with all the exertion of which I am capable to lead a decent life and to keep out of trouble. I couldn't work, I borrowed, borrowed, borrowed, until I couldn't do anything else, and I committed this crime. I plead guilty." He was sentenced to one year in the penitentiary.

The general impression concerning Johnson was that he was "giving the judge a story"—using the common vernacular.

(Since writing the above I have learned of Johnson's death by consumption, in the prison where he was serving out his sentence.)

The veteran detective, Philip Farley, speaking of Johnson twenty years ago, said:

"There are thieves who, during their careers, have stolen millions of money, and who are abject, miserable, skulking beggars to-day, either breaking stones in some prison-ground or shadowing the haunts of younger men, craving the means to buy bread. A man known as Chauncey Johnson at one stroke stole half a million, and if he were arrested to-morrow it is doubtful that he could find any one to go his bail for a hundred dollars. The mystery that shrouds the doings and the days of these people is a cloak of shame, and sin, and discontent, and never-ending watchfulness and torment. There is nothing heroic behind it; nothing loyal, nothing true, nothing generous, nothing noble, nothing hearty; all is selfishness, cunning, craving, mocking, traitorous and mean. It is a cloud on which no sunshine ever breaks, unless the light of grace should strike there; and it is a cloud that wraps close in beneath its folds sorrow, sadness, tears and suffering. Lift the poor thief when you meet him. Do not kick him further down. There is still some man in him. They are the most grateful of all men, probably because they feel they want most, and never forget a kindness done them. The older they grow the more pitiful they become, and the more dependent and wretched. When years roll in on them, and at the time when other men are enabled to rest from work upon the fruit of their years of toil, the thief has but arrived at a more extended notoriety, and the number of hands stretched out to grasp him, to satisfy the law's demands, is ever increasing. That is the only wealth he piles up for himself in the future, and beneath its weight he finally falls."

The hard characters of these districts are not all red-handed bandits. Here is one whose features recently appeared in print. He is a specimen, perhaps a little extreme, of many similar characters who wander about, roosting on park benches or in hallways, begging occasionally, occupying seven cent beds, and occasionally regaling themselves with twenty-cent course dinners. This man denied that he was a tramp, and claimed to be an Englishman

Weary Willie.

and a gentleman, and that his resemblance to Lord Tennyson in features was only equaled by his resemblance in mental powers. When asked to give his home address, he said: "The wide world is my home, the birds of the air are my friends, and my own thoughts are my companions." (How like the great poet!)

Although the difficulties in the way of reformation are almost insurmountable, it happens occasionally that a criminal, who is anxious to redeem his past, falls in with such practical relief and makes so clean a surrender of his old self that he succeeds. The difficulties in the way of reformation are not all on the outside, for the inner temptation to return to criminal ways is exceedingly strong even with the best resolved. There was a man who finished a term of imprisonment at Sing Sing, and left that institution with the resolve to forsake his evil ways. He went to a merchant on Broadway, of whose common sense he had heard, and applied for a position in his store. The merchant asked for his references, and he said frankly: "I have none; I am fresh from prison." "What was your crime?" was the question. "Forgery," was the answer. After some further conversation the merchant said: "I will give you a chance. You have told me your past, and if you injure me it will be my own fault." Years have passed and that man is still in the same establishment; his past is not known to any one but his employer, and he has made a new record for himself.

A well-known and philanthropic restaurant keeper gave employment to quite a number of men as they were discharged from prison, and found them satisfactory servants; but when a safe was blown open in a neighboring establishment the skeptical police insisted that his reformed criminals were the culprits, and, though they did not prove it, his charitable scheme received a severe set back.

## NEW YORK CITY LIFE

*News Item, December, 1896.*

"'Kid' McCoy, once a notorious burglar, is in hard luck. According to his own story, he has been leading an honest life for several years, but it has not paid well. The wolf is at his door, and unless he is assisted he and his wife and babes will be turned out of their homes. 'Kid' is tender-hearted, though he has led a life of crime. No one to look at him would suspect he was a professional criminal. He is a tall, curly-haired fellow, about forty years old. Sergeant Kelleher received a visit from 'Kid' last night. The reformed burglar wanted to see if he could not get a certificate of good character to save himself and family from being evicted from their home, on the third floor of Number 27 Frankfort Street. 'Kid' cried as he told his story. He said that since being released from State prison eight years ago he had reformed. He married and has two pretty children.

"'I don't care for myself. Trouble never bothered me much. I am tough and can stand anything except to see my wife and children suffer for no fault of theirs. I have not a cent in the world. My landlord has learned that I was once a burglar, and as I owe him a little rent he has obtained a dispossess warrant against me. My wife is a good Christian. She goes to church regularly. My children have been baptized. I am not such a bad man myself. I don't pretend to be an angel, but I can swear that I have not turned a dishonest penny in a great many years.' The landlord had

'Kid' summoned to the Center Street Civil Court yesterday afternoon. The Judge, after listening to the testimony, granted a dispossess warrant, and 'Kid' was given until next Monday to get out. If he is not out by that time he will be evicted. 'I am sorry that I cannot do anything for you,' said Sergeant Kelleher. 'I know nothing about your career except from hearsay. If you want a character recommendation you will have to come around and see Captain O'Brien to-morrow. He knows all about you. I have not the least doubt that if he gives you a good reputation the Judge will extend the time for you.'—'There is not much use in my striving to be honest,' said McCoy, sadly, as he left. 'If I am evicted my children will be lost to me.' The picture of 'Kid' is in the Rogues' Gallery, labeled plain John McCoy. Thieves conferred the name of 'Kid' upon him when he was a stripling, trying to earn a reputation and dollars by questionable ways. He was last convicted in Delaware of safe burglary under the name of John Martin. He has served several terms in different States for various crimes. He has tried to make a living by selling a lock he patented. He carried about with him a small model of a safe door, and explained the merits of his device by practical illustration of its working. He says the lock is so constructed that no burglar can open it."

When we entered this awful region we passed by the peaceful and health-giving old "tea-water pump" and its delightful sylvan surroundings, and as we went down Roosevelt Street we entered the serene and quiet Wolfort's Meadow, which was once owned in common by those quiet good citizens, Rutgers, Roosevelt and Bancker, and was not divided by streets nor subdivided into lots until 1750. In working our way north we passed by Cowfoot Hill at Franklin Square, and then by the orchard of cherry trees, the luscious fruit of which was famed in old New York. The view of the East River from Cherry Hill in those days was the sweetest and prettiest picture that could be seen upon Manhattan Island. May we hope that the development of civilization in New York has reached such a point that hereafter no similar place of beauty shall be so desecrated by the diseases, the deformities, the crimes and the degeneracies of humanity.

---

# CHAPTER NINE

## *NEW ISRAEL: A MODERN SCHOOL OF CRIME*

Americans cast out—The Spirit of Rebecca Fream—The Female Pullers-in of Division Street—Allen Street Church—Benighted Israel—Schools of Crime—Ignorance and Vice—Max Hochstim's Beauties—Walhalla Hall—Balls—Tenth Ward Politics—Florid Speeches and Iridescent Parades—Synagogues—Quaint Customs—Incidents of Daily Life—Fire Bugs—Hester Street—The Russian Element—Bone Alley—Swindling each other—Mandelbaum—Big Thieves—Police Partners—Autobiography of a Protected Burglar—White Slaves—The American Spirit discovered in New Israel—The sad Story of Kaele Uchital—A Type of the Police Wolf—The Pimps—Attacking the Representatives of Law and Order—A Diversion toward Kip's Bay—Following the old Inhabitants of the Tenth Ward—Struggles for the Defense of American Institutions—A Faithful Church—The Rise of Croker—O'Brien Boru—The Shipyards—Grand old Ship-Builders—The Dawn of Commerce—Famous and Noble American Names and their High-sounding Successors—A Mysterious Bill of Fare—Catherine Market—Back to the old Fort—Some Natural and Pardonable Reflections

HAVING explored the Fourth Ward till we are tired of the task, we have made our way to Chatham Square and are now ready to plunge into the depths of New Israel. We will find that this section of the City, while brought into conformity with the others by its street lines, its types of buildings, and its general methods of travel, traffic and trade, has characteristics that separate it sharply from the other districts that have been mentioned in the preceding chapters. As we start down Division Street we will try to remember that we are going into a ward which once was as distinctively a native ward as the Old Ninth; but we shall look in vain for native Americans or old-time New Yorkers, unless we run across a few faithful old Methodists of the Allen and Forsyth Churches, or Presbyterians of the Allen Street Church, or some strong-minded person like Rebecca Fream, who resolutely defies the onrushing waves of foreign immigration and refuses to be driven out of her home by the billows of foreign customs and manners, even though they make life most uncomfortable for her.

REBECCA FREAM.

We became acquainted with the "puller-in" on Baxter Street, and we will find his sister on Division Street. The southern side of the street is lined with Hebrew millinery and cloak stores, containing gaudy goods of the cheapest character, and every one of these establishments has its representative on the sidewalk, ready to seize any woman that passes by and to force her into the store that she represents. One or two of these stores have real wax figures in the windows on which the cloaks and hats are exhibited to view, but most of them use battered cardboard representations of female heads which are thrust into the necks of the show-window cloaks. These cloaks and hats are not exhibited on the forms of the "puller-in," for they are generally accoutered in shabby clothing, and when it rains they make a most disreputable appearance. A gentleman from the country, with a lady under his escort, strayed through this street one wet evening, and one block of it drove them to take refuge on the elevated railroad. The first outpost said, "Buy the lady a new hat." She wore a very expensive and becoming bonnet; but the earnest agent paid no attention to it, as she pointed to the gaudy head-dresses in the window. The picket in front of the next store said, "Make your lady look handsome with one of our beautiful new hats." The lady, who was not expecting any such demonstration, began to blush and grow angry, but her troubles had only begun. The next outpost seized her by the arm and tried to turn her haughty footsteps into the store. She tore herself away only to encounter another, twenty feet away, who put both arms about her in the most sisterly way and advised her of her great opportunity to invest cheaply in much-needed apparel. When the next store was reached a youth tried to put his hand into the gentleman's pocket. Then they realized that a rapid retreat was in order and they made good time for the railroad. This was but an introduction to the urgency of the merchants of New Israel. If we had nothing worse here, we could well refrain from fault-finding. One would little think that Division Street was once the home of the Quakers—yet the little houses with dormer-windows were nearly all occupied by those gentle people.

Turning out of Division into Forsyth Street the pilgrim comes unexpectedly on a church, the second Methodist society in New York. It was founded in 1789, one month after the inauguration of President Washington, by Major Thomas Morrell of the Continental Army. Bishops Asbury and Coke preached in it frequently, and Washington took an interest in it, on account of his faithful friend Morrell. Washington Irving attended it in childhood. There the Missionary Society of the Methodist Church was organized (and the church now is in a foreign country). A graveyard surrounded the old church. When the Jewish wave swept over the neighborhood, it almost carried the society out of existence, but some wise heads conceived the plan of moving the building to the rear of the plot, and erecting tenement houses on the front; and now the church is in the middle of the block, and the Jews in its tenement houses help to pay its expenses. The Allen Street Church was not so fortunate. It had to sell its building to the Jews, who use it for a synagogue, and the remnant of the once powerful and influential American congregation worship in a little memorial building in Rivington Street, doing what they can to hold up the banner of Christ in the midst of teeming multitudes who hate His name. I have heard the faithful little congregation of old-fashioned Americans, with a few Jewish converts, sing the battle hymn of the church, and have been profoundly moved as I watched, and listened, and remembered, and thought.

**Stand up for Jesus.**

1 Stand up, stand up for Jesus,
  Ye soldiers of the Cross;
Lift high His royal banner,
  It must not suffer loss.
From victory unto victory
  His army shall He lead,
Till every foe is vanquished
  And Christ is Lord indeed.

2 Stand up, stand up for Jesus,
  The trumpet call obey;
Forth to the mighty conflict,
  In this His glorious day:
"Ye that are men, now serve Him,"
  Against unnumbered foes;
Your courage rise with danger,
  And strength to strength oppose.

3 Stand up, stand up for Jesus,
  Stand in His strength alone;
The arm of flesh will fail you;
  Ye dare not trust your own:
Put on the gospel armor,
  Each piece put on with prayer;
Where duty calls, or danger,
  Be never wanting there.

4 Stand up, stand up for Jesus,
  The strife will not be long;
This day the noise of battle,
  The next the victor's song:
To him that overcometh,
  A crown of life shall be;
He with the King of Glory
  Shall reign eternally.

Perhaps there is no part of our City where the workers toil harder and more continuously than the poor people do here. The multitudes are almost beyond numbering, and their abilities are restricted to a few kinds of work, which, because of the vast numbers that are anxious and even clamorous to get it, are let out on starvation wages. Here are the sweat-shops, where men and women labor far into the night, without holidays or vacations, at the lowest possible wages, barely sustaining life with the utmost expenditure of force and the most unremitting application. Ignorance, prejudice, stubborn refusal to yield to American ideas, religious habits and requirements, clannishness, and hatred and distrust of the Christians; these combine to hinder every device for raising the condition of the poor of this great Jewish district. The people huddle together and live in such restricted quarters, and in such unsanitary conditions, that the wonder is that they are not carried off by a plague. Often two rooms serve for the accommodation of a father, mother, children, and two or three boarders. The boarders are an important institution in this life.

They are Hebrew immigrants without family ties, who live cheaply by accepting the bare shelter that protects them from the night air, and the meager subsistence that prevents starvation. At night the floor is covered with the sleepers, who are fortunate if they have mattresses to interpose between themselves and the boards. There is no part of the world in which human parasites have greater feeding and can be found in more overpowering numbers. They match their human pasturages in thrift, in activity, in attention to business and prolificity. It is perfectly obvious that the privacy and the retirement which are essential to decent living are unknown in these Hebrew homes. All of the family participate in the entire drama of life from advent to decease. Could the farmers of Long Island secure the fertilizing elements which go to waste in this part of New York their farms would take on a productivity that would discount all of the important results attained by bone-dust, ashes and phosphates. The life of these people is intensely religious, though consisting mostly of the forms and ceremonies which have descended to them from the centuries of the past. Their little synagogues are found everywhere, and the people throng to them on all the religious occasions, which are frequent and many. The ignorance and the dirtiness of New Israel are not its only dark features. It is a distinct center of crime. It is infested with petty thieves and housebreakers, many of them desperate; and the criminal instincts that are so often found naturally in the

Russian and Polish Jews come to the surface here in such ways as to warrant the opinion that these people are the worst element in the entire make-up of New York life. In all of the despicable oppressive crimes that have been perpetrated against the defenseless foreigners of this section of New York, through the instrumentalities of a corrupt police and police court, I have not yet heard of a single instance in which the means of oppression or injury was not also a foreigner, who, for some base pittance of reward, betrayed his own countryman into the hands of the oppressors.

In his report of the work of the past year to the New York City Mission and Tract Society, John Jaeger, superintendent of the mission at Number 136 Chrystie Street, speaks thus of the conditions which prevail on the lower east side of the City:

"My field of labor is in the darkest section of New York City, where the population is more dense than in any of equal size in this City or in the world. It embraces that part known to the police as the Eleventh Precinct. This precinct is only nine blocks square, but it contains more inhabitants than the city of Albany. It starts at the beginning of the Bowery and extends east along Division to Clinton Street, then north to East Houston Street, then back to the Bowery and to Chatham Square. Within these narrow limits we have people from every quarter of the globe—Americans, Irish, Germans, Italians, French, Hungarians, Englishmen,

Chinamen, and a dozen other nationalities—but Polish and Russian Jews form the majority of the population. In some of these sections in the tenement houses you will find four or five families on a single floor, and often two or three families in a tenement apartment. Besides these classes, that form the regular inhabitants of the section, there is a large percentage of 'floaters' or 'transients,' who form the population in the lodging houses. It is within the narrow limits of this section that we find the cheap lodgings where men and women who manage to secure five, ten or fifteen cents find shelter over night. This is eminently the section of crime. During the last year an enormous percentage of the population of this precinct was detained in the Eldridge Street station, charged with some violation of the law, five thousand of these being women. There is hardly a 'crook' or 'confidence man' in the whole country who has not at some time or another been an inhabitant of this section. The riff-raff of the world, coming to New York, seeks the Bowery and drifts in here. One-half of the prisoners that appear in the Essex Market Police Court come from it, although four other police precincts send their prisoners to this court. Twenty murderers were arraigned for trial from this precinct last year, and perhaps there were as many more whom the police failed to apprehend. And yet among the people we find quite a percentage of the population who are by poverty and unfortunate circumstances compelled to live in this section; honest, struggling poor, who try to do their best and seem content in the struggle for mere existence. Among these are a large number of children, who early in life are brought in contact with the conditions I have heretofore described. During the past year we have had an aggregate

Harry Joblinski and two of his pupils, Bernard Scheuer and Joseph Otterman.

attendance at the mission of 26,235. Of these 15,000 asked for prayers, and over 1,000 came forward. A large number of them simply pass through our hands and are never heard of again by us, while occasionally we hear from others who are standing loyally by their confessions."

Mr. Jaeger's mission is surrounded by disreputable cafes, and the unspeakable "Palm Garden" is just opposite him.

Schools for thieves there are, that equal Fagin's, though in them the tutor's name generally ends with "ski." Two little boys, Bernard Scheuer and Joseph Otterman, were recently arrested, and one of them confessed to eleven robberies of stores. They said they were taught and forced to steal by Harry Joblinski, who had been similarly charged before. Some days later, Harry Rosenfield, ten years old, of Number 7 Allen Street, made the same kind of a confession, and said that Joblinski had fifteen boys in school. This precocious youngster admitted getting fifteen pocketbooks in one week. The king of this district has already been referred to. His name is Solomon, his nom de plume is "Silver Dollar Smith," his political name is Charles S. Smith. He is an "Honorable"—that is, he has represented the district in the Board of Aldermen and in the Assembly of the State. The throne room is the Silver Dollar Saloon, now a "Raines Hotel," just opposite to the Essex Market Courtroom, which he used to dominate with his burly presence. His chief counselor and executioner was Max Hochstim, a man of the same instinct, but cast in a smaller mold, and one who aspired to public office, but never got beyond public prison. The great "Silver Dollar" made his combinations with political dignitaries and various officials of that district, some of whom possessed fair reputations, but for some reason permitted their names to be associated with his, and thus gave him apparent power. Barney Rourke was his chief of politics, and he could always cast the vote of "de Ate" Ward to the strongest bidder. This section, according to the police division of the City into precincts, is known as the Eleventh Precinct. It was made famous by the administration of Captain McLaughlin

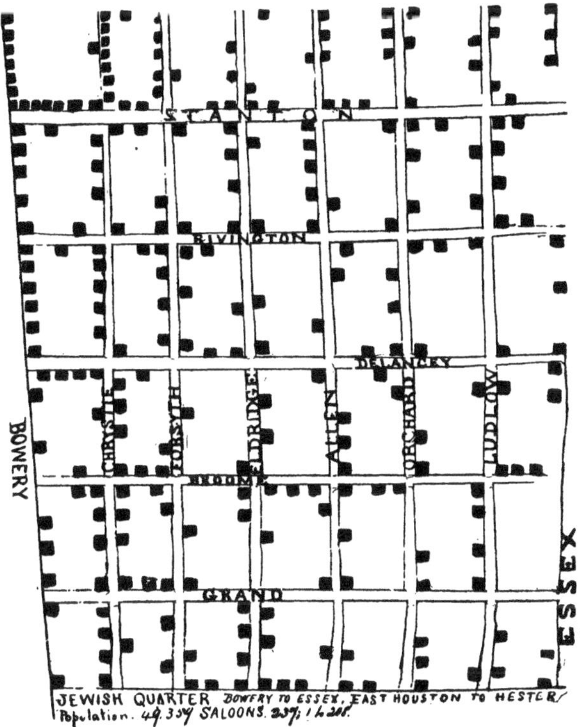


Comparative Map Showing Saloons.

and by the management of Captain Devery. It was the ground upon which the Society for the Prevention of Crime worked steadily, until by its revelations of official corruption and rottenness there, protected by the departments of the City, it caused the appointment of the Lexow Committee and its exposure of the general criminality of the departments which it investigated. The condition of the Eleventh Precinct, under the captaincy of Devery, was the cause of the Lexow investigation, and the

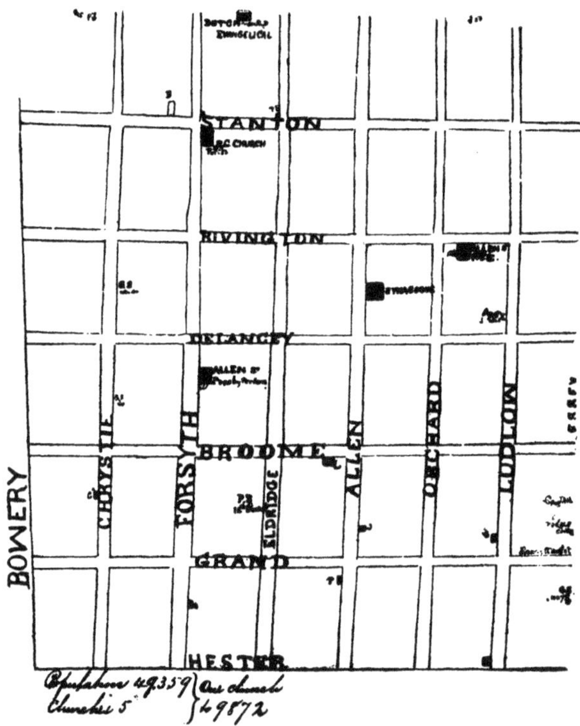


Comparative Map Showing Churches.

principal cause of the overthrow of Tammany Hall in 1894. Its streets were dotted with disreputable saloons and disorderly houses, which were carried on without concealment and in open defiance of law and decency, and the gang in Essex Street fattened on the proceeds of rampant and unconcealed crime. The organization at the center of the Eleventh Precinct was held together by the protection which it obtained through the corrupt agencies that were in operation all over the precinct, and that bound the unfortunate inhabitants in a serfdom as galling and complete, under the Stars and Stripes, as ever it was under Russia's Cross. The picnics of the gang were hilarious affairs, and turned immense treasure directly into their strong box, because every one of the large number of persons engaged in illegitimate operations was compelled to buy tickets at five dollars apiece, in order to stand right with the Royal Court.

Let us now exhibit an important memento of those days; to wit, an advertising card of the great picnic of 1894, which occurred in the midst of the investigation:

*GRAND* *ANNUAL*

OUTING

OF THE

**MAX HOCHSTIM ASSOCIATION,**

TO

DONNELLY'S BOULEVARD HOTEL,

COLLEGE POINT, LONG ISLAND,

*MONDAY, AUGUST 6th, 1894.*

**Steamer leaves foot of Broome St., East River, at Nine O'Clock, A. M., sharp.**

**TICKETS,** **FIVE DOLLARS.**

BERNARD (BARNEY) ROURKE, *President.*
Hon. T. D. Sullivan (Dry Dollar), *Vice-Pres.*
Fred. J. Seelig, *Vice-President.*
E. J. Sparenberg, *Vice-President.*
Martin Engel, *Treasurer.*
Julius Simon, *Financial Secretary.*
Benson M. Levy, *Recording Secretary.*
Aaron Herzberg, *Corresponding Secretary.*
John J. Driscoll, *Sergeant-at-Arms.*
Wm. Hofer, *Sergeant-at-Arms.*

CHARLES SMITH (THE SILVER DOLLAR), *Chairman Arrangements.*

Hon. P. J. Keenan,
Hon. Joseph Koch,
Hon. P. J. Scully,
Hon. H. M. Goldfogle,
Hon. John F. Ahearn,
Hon. Geo. Kraus,
Hon. S. D. Rosenthal,
Hon. J. E. Brodsky,
Hon. Jacob Mittnacht,
Hon. Edward A. Eiseman,
Hon. Christian Goetz,
Hon. Samuel J. Foley,
Hon. William Clancey,
Hon. Philip Wissig,
Hon. Philip Benjamin,
Hon. Joseph Dunn.

Edward Miller,
Nathan Miller,
Henry J. Goldsmith,
Louis Green,
Chas. Engel,
Harry Rosenthal,
Chas. Wolfman,
Bennie Spanier,
Adolph Silverstein,
Josh Cooper,
Morris Cooper,
Israel Goldstein,
A. Hanover,
Timothy J. Sullivan (No Dollar),
Chas. L. Feinberg,
George Dauer,
Samuel Wolkenberg,
A. Lotary,
John Burke,
Samuel Swartz,
Edward Lotary,
Max Greenfield,
Sam Klatsko,
Max B. Engel,
Sol. Peyser,
S. Shinkman,
George Greenberg,
David Katz,
Abe Weiss,
Barney Simon,
David Gureran,
Adolph Frish,
Herman Sacharine,
Philip Hofer,
Louis Shaffer,
Wm. I. Leavey,
Edward Butler,
Walter Keech,
Hyman Sugar,
Jos. J. Colligan,
E. Beyer,
S. Hapner,
James McManus,
Chas. Hefner,
Morris Isaacs,

Sam. Engel,
Max Berman,
Abe Miller,
Henry H. Swartz,
Henry Loewey,
David Benjamin,
John Frederick,
Oliver F. Washburn,
Chas. Solomon,
S. Rinaldo,
J. Pomeranz,
Anton Smith,
Issy Putter,
Morris Bruckman,
Abe Lent,
Louis Pilzer,
Jacob Pilzer,
Jos. Ecker,
Louis Ullman,
Max Tischler,
Joseph Segall,
Jacob Blum,
Philip Feldman,
Chas. Kramer,
Abe Fink,
Adolph Schleisinger.

NATHAN S. LEVY, *Chairman Reception Committee.*

Morris Swabinger,
Harry Abrams,
Morris Swartz,
Louis Rothstein,
M. Solomon,
Chas. Wernberg,
Paul McCarty,
Jacob Stiller,
A. Baum,
John Baker,
Adolph Krumholz,
B. J. McCann,
Louis Oberman,
Nathan Neuman,
Samuel Schweit,
M. Feldmans,
Jacob Hertz,
Israel Perlidick,
Samuel Erller,
Wolf Brod,
Max Karp,
Chas. Weber,
Barney Weber,
I. Smith,
Morris Klein,
H. M. Brodsky,
Frank Malizia,
Francis DeKanis,
Weinstein Kalish,
Sol. Rosensweig,
Jacob Heller,
David Kernheiser,
John Needles,
Samuel Dunklebum,
Patrick O'Brien,
William Ackerson,
Richard Ackerson,
Joseph Seelig,
Michael Coleman,
M. Yuckman,
Isaac Fuchs,
Louis Marx,
Jacob Wolf,
Richard Losier,
John Stiger,
John Leipziger,
Michael Cohen,
Albert Seaman.

The Association will assemble at Headquarters, Number 47 Delancey Street, at eight o'clock A.M. sharp, and march in a body to the boat.

A number of the gentlemen whose names appeared in the heading of the card disclaimed any connection with the association. They were Philip Wissig, John F. Ahearn, H. M. Goldfogle, P. J. Scully, John E. Brodsky, Joseph Koch, P. J. Keenan, Samuel J. Foley; nevertheless the cards remained prominently displayed all through the Tenth Ward without interference, and the brothel-keepers were impressed accordingly with the power of Smith, Hochstim and Engel.

It will be seen that on it are the names of some men who are prominent in local politics, and quite a number who prefix "Honorable" to their names, but those who are familiar with Tenth Ward affairs, and who run their eyes over the list of peculiar names that follow, will wonder at the audacity and the disregard of public opinion which grouped those names together. We have the record of a large number of these worthies, some of them pimps, gamblers, thugs, fighters and dive-keepers, representing undoubtedly the ruling power of this great district; and it is enough to fill a true New Yorker with indignation, and with shame at his own supineness, which so long contributed to the support of the oppressive and corrupt power that ruled the Eleventh Precinct, and made it not only a shame to free America but a blot on civilization. Many a poor foreigner left the oppressions of Russia and Poland, his heart beating at the thought of free America, and, when he settled down here, found that the blue-coated representatives of government, and those who exercised judicial power, were not only oppressors but robbers. While we wondered at the growth of anarchy, and heaped our condemnation upon anarchists, and filled our hearts with wrath toward those rapidly-growing companies of foreigners who expressed their hatred of all government, including our own, our local and official representatives, who, in their uniforms and official characters embodied the Constitution and all American institutions, by their villainous conduct were filling the common people of the ward with a just resentment and a just hatred of a government which was so distinctly and plainly wicked and oppressive. It was a great thing for this district and for New York, as a City, when the organized power of this combination of robbers was broken and the ignorant foreigners of the district were shown how to defeat their oppressors, were led and inspired in their successful movement, and were brought into understanding and sympathy with the elements of truth and justice that reside in the mass of our citizens.

Walhalla Hall, at Orchard Street near Grand Street, is the best known public gathering place in all New Israel. There public meetings are held, strikes are organized and managed, conventions manipulated, and marriages are celebrated. Balls and dances attract the gay youngsters of every class, style and description. Some of the associations which have had their "grand annual receptions" there, this year, are "The East Side Dramatic and Pleasure Association," "The Pete Hill

Association," "The East Side Crashers," "The Lady Liberties of the Fourth Ward," "The Bowery Indians," "The Crescent Coterie," "The Lady Flashers," and "The Jolly 48." Recently a ball was given by "The Eothens," a literary, dramatic, social and dancing club, of which Reddy McDevitt is president. According to a veracious account of the affair—

"Daisy Gorona, a pretty, black-eyed Italian, who dances with the grace which most of her countrywomen exhibit, was the belle of the ball. Her father is a butcher, whose shop is in Baxter Street. Her 'steady' is Jim Clarke, who is trying to be a conductor on the Third Avenue cable line. James Sullivan, who says he is a driver, and who gives his residence as Number 19 Delancey Street, was a guest at the ball, and his fancy was taken by the grace and bright eyes of Miss Daisy. He was dressed in the style most approved by the Bowery tailors, and he found favor in Daisy's eyes. The ball went along harmoniously till midnight. Then President McDevitt mounted a beer keg which lay in one corner of the room, and made the ceiling echo with his shout for order. 'Now's de time,' he cried 'now's de time fer de prize spieling. De Eothen Club gives a box of cigars to de best gent spieler and a fan ter de best lady spieler. I'm de judge. De band will please play "My Pearl is a Bowery Girl."' A rush for partners immediately followed. As Daisy Gorona was admittedly the best dancer in the hall, ten or twelve men started on the run to claim her hand for the dance. Jim Clarke, her 'steady,' thinking the ice cream he intended to buy for her this summer pledged her to him, was a laggard, and Sullivan, the loud-trousered guest, won the girl. Moreover, he won the prize, for he and Daisy 'outspieled 'em all.' But President McDevitt's award did not meet with approval. In a moment fists were flying. 'Get on out of here!' shouted the president. 'Do your fighting in the street!' One man was thrown downstairs, and the rest followed. The sidewalk was a mass of fighting men when Acting-captain Hogan and Detectives Cohen and Monahan, of the Eldridge Street station, approached. Suddenly Clarke yelled that he had been stabbed, and the blood trickled down his arm from a wound made by a pocket-knife. The crowd was so thick that it was impossible to tell who the assailant was, and the police were unable to make an arrest. Sullivan remained on the outskirts of the crowd and took no part in the fight. His attention was soon attracted by the handsome diamond pin, the pride of the Eldridge Street station, which reposed in Detective Monahan's necktie. He edged his way to the policeman's side and his hand softly grasped the diamond. It was fastened by a small gold chain, however, and did not respond to the

The Tough Couple.

touch. Monahan paid no attention to the attempt at robbery, and Sullivan grasped the tie in his left hand and tried to break the chain. Then the policeman's arms were around him and he was placed under arrest. In his pockets were found a gold watch, which had evidently been wrenched from a chain, and $110. At the station he was recognized as an old-time pickpocket, and he was held for trial in $1,000 bail in the Essex Market Police Court. As Sullivan was being led away, Daisy Gorona came out of the hall and heard the story of the arrest. 'Only a pickpocket,' said she, 'and I t'ought he was a swell.' Then she caught sight of Clarke, who was nursing his bleeding arm. She ran up and printed a kiss on his cheek, with the remark: 'My "steady" is the best, after all.' This ended the ball."

The ball of the "Soup Greens" was another flamboyant affair. Among those present were President Mollony, Vice-president Nolan, Bug Connors and Katie Riley; Limpy Farrell and Maggie Nolan; some members of the Lady Barker's Association; Mixed-ale Marty Donahue, with Mary Ellen Hogan, Slimmy Maher and Slob Cullen; and they danced until daybreak.

Pickpockets and petty thieves resort to Walhalla Hall.

The only rival of Walhalla Hall is New Irving Hall, at 214 Broome Street. This news item will show its claims.

"Five members of the William J. Sullivan Association—Duck Reardon, Chuck Connors of the Fourth Ward, George Leary, Jerry Leary and Arthur Hassett—and Mike Walsh, a tugboat hand, were arrested by Captain Thompson and detectives of the Oak Street Police Station yesterday.

"The Cherry Hill gang announced that they would appear in evening clothes at the Sullivan ball in New Irving Hall to-night, and the five men named, representing the Batavia Street gang, cast about for means to parallel this display. They were all broke but Reardon, and his assets wouldn't guarantee evening clothes for the crowd. In this extremity, Vice-president Hassett and George Leary, assistant sergeant-at-arms of the Sullivan Association, captured a watch from Herman Segal's jewelry shop at 58 New Chambers Street, and raffled it off on Saturday evening in Coyne's saloon, 1 James Street. Jerry Leary threw forty-five and took the watch. Then it was found that the proceeds of the raffle were insufficient to hire the desired flash clothes, and the whole gang adjourned to Segal's shop at 5 o'clock yesterday morning. A front window was smashed, and forty four gold rings, worth from $3 to $45 each, were taken. Segal reported the robbery, and Captain Thompson, with Detectives Galvin, Mullarkey, Gilhooly, Barlow, McCrary and Touwsina captured the members of the Sullivan Association, and Walsh, who had bought one of the rings from Reardon. The prisoners were brought before Magistrate Cornell in the Center Street Police Court this morning. There it appeared that the particular Chuck

Connors under arrest was not the only celebrated Chuck of Bowery and Chinatown fame and song, but quite another Chuck, an amateur pugilist over in the Fourth Ward, and not related to his famous namesake. George Leary of 43 Market Street, who stole the watch, was held in $300 to answer. Duck Reardon, the bogus Chuck Connors, Walsh, the tugboat man, and Vice-president Hassett, were held in $1,000 bail for examination. Jerry Leary, who threw forty-five and won the watch, was released last night by Captain Thompson, as no charge could be made against him."

New Irving Hall is much used by the Bowery and Five Points' tough citizens for their balls.

The ball of the Robert F. O'Toole Association is a sample. It occurred on December 3, and lasted until five o'clock in the morning of December 4. O'Toole is Mike Callahan's bartender; so the combined efforts of the Callahans, the Lavelles, Chuck Connors and the Chinatown girls, went in to make the ball a success.

The ball now anxiously awaited is that of the "Limburger Roarers," announced for January 30.

These are types of the frequenters of the East Side balls: Miss Josephine Irving is the "belle" of the "Lady Locusts," and "Nigger Joe" and Samuel Clark are rivals for the privilege of being her "steady." "Nigger Joe" is an Italian athlete and boxer, while Clark is simply an ordinary tough. Josephine's beauty and the rivalry of Joe and Sam broke up the recent ball of the "Lady Locusts" and landed the participants in jail. Clark told the judge, "It was me love for Josephine that drove me to bust up the ball."

The politics of the Tenth Ward were always ruddy, and many have been the exciting and the humorous campaign experiences. In the recent campaign, General Michael Kerwin and Charles H. Murray, the ex-police commissioners, led a valiant McKinley and Hobart night parade, in which a big man named McGillicuddy was very conspicuous as the custodian of the fireworks. When they reached the Tenth Ward Athletic Club in Canal Street, and the band was doing its cheerful best, a mighty howl burst from the billowy depths of McGillicuddy (according to a veracious reporter):

"Holy smoke! I'll be burned alive! Wow! Put me out! Me pockets is full o' red fire 'n rockets 'n Romin candles. Fer hev'n's sake put me out. Me leg's afire 'n me pockets is full o' skyrockets. Fur heav'n's sake ketch me before I go up! Me panse is afire, and they is dynamite in me close."

A policeman rushed through the crowd that was waiting to see a human skyrocket, knocked Michael down, rolled him a few times in the gutter, and then stood him up, a sorry picture, in a one-legged pair of trousers and with a pained expression on his face. Kind friends removed from Michael's pockets three rockets, four packages of red fire, a dozen Roman candles and a few pinwheels. As he walked away he muttered: "They'll pay dear fur me vote this year." Then the parade started again, and for half a block there wasn't the least sign of trouble. But somebody who didn't know a thing about the aiming of skyrockets began to shoot. General Michael Kerwin, who was riding a horse, fell on its neck and escaped, but "Sam" the butcher was not so fortunate. The rocket struck his hat. "I'm killet deadt," he screamed, as his silk head-gear went sailing through the window of a house across the street. Not a thing happened for another half block. Then Moe Gardner, the butcher, stopped his horse and reached to shake hands with his friend "Ike" Butler, the butcher. Moe and his horse were enemies, apparently, and so Moe landed on the pavement. Patrick McShike, the peddler, had a restive steed that kicked over the cart of an Italian, who swore he would have money or a life; a long argument followed, and a policeman settled it. The parade then went on, and at last it reached the reviewing stand at the rooms of the Lincoln League, 272 Grand Street. Commissioner Murray was there, the biggest man of the lot, but he could see little, because red fire on slates at every window was sending dense smoke into the room.

A gayly decked bicycle came to grief in front of the reviewers, a car was stalled, there were three fights, a man asked for three cheers for Bryan and was carried home, and, as a butcher in blood-stained frock went by, somebody cried: "Three cheers for 'Tim' Campbell."

Among the alien spellbinders who occasionally stray into these wards to charm Yiddish votes into Tammany columns, is the Irish barrister Tommy Nolan, a good-natured giant, beside whose charming tongue-treacle the honeyed words of a Brady would seem like glucose. Here is a report of his great speech for William J. Bryan:

" 'Friends and fellow Democrats, draw around. Draw around and hear the truth. Let us consider the silver question, bearing in mind the advice of the past.

" 'If young folks would mind
What old folks would say,
When danger threatened
They would run away.

" 'And again—we are threatened with danger today. Let us consider what course was pursued by the ancient peoples. From Thucydides and Tacitus, and many other historians, we learn that the Athenians and Posterians, to say nothing of the Phœnicians and Egyptians, used silver coins. The ancients were in favor of free silver, and so am I. (Great applause.) And, mind you, I'm speaking intelligently now. Let us not be deluded by the emanations from the paraphernalia of deception.'

"'Hurrah! Hurrah for the Counselor!' yelled the audience. 'No, no!' said Mr. Nolan, modestly. 'Let us hurrah for our candidates.

"'Bryan Boru
And Sewell, too!

"'That's my motto and I'm proud of it. Let me tell you of the great wrong that was perpetrated upon defenseless silver. In 1783—' Here Mr. Nolan stopped, walked across the platform, poured about a pint of ice-water into a glass and slowly drank it. In sheer good nature he winked at the audience, thus showing that ice-water is his only tipple—perhaps. 'And again,' he resumed. 'As I was saying, in 1873—'—'You said 1783, Tom,' yelled a voice.—'What matter?' asked the Counselor. 'What differs a matter of ninety years in the great onward and irresistible march of the problem of free silver? Come, answer me that, now!' 'Hooray!' roared the crowd. 'Our enemies,' cried the orator, 'are in no better position to answer our arguments than a fish out of water. They can't trust themselves to—'

"'What's the matter with the Counselor? Hooray!' yelled the audience. Thus did the orator play upon their sensibilities as he chose."

Mr. Nolan is a great hand to try "accident cases." John M. Scribner, with a Gibraltar forehead and head as smooth as an ostrich egg, representing the Dry Dock Railway Company, was his antagonist in such a case. Nolan went on to describe the accident and the physical injuries of his client:

"Gintlemin," said he, "ye must undershtand how this sad accident happened to my unfortunate client. The sand car was going around the curve. Me

COUNSELOR NOLAN.

poor client was shoveling the sand into the hopper. The dhriver shouts 'Hould on!'—but phwat would he hould on—the air? He was pitched out into the shtreet, and landed on his head, and likewise he bushted his thracheal gland. Now, gintlemin, this thracheal gland is a very important iliment in the process of digistion, and his digistion has been ruin'd iver since the fateful day. But, gintlemin, that was not the worsht of it. He fell on his poor head, and the injoory—how can I describe it? Ah, friend Schribner, yer have a beautiful head, will ye lind me the loan of it, while I diagramate the awful injoory upon it?" He reached out his great gentle hand—Scribner angrily retreated, the jury and the spectators "snickered," and he said: "Ah, niver mind, friend Schribner isn't willing—sure I am not so great a man. I didn't defind Jake Sharp, who put up the money for the boodle aldermen."

Speaking of eloquent lawyers may we be pardoned for digressing long enough to recount a sweet story about the lawyers Choate and Lauterbach? They had worked together on a case. When they won it, they consulted about the fee. Lauterbach suggested five hundred dollars apiece. Choate said "Leave it to me." Some time afterward Choate sent for Lauterbach and handed him a check for one thousand dollars as his portion of the fee. Lauterbach was astonished, then recovered and said: "Choate! Choate! Almost thou persuadest me to be a Christian."

The young Jewish lawyers of this district, who may be seen about the two local courts, buzzing like flies at a meat shop, don't need to take lessons from Choate or Lauterbach in the charging and collecting of fees, and the neophyte among them could whip the eminent lawyers together, at the Essex Market or the Clinton Street Court.

There was a little Irish judge who once got himself elected to the justiceship in this district. He was a good lawyer, a humane man, and very popular throughout the Ward, which, considering its prevailing nationality, seems strange; but he justified the confidence of his Semitic friends by marrying the sister of the principal practitioner in his Court, a wealthy Hebrew widow. This was an uncommon, but a happy mating, and it proved to be all that was hoped by the friends of the contracting parties, and opened the way to higher honors for the thrifty little judge.

The term "shyster" had its origin in the Essex Market Police Court fifty years ago, when Justice Osborne dispensed (with) justice. There was a Clinton Street lawyer named Scheuster, whose practices were reprehensible and were obnoxious to the judge, and when another lawyer played a mean trick the judge would call it "Scheuster practice." Soon those lawyers who emulated him were called "shysters."

There are three hundred synagogues in New Israel, and in them all, the Talmud is read three times a day. In many of them schools are maintained for teaching the children in the Hebrew tongue, and occasionally some effort is made to familiarize the people with the English language, though their efforts in that direction lead to some strange pronouncing and some peculiar notions concerning things in general. The "chedars" or boys' schools are conducted as of old. The boys read one after the other at top pitch and break-neck speed and without a pause, and the noise of the performance can be heard in the street.

"No customs of the Polish Jews are more picturesquely strange than those concerning death. The body is put on the floor and covered with a sheet. Candles are placed in a semi-circle around the head, and all the looking-glasses in the room are covered up, so that the corpse may not be reflected in them. Should the white form on the floor be shown in a mirror it would bode ill. Two watchers, women or men, according to the sex of the dead, stay by the body, never leaving the room for an instant. This is to guard against evil spirits. Watching over the dead being a toilsome task when it must be continued over forty-eight hours, there are professional watchers who drive a good trade for small fees.

"On the day of the burial the body is curiously clothed. Be it of man or woman, the grave clothes are alike, a single garment of white. It is really nothing more than a great sack, with two holes for the arms, pulled on over the head and tied at the feet, completely incasing the body. Over each arm a smaller sack is slipped and tied below the finger-tips. The corpse is then placed in a coffin made of six plain boards, unpainted, unlined, without a single ornament. Under the head a pillow of earth is laid. Just before the coffin is closed there comes the ceremony of breaking a plate, three of the pieces of which are laid with reverence on that part of the sack that covers the head, two just over the eyes, the third over the mouth.

"This is the tradition which explains the custom: The Polish Jews believe that some day in the ages to come all the sons of Israel, dead and alive, will be summoned to Jerusalem to refound the city and to live there in eternal bliss. The dead will travel, so the tradition runs, through the earth in a straight line from their graves. Some of them will have been buried for thousands of years, their bodies will have long since become dust, and yet it is part of the Promise that they shall appear at Jerusalem the New as they were on earth. The bits of broken plate are to indicate their features and to aid the God of Israel in recreating their bodies.

"Quite as strange are the mourning customs. A widow, widower, father or son, must mourn seven days after the funeral, sitting immovably on a low stool or on a pillow on the floor, and barefooted. No work can be done, nothing of any sort, during these seven days, and the garments must be rent (this injunction is generally carried out by the Jews of this country by tearing out the buttonhole of a coat) and ashes must be sprinkled on the shoulders.

"An Orthodox Polish Jew offers up prayer three times a day (two hours in all) continually during his life.

"A younger brother is expected to marry the widow of the elder, as in Old Testament times. It is seldom among the Orthodox that this is not observed. The man may, however, avoid it by 'absolving' the woman, or releasing her. He goes to her house, and in the presence of ten witnesses (ten is the necessary number among these people in matters of religious law, or of vital importance, ten making a synagogue 'quorum'), puts ashes on her head and takes off her slipper or shoe. The woman is then free to marry as she will.

"At weddings the most curious rite is the 'marseltoff,' or the 'congratulations' to the newly wedded pair. Each guest takes a piece of crockery in his hands (a stock of old and cracked cups, saucers and plates has been laid in), and, raising his arms over his head, smashes it down on the floor with the cry already given. The din is prodigious, but no Polish Jewish couple is well started in life without it. Of course, if the ceremony takes place in a synagogue, these congratulations are left until the bride and bridegroom have entered their new home, which they do immediately. Another custom of the ceremony is for the bride to drink out of the same cup as her husband; and there is also the rule that on the day of their marriage both contracting parties shall eat nothing. The ceremony generally takes place in the evening, and this makes necessary a fast of twenty-four hours.

"In the matter of keeping their Sabbath these Hebrews are rigid according to the full letter of the law. As to the spirit of it, there are some curious evasions. The law and their customs make strange provisions. No work of any kind may be done on the Jewish Sabbath; nothing must be cooked, nothing can be carried in the pockets, not even a hand·kerchief. If it is absolutely necessary for a man to take a handkerchief with him, the only way allowable is for him to tie it about his wrist. Letters or telegrams cannot be received or opened on this day, and no fires can be lighted. Nor can a man or a woman touch money for any purpose whatever. It is said that if an Orthodox Polish Jew, walking along the street on the Sabbath, should see a piece of money on the sidewalk he would not dare stoop and pick it up.

"The evasions practiced by some of these people are shrewd in the extreme. They will not open a letter or a telegram themselves on the Sabbath, but they will get some Christian to do it for them, and have him read the contents aloud. They will not touch a piece of money, but, laying some on a convenient bureau Friday afternoon, they will be able to push the coins needed on a large knife blade, and in this way hand them over. They would not, under any circumstances, do work about their rooms on the Seventh Day, but they argue to themselves that it is not wrong to get others to do it for them. There are a number of Italians who make a good living by doing work on the Sabbath for the Polish Jews. Each of these Italians has arrangements with from twenty to thirty of these families, and for a few cents per household, visits each several times during Saturday, building fires and performing other domestic labors.

"Few of the women can read, though the girls are becoming educated in the public schools. The drag-net is too complete for them to escape. Each house is ruled over in a patriarchal fashion by the father, who has absolute control over the marriages of his children. There is a time in the year when the Jewish head of the family puts on all his traditional dignity and authority. It comes in the spring, and for this occasion each household has a miniature throne of chairs and pillows built up, on which, clad in a long, white robe, sits the father."—"Tribune."

At accouchements, all the old women of the neighborhood gather in the room, and when the mother begins to express her feelings, they turn their faces to the wall, and knock their foreheads forcibly against it, crying in chorus, Ja-wohl! Ja-wohl! Ja-wohl! until all is over. The eighth day rite is performed on infants in the presence of the whole family and its friends, and frequently curious tricks of magic are exhibited to interest and amuse the company.

The feast of Tabernacles is widely observed. Little booths are built in backyards, and there the families eat their meals, and the old men pore over their sacred books. The tops of the booths are covered lightly with boughs, and if the weather is inclement there is lack of comfort, but they persist nevertheless in their devout observances.

The feast of lights is celebrated during eight

days. Hanuka, as it is called, commemorates the dedication of the second temple at Jerusalem, 2,248 years ago. There is a sunrise service in the synagogues, at which "Muos Schur Jeshuossi" (the promise of the Messiah) is chanted. This is chanted again at evening about the supper table, and then colored candles (Hanuka lichtshee) are lighted, and the children's fun begins. It is a jolly holiday. Its greeting is "Gut Jontif."

The "cleaning time" of Passover is an institution that breaks the hearts of the street cleaners. Said an inspector: "I had rather undertake to keep clean any three other districts in town. We carted off over three thousand mattresses, to say nothing of all the broken pots, saucepans and cooking utensils that you can imagine. Lounges there were without number, and old sofas, settees and chairs. We used one hundred and five carts. It went on for eight days. On Thursday night, at eight o'clock, though we had worked hard, two streets remained untouched. I would rather contend with two big snowstorms than this avalanche of rubbish. A man was going through Norfolk Street and was astonished at being overwhelmed with a mattress thrown from a window. These mattresses are so filthy that even the Italians will not take them."

### Incidents of Daily Life in New Israel.

"THEY WERE TOO FAT TO PASS.

"Sholem Rudman and Mrs. Mary Powers both live at 52 Jefferson Street. Both are extremely stout and the stairways in the house are narrow. Mrs. Powers was coming down the stairs with a pitcher. Rudman was on his way up with a basket of coal. They met half way. 'Go back, Mrs. Powers,' said Rudman, 'I have got a bigger load than you.' 'You back down,' said Mrs. Powers. 'I won't,' replied Rudman. 'You are no gentleman, or you would back down and give a lady like me the right of way,' said Mrs. Powers. Then they tried to pass. The pitcher was broken, the coal was spilled, and the two combatants were wedged together in the hallway. The tenants extricated them. Rudman was arrested and fined."

"A cry of fire caused a panic among six hundred men and women of the congregation Abshe Skoller, during the holding of Jewish New Year's services in Pollack Hall, at Number 174 Allen Street. Although the excitement lasted only a minute, a serious loss of life probably would have resulted had it not been for the presence of mind of Policeman Gick, of the City Hall Station. He jumped between the frightened people and the stairway and compelled the congregation to return to their seats. Little Sallie Rusack, the eight-year-old daughter of one of the officers of the congregation, was the innocent cause of the trouble. She and her four-year-old brother Joseph sat on the window sill. The other window sills were crowded with children, and even the stairway was packed with the little ones. Sallie slipped and fell to the floor. Her brother shouted:

'Oh, papa! mamma! Sallie has fallen out of the window!' Praying ceased instantly. All jumped to their feet. A woman shouted 'Fire!' threw up her arms and fainted. Then there was a wild rush for the stairs. Policeman Gick saw them coming. He drew his club and cried, 'There's no fire! youse people will all be killed if you try to get out at the same time. Git back there.' The people returned, trembling, to their seats. The singing was resumed and the excitement was over."

"What is that?" said Judge Goldfogle in the Clinton Street Court Monday, as a stench came up the stairs leading to the court-room. "Fresh air! Open the windows!" But the stench became denser, and it was found to proceed from Moses Borachek, a heavy man, with a gold watch-chain on his waistcoat, who was coming up the stairs as a witness. As Borachek stood before the judge the latter lighted a strong cigar and asked his name. When he learned it, he said: "The idea of a man with a gold watch being as dirty as you are. I wouldn't let you kiss the Bible for a thousand dollars. Get out, and don't show yourself until you are presentable." Yesterday the judge was amazed when a man in a new suit, clean linen and a broad smile said, "I'm Borachek." "Well," said the judge, "that's what you should have done yesterday. Go on with the case."

The firebugs form a definite feature of life on the East Side. Many of the miserable Poles and

Russians make a business of effecting insurance and then setting fire to their stores and homes, and defrauding the insurance companies, regardless of danger to human life. For several years past there has been a relentless warfare against these men by the insurance companies and the district-attorney's office; and Vernon M. Davis has made a splendid reputation by his earnest, patient and able prosecutions, which have broken up several organized bands and placed some of the conspirators in State Prison on life sentences. This is a confession made in the case of Isaac Zuker, the wealthy Hebrew merchant, who, it was charged, employed "mechanics" to set fires at twenty-five dollars each, regardless of the fact that men, women and children of his own race lived and slept in the buildings where he had his stores:

"Gustave Myers, on the advice of his attorney, Benjamin Steinhart, of Howe & Hummel, made a detailed statement of Zuker's fire on Division Street. Myers said that about six months previous to the fire—some time in July, 1891—he had a talk with Zuker in the latter's store at Number 264 Division Street. Said Zuker: 'I am going to burn this shanty down; if I don't, the Health Board will condemn it. I am going to make a fire in this little back room. I will take the plastering off so the fire can get into Blum's place, next door. Blum's shanty must come down, too. I have made a deal with Blum. He has a thousand dollar insurance in the German-American Fire Insurance Company.'

Myers testified that Zuker then showed him how easy it was to build a fire. 'We had another talk about the job,' Myers testified, 'and Zuker said to me: "I am going to get twenty gallons of kerosene oil and move the gas-meter out here. Both together will bring this shanty down and cover up our tracks. I am going to move my family out." About three weeks later, Zuker's family moved out. We talked again about the fire, and I asked him how he was going to keep people from seeing the kerosene oil. He showed me a tub and a small barrel, and said he was going to build a partition so people could not see in the back room. He said the business had to be done before January. I asked him if he was going to do the job himself. "No," he replied, "because the people around here know me too well. I am going to get Schoenholz to do it for twenty-five dollars. I guess he's safe."' Schoenholz is serving a sentence of forty-eight years in Sing Sing. The prosecution alleged that Zuker was at the head of the organized gang of incendiaries who fleeced insurance companies.

"Continuing, Myers said: 'The night of the fire, January 4, 1892, I met Zuker on Grand Street. He was excited, and told me the fire was coming off that night. He wanted me to go up to see what was the matter with Schoenholz. He was afraid something had happened and was very nervous. "Go up and see Schoenholz," he urged. "He's in Division Street, at my house. Get the key of the store from him.'' I told Zuker I wouldn't go because the thing might explode while I was around. As people knew me so well, I might be suspected. As we walked up Grand Street Zuker said: "I don't hear the engines. If that thing don't go off and they find the kerosene in there, I'll have to get out of New York.'' When we got to Attorney Street, we heard the engines, and saw the smoke, but Zuker thought there was more smoke than fire, and was afraid there was not much damage. At Ridge and Montgomery Streets we saw Schoenholz talking to a man named Louis Warschauer. Zuker wanted me to go over to see Schoenholz, but I refused, and left him and went home.' ''

During the last four years Mr. Davis has convicted seventeen firebugs. The first was Samuel Mantol, convicted May 25, 1892, and sentenced to imprisonment for nine years and eleven months. Then followed these convictions:

John Buchholz, convicted August 11, 1892, sentenced to twelve years and six months' imprisonment.

Meyer H. Rothbaum, convicted November 3, 1892, sentenced to twelve years and five months' imprisonment.

Morris Isaacs, convicted March 29, 1894, sentenced to eight years' imprisonment.

Jacob Kaiser, convicted October 4, 1893, sentenced to seven years' imprisonment.

Ida Lieberman, convicted March 1, 1895, sentenced to six years and eight months' imprisonment.

Sarah Silbermeister, convicted January 25, 1895, sentenced to twenty-five years' imprisonment.

Max Grauer, convicted March 1, 1895, sentenced to thirty years' imprisonment.

Morris Schoenholz, convicted recently and sentenced to forty-eight years' imprisonment.

Adolph Hirschkopf, convicted recently and sentenced to life imprisonment.

Henry Gottlieb, recently convicted and sentenced to ten years' imprisonment.

Harriet M. Raisbeck, convicted recently and sentenced to one year and six months' imprisonment.

Louis Rothman, convicted recently and sentenced to fifteen years' imprisonment.

Isaac Zuker, convicted recently and sentenced to thirty-six years and six months' imprisonment.

Life was lost in the fires set by Schoenholz and Hirschkopf. These people and several others, who have not been apprehended, formed an organization of one nationality, whose business it was to make fires for the purpose of defrauding insurance companies. They set at least three hundred fires, many of them at night, and in tenement houses, located in the crowded district of New Israel. Zuker, the head of the combination, and who became quite wealthy by his operations, came to this country from Poland in 1878. He began his life in America as a peddler in front of 49 Vesey Street. He saved money and opened a little clothing store, which he set on fire. His success in that venture led him to form the combination which has been broken to pieces. The headquarters of this desperate conspiracy was at the saloon of "Old Man" Isaacs on the corner of Delancey and Suffolk Streets. Among the places in New Israel fired by these people were 25 Pitt Street, 424 Grand Street, 178 Canal Street, 264 Division Street, and 129 Suffolk Street where Lizzie Jaeger, a child of seven years, perished.

New revelations of this remarkable development of crime occur almost daily; and it now seems certain that the conspiracy includes many scores of members, operating in various cities. The opportunity to recover money on fraudulent insurances is the occasion of the cunning and ruthless villainy which these criminals have displayed. We are reminded of the writings of a Frenchman who made a sojourn in London some eighty years ago, and who had occasion to notice the practical operation of fire insurance then coming into use. He wrote:

"Fire! fire! fire!—Such was the frightful cry which about midnight aroused me from my bed just as I was going to get into it. I threw on my gown in haste, and ran into my little saloon, which looked into the street, where I saw the flames issuing with violence through the windows of a neighboring house. The proprietor of the house on the other side of the one in which I lodged—though he had comparatively nothing to fear, as he was further from the fire—was nevertheless very busily engaged in removing his furniture; and I could not conceive the reason of the tranquillity which reigned in our own dwelling. 'These good people are asleep,' thought I, 'or they are not acquainted with the truth that—Tua res agitur partes cum proximus ardet.' I thought I must sound the alarm; and accordingly played one after the other the two bells with which my room was furnished. My hostess ran up immediately, and asked in the most calm and tranquil tone—'What do you want, sir?'—'Why, to advertise you of the danger which threatens your house. Don't you see the fire is in the next house?'—'Oh! is that all! We knew that before. My husband and myself had not gone to bed. You had better pack your things in your trunk; for it is possible that the fire will be communicated to this house. It sometimes consumes three or four before they can get it under.'—'But what means the tranquillity in which I see you? Why don't you take yourself the good counsel which you offer me?'—'Oh! I have nothing to fear. You see by the sign over the window that my house is insured. It is very old; and if it is burned they will pay me; so I run no risk.'—'That is very well for the house. But your furniture?'—'Is insured too. I am in no uneasiness. I have only prepared a little packet of linen, which we shall carry out at the last moment.'—'All London is insured then?'—'Yes; and life too. You can get yourself insured for sixty or sixty-five years;

and if you die before that age, the contracted sum will be paid to your heirs.' At this moment the rafters of the burning house fell in, and the fire seemed to acquire a new force. 'I hope nobody has perished!' exclaimed I.—'No,' she said. 'Do you see that large man in an overcoat, with arms crossed, leaning against the wall of the other side of the street, in front of the house which is on fire? It is the owner. I see close by his wife, his three infants, and his servant, who were the sole occupants of the house.'—'I need not ask you whether his house is insured; his air of tranquillity convinces me of that. He reminds me of an ancient philosopher, who warmed his hands over the burning ruins of his house saying, it was the last service which it could render him.' At length the fire was mastered. 'It is a fine thing, this insurance,' thought I, in returning to my bed; 'but it may be the cause of great mischief, by making the owners of houses less solicitous about fire, and less careful to take the proper measures to prevent it. Is it not possible, also, that villains may get their houses, their goods, and their merchandise insured, and then set them on fire with their own hands in order to receive the stipulated sum of insurance?' —In the morning I suggested this reflection to my hostess. But she answered that, in the first place, the crime was punished with death (about eighteen months before a man had been hanged for it); and that, on the other hand, after having given an insurance, the company causes your house, your furniture, and your goods to be estimated, and may renew that estimation as often as they please. This answer satisfied me but imperfectly; for the day after the valuation the insured might cause to disappear the best part of his furniture and goods; so that no estimation can completely prevent the rascality of which insurances are the occasions."

The original Jew seems to have been Asser Levy, whose name appears on the list of great citizens. He kept a tavern and was a butcher. In 1665 he and Arent Isaaczen lived in De Hoogh Straat. Some of his fellows were Abram Costa, Jacob Hendricks, Isaac Meza, one Melhado, and Abram Lucas. On September 12, 1685, the Common Council decided that no Jew could do any retail trade, though he might wholesale with the governor's permission; and on September 14, the Council refused to permit the public exercises of the Jewish religion. However, there was no interference with the observance of their rites in their homes, and in house-to-house gatherings. Their first regular service was held in 1696, when there were twenty families. Samuel Brown was rabbi. The first Jewish graveyard was started in 1728. In 1729 the first synagogue was opened on Mill Street near Beaver. It was attended by Spanish and Portuguese Jews. Its successor is the Congregation Shearith Israel (the Remnant of Israel), whose church is at 19th Street near Fifth Avenue. The second congregation was established on Crosby Street near Spring.

The biggest sight of New Israel is Hester Street. There are many little market-places, but that is the big market-place. On Fridays and on certain evenings a journey through that street is an experience never to be forgotten. There is no pen that can describe it, no pencil that can depict it, no Hungarian rhapsody or Wagnerian mystery that can re-

Going on the Roof to Bed.

A Favorite Spot.

produce its babel of symphonic and dissonant sounds, no panorama that can keep up with its shifting scenes. The stores cannot hold the goods, the sidewalks cannot accommodate the buyers, and the streets cannot contain the mass of carts that are pushed upon, into, and toward its asphalt pavement. The great thieves that once dominated the

43 AND 45 HESTER STREET.

New York, Vol. Three, p. 200.

street are gone; there is nothing to keep them, and no place for them to rest, and think, and hide and plan. Billy McGlory, the fiend, the king of dive keepers and the ruiner of an army of girls, once kept his Armory Hall at 158 Hester Street, but he is gone. Now the neighborhood is "Goose

A Courtship on the Roof.

Mrs. Cohen and her Baby.

Market." Russia, Poland and Hungary seem to have poured their Jews into this little street, and it is not America—it is hardly New York. In the busy blocks, every foot of available space is occupied by stores, stands, boxes and carts. The visitor may stand at one point and see without moving, not only a bewildering variety of stores, but sidewalk merchants and push-cart venders, who are selling and crying at once in their own jargon—bread, ribbons, meat, candles, fish, eggs, clothing, handkerchiefs, hats, shoes, matches, pins, poultry, onions, lemons, vegetables of all kinds, coal, wood, beans, rice, shoe-laces, buttons, sausages, candies, crockery, tin ware, notions. Soda water is one and two cents a glass, beer is three cents, whisky is five cents. Their motto is, "Poor quality, small prices, quick sales and many of them." At night the oil lamps flare and flicker, and fill the air with smoke. Such faces, such names, such voices, such sounds and smells, such intense haggling, bargaining and trading! There is more shouting than on Mulberry Street, and there is no laziness: all is animation and business. The amount of money invested by purchasers is small, for the people are poor. They live on the plainest and poorest provisions, and they crowd into small and unhealthy apartments. How they suffer in the torrid days of the summer! In winter they bundle up and huddle together.

Death in the Tenements.

Both summer and winter cause intense suffering

among the poor people of this ward. An instance of suffering in winter is the death of Louis Bressler in December. Pelham Street is full of sweat-shops. Bressler worked for Abraham Perlman, and Samuel

Pushed Out into the Cold but Came Back to Die.

Boloffsky. The night was very cold. The watchman heard a knock at the door, and looking out, saw Bressler's shivering form. He said, "For God's sake let me in. I'm so cold." The watchman pushed him out and went back to his stove.

An hour afterward he heard groans, and going out, he saw the man crouched on the stairs, but then his face was pale in death. The verdict was death from exhaustion, cold and lack of food. While the little group was looking at the body, Perlman and Boloffsky appeared. The policeman said, "Here's a dead man, do you know him?" Boloffsky bent over him and said, "Vhy, dat man vorks for me." The employer then found a piece of dirty cloth and wrapped up the body, and presently the dead-wagon carried it off. That was the end of it. In the same month Mrs. Cohen, of 162 Ridge Street, was arrested for selling matches without a license, and was fined five dollars by Magistrate Mott. She said her husband had deserted her and she was selling the matches to get a few pennies to buy bread, and that she did not have enough money to buy a license. She was hustled off to prison, but she made so great an outcry that one of the officers listened to her, and then it appeared that she had left at home, locked in her room, a baby eleven months old. The Magistrate permitted her to go with the policeman to get her baby, and sure enough they found it, crying with hunger. Mrs. Cohen and her baby had to serve five days in prison, one day for each dollar of the fine. Were they not entitled to a halving of the term? In the Fifth District Court, on Clinton Street near Grand Street, the dispossess cases of several wards come up. They are always heartrending, but are especially so in cold weather.

There are men whose thrift shines out in this mass of industrious people, and some of the Hester Street immigrants have grown quite wealthy. A conspicuous example is the Polander, Louis Krulewitch, who began life in New York as a peddler thirty-three years ago, and who now owns eighty-two houses, and is worth over $2,000,000. He is called the "East-side Crœsus."

Dispossessed.

On the northwest and southwest corners of Hester and Chrystie Streets are houses nearly a hundred years old. For fifty years they have been noted resorts for thieves and prostitutes. Among the former propriotors were Elias Randel and Jim McManus, who were quite famous in their day.

Number 64 Chrystie Street is kept by Jersey Jimmy. It has long been a notorious place, and its frequenters are a hard lot.

Crowded as Hester Street is, there is another spot in New Israel which has a denser population; indeed, it is called "the most crowded place on earth." It is "Bone Alley," in the block bounded by Houston, Willett, Pitt and Stanton Streets. The block contains sixty-three houses, three hundred and sixty-three families, and sixteen hundred

Some Glimpses of Bone Alley.

and fifty inhabitants, composed of Italians, Germans, Hungarians, Poles and Russians. On the block the death rate is 26.06 per cent; in the alley (containing one hundred families) it is 47.97 per cent. It is a dirty spot too. Before long it will be replaced by a park. How incongruous in these surroundings are the names of the streets, which are supposed to honor four eminent public characters. The Jews are generally credited with a willingness to "spoil the Philistines," but one of their strongest characteristics as a people is fidelity to each other. In this great Jewish colony the unpleasant characteristics of the race are exaggerated, and their virtues are conspicuously deficient, or at least they have conspicuously large exceptions. Their life is full of miserable impositions and swindles, perpetrated by Jews on Jews. The young lawyers that practice in the local courts are noted for their sharp conduct and their money-making schemes, which are applied with impartiality to Christians and Jews. The doctors are not behind the lawyers. There are many young doctors who have recently been admitted to practice there, who put that learned profession to shame every day. It may be that these people, who must live by their wits, are compelled to prey on each other, because there are not Christian martyrs enough to go round. Cases are reported to the Society for the Prevention of Crime almost weekly, where poor litigants have paid counsel fees for services that were never rendered, or for services that when rendered were obviously designed to benefit the other side. As for the doctors, let one illustration suffice.

There were two doctors who worked together under an agreement to divide their fees and their plunder. They were men of some standing. One of them went out in the guise of an oculist, visiting the people from floor to floor in the tenement houses and inquiring about their eyes. He found a woman with inflamed eyes and defective sight, and after examining her, apparently with great care, said to her, in substance: "My poor unfortunate woman! You are indeed in great trouble. I see your bad eyes, and I wish I could relieve them. I can help them a little, but I cannot cure them, for I am only an oculist. Your trouble is in your brain. The pain in your eyes comes from your brain. If your brain is not cured you will become crazy, and that will be worse even than having sore eyes. You have a very rare and terrible complaint, one that is not often seen, and I do not believe that even a good doctor can help you. You are almost sure to lose your mind." The effect of this startling information upon a nervous, ignorant woman may be imagined. In a moment she was on the verge of hysterics. Then he started to leave the apartments. As he was going, he seemed to recall something, and said: "Oh! how fortunate that I thought of it! After all, you are in great luck. I just remembered that the celebrated Dr. ———, a most eminent physician from our own country, has just arrived in New York, and is visiting some friends. He is not here for business. He is a rich man. I don't know whether I can get him to see you. I think of all the doctors in the world he is the one that can relieve you. Shall I speak to him and see if he will come?"

The bait was snapped up quickly, and the next day doctor number two arrived and played the part of the eminent professor from Russia. He accepted a little token of the woman's appreciation, amounting to several hundred dollars—it was all she had; —and gave her a little humbug treatment. The woman is grateful to him yet; for did not his providential coming and his splendid treatment save her from insanity? This story came into publicity through a quarrel between the two doctors over the division of the money wrung from the woman.

New Israel has always been a stronghold of the "fences" (those places so necessary to thieves for the conversion of their plunder into money). The most noted of all these places was the one which was kept by "Mother" Mandelbaum at 79 Clinton Street. That place was of the most innocent appearance, and the neighbors in those days, when there were many people owning their own homes, traded with the widow to help her along, never suspecting that her little "notion business" was merely a cover for gigantic thieving operations. Her connections extended throughout the United States and even into Canada, Mexico and Europe. She employed famous criminal lawyers on yearly fees to look out for her, and they did it thoroughly. She made her connections in such a way that until Peter B. Olney became district-attorney there was no interference with her illegal transactions. Her real business was done in a little frame wing of the main building, about twenty-five feet long. Its first floor was known as "Little Germany," and was fitted up sumptuously and furnished with costly appliances for the entertainment of guests. There were many unique assemblies about her table, for she gave "swell" dinners to her thieving associates, many of whom were eminent in their profession, and these dinners were free from any danger of police interference. There, crooks became politely hilarious and eloquent, and enjoyed themselves for the hour with all the freedom of perfect safety. At the outset of her criminal career she received the plunder in these apartments, but in the later days she used her home simply as an agency, and transacted her business with great care and exactness by means of messengers, orders and telegrams. She stood by her friends and often furnished money for the defense of criminals in distant parts of this country, and even in other countries. Her special friends were "George Leonidas Leslie" (George Howard), "Michael Kurtz" (Sheeney Mike), "Billy O'Brien" (Billy Porter), "Jim Brady," "Shang Draper," "Red Leary," "Kate Leary," "Big Frank McCoy," "Jimmy Wilmot," "Jimmy Hope," "Ed. Goodie," "Jim Casey," "Joe Dollard," "Johnny Dobbs," "Abe Coakley," "Sam Perris," "Jimmy Dunlap," "Oscar Decker," "Tom McCormack," "Piano Charley," "Pete Curley," "Butch McCarthy," "Bill Connors," "Jack Rand," "Bill Train," and "Ike Marsh." Her "gang," while in their period of power, committed eighty per cent of the bank robberies in the United States. Those familiar with the criminal history of our City will recognize in these names the princes among the thieves of twenty-five years ago, including bank robbers, burglars and swindlers. Kate Leary died in December, 1896, a poor old hag in a hovel on Coney Island, but in "Mother" Mandelbaum's day she was beautiful and ambitious, and was possessed of a rude culture. She delved into esoteric Buddhism and lectured her fellow criminals. She acted as a decoy for well-dressed men, whom she would lure to her den, where Leary, Draper and McCoy would capture their valuables. She married Leary by a formula of her own, and Billy Train, who was present, ran out, knocked a man down, took his pocketbook, purchased champagne and chicken, and brought in the wedding breakfast. The detective bureau and its chief made no trouble for Mrs. Mandelbaum, but Mr. Olney, the district-attorney, did, and he was roundly abused by the police detectives, because he spurned their services and employed Pinkerton detectives. A case was worked up with the assistance of attorneys in New York (S. D. and D. J. Noyes), who represented people that had been robbed by Mrs. Mandelbaum's "pals," and it was so strong that Mrs. Mandelbaum forfeited her bail and fled to Canada, where she died a few years ago. The freedom of this woman, while the greatest detectives of modern times ran the detective bureau of the police department, was paralleled only in the case of Madam Restell, the world-famous abortionist, who occupied the beautiful house on the northeast corner of Fifty-second Street and Fifth Avenue, conducting there a revolting occupation, fattening on blackmail, while even the children knew of her doings. The remark was common among the boys living in the neighborhood, who, little understanding the remarks of their elders, repeated them with awe as they passed the corner—"That house is built on babies' skulls!" She began her evil career in Greenwich village. Archbishop Hughes denounced her from the pulpit of St. Patrick's Cathedral. Later, when he tried to buy the corner of 52d Street and Fifth Avenue for the Episcopal residence, she bid it up, and secured it. She became a millionaire. Anthony Comstock finally brought her to ruin. He found evidence and used it relentlessly, and when she saw that she could not escape prison she killed herself. Many persons have practiced her abominable calling without any effectual police interference. The most famous after Restell was Dr. Rosenzweig, who killed Alice Bowlsby by an operation conducted at 687 Second Avenue.

Dr. Whitehead testified before the Lexow Committee of methods by which abortionists secured protection from criminal prosecutions. The public advertisements of these days show that the same class of practitioners are at work in the Tenth Ward and elsewhere. In the recent past, grand juries have listened to revelations by former burglars of New Israel, of partnership relations that existed between them and police detectives, who on some occasions watched while they operated, so as to prevent interference by green policemen, and then divided the plunder. These detectives, when publicly questioned, admitted very close and intimate dealings and relations with burglars and hundreds of interviews with them, but claimed that they cultivated their acquaintance so that they might be informed of the illegal operations of other thieves.

Extract from testimony of detectives in Police Court, March, 1895:

"Q. How long have you know S. (the burglar)? A. Since the day of the arrest in Madison Street. I believe it was in October, 1891.

"Q. How many such people are you acquainted with? A. I know a great many of them.

"Q. And you recognize that as one of the established methods of the police department, cultivating the acquaintance of criminals that you may catch other criminals? A. It is absolutely essential to our business.

"Q. How many times did you see S. (the burglar) in those two years? A. A thousand times.

"Q. Did you have transactions with him? A. Police transactions, yes, sir.

"Q. Did you ever write him? A. I think I wrote him letters when I wanted to see him.

"Q. How did you address him? A. J — S —.

"Q. Friend Jo? A. Yes, sir; it requires a little 'jolly' to keep these people in line.

"Q. You used to meet him in a restaurant? A. Yes, sir; he came to my house a hundred times and knows my children and wife. I always received him with the utmost courtesy and acted to him like a man should act to anybody. He sat at my table. I let him eat there when he was hungry. I have sat in public restaurants with him many times.

"Q. This place, 'Lyons' (a Bowery restaurant), where you say you met him, do you meet other thieves there? A. Oh, yes, sir.

"Q. Did you give him your address in writing? A. Oh, yes, I told him to send any letter, because I told him any time he wanted to see me that he could either write to the post-office or police headquarters; that if he had anything he wanted to give me *urgently*, if it was in the afternoon, to direct it to the post-office box, because every afternoon I am downtown.

"Q. Then you recognized he might have something to give you *urgently?* A. Yes, sir."

And so the detective went on. He has dropped out of the force since its partial reorganization. The "side-partner" of this detective testified:

"Q. How many of these burglars and thieves are you dealing with now? A. I can't count them —a great many.

"Q. You use them *of course* for no other purpose than to get information against other thieves? A. *Well, yes.*

"Q. That is one of the methods of your office;

you cultivate the acquaintance of these crooks for police reasons? A. Yes, sir.

"Q. What is your special line of work? A. I have no special line to work on. I usually get anything I can.

"Q. You have a roving commission? A. Yes, sir.

"Q. Mrs. O.'s is in Chinatown, is it not? A. Yes, sir. You might term it so.

"Q. Do you call at her place? A. To meet my brother officers once in a while.

"Q. Mrs. O.'s place is frequented by women who live in Chinatown? A. Some of them.

"Q. A great many of them? A. I don't know—a great many of them.

"Q. Do you report your calls on Mrs. O. at headquarters? A. No, sir.

"Q. Your calls are of a social nature? A. Yes, sir.

"Q. Do you know that Mrs. O. collects from the Chinatown women? A. *No, sir.* (Of course not!)

"Q. She boards these women, does she not? A. She might board four or five."

Let us read a very little of the story of this burglar S., who had such extensive dealings with these two headquarters' sleuths, as he told it in legal proceedings. It will illuminate not only recent police methods, but an important phase of the criminal life of the Tenth Ward. The account has never before been published.

"I was born in Poland. I came to the United States in 1889 with one thousand dollars and began business as a barber. I became acquainted with a woman named E—— H——. A man named J—— H——, who claimed to be her cousin, acted as schatchen (match-maker). I paid him seventy-five dollars for his services. I went to live with E——

A Schatchen.

H—— on Orchard Street, and then I found that she was the wife of that J—— H——. She got possession of my money and everything else that I had, and I began to drink and fell into the company of the burglars, pickpockets and 'flim-flam' men, and then began myself to be a burglar. I was caught in my first act and got out of prison in October, 1891. I was going to leave the country, but I met a man who was discharged from prison a week later than I, and we resolved to commit another burglary. We went to a house on Madison Street, and while breaking in the door were caught by three police detectives. The next morning, on our way to the Tombs, the detectives took us into a saloon, and we asked them to let us go, which they agreed to do for five hundred dollars. My friend could not raise more than sixty-five dollars, and they refused to let us go. In court he told the judge that the detectives asked us for five hundred dollars to let us go, but he was not believed. I kept quiet. I got a friend, a lady, to help me, and she paid some money to the detectives. We were indicted. My friend was sent up for a year and I was discharged. After being discharged, I went to the detectives to get some trinkets that had been taken out of my pockets. They told me that, since I was smart enough to keep my mouth shut, I could do everything in the world if I would only do the right thing by them. They gave me their address, and informed me that, should I get into trouble, I should send for them. I saw them again, and told them I had a place where I could make a couple of hundred dollars, and that they must come along with me, in order that I might be protected. We went to — —— Street, a Chinese laundry. I grabbed a box from the Chinaman's drawer. It contained something like fifty dollars. This money I divided with the detectives in a saloon at the corner of Essex and Grand Streets. Then I located a place at — —— Street, where there was living a rich man. I went to the detectives and told them that if they wanted to make some money they should go along with me. We went to the place in the night time. The detectives stood guard on the corner of Pitt and Broome Streets; for the purpose that, should there be an outcry, I would run into their hands. I got in through the window. I got watches, diamonds and cash to the amount of five hundred dollars. The next morning I pawned the goods and divided the money with the detectives. At Number — Norfolk Street a man kept a saloon. I met a boy pickpocket who had some money, and I informed detective —— of this, and suggested that he arrest the boy and give him a bluff, and we would get some money out of him. The detective arrested the boy and took him as far as Houston and Chrystie Streets, where I met them and told the boy that it was best to square it with the detective. The boy told me to run quickly to the saloon and tell his friends that they should raise money enough to get him released. I got fifty dollars, and the boy was never taken to headquarters, and I divided the money with the detective. I noticed a jewelry store at — Houston Street. I informed the detectives and made arrangements to meet them. We met, and they went with me and tried the key in the door, so I could open the door the next morning. Two or three days later I went with two detectives and stationed one at the corner of Ridge and Houston Streets and the other at the corner of Pitt and Houston Streets. When the man went out for dinner I opened the door and robbed the place of about twenty-five watches. I sold some of them to ——, who keeps a dive at 41 E—— Street, and I pawned some of the goods, and I divided the money with the detectives. A man named —— lived at — R—— Street. I told him how I could make a couple of thousand dollars, and invited him to go with me at night time. He accepted my invitation. I gave him a lot of burglar's tools to carry. I had arranged with detectives —— and —— to wait outside on the street. The man walked a little behind me. The detectives jumped on him and kept him at headquarters two days. I went and told his wife that by paying a sum of money he would be released, and if not he was liable to get a couple of years. His wife raised fifty dollars and paid it to the detectives in a saloon near the Tombs. The burglar's tools were not shown to the judge and the man was discharged. The same day a crank went into Russell Sage's office and threw a bomb, and while the crowd had collected there two pickpockets were caught by Detectives ——, ——, and ——. They were held for trial, and I saw the detectives and gave them money to release them, and when the time came for trial only one detective appeared, and his evidence was not sufficient to convict them."

There were thirty-three of these cases, and several of them were sustained by corroborative proof. Some of them involved members of the Max Hochstim Association, who were always on hand when any money was at stake.

The purpose of the thousand meetings which the detective conceded to have occurred after the burglar's release from prison in 1891 is easily seen.

The Eleventh Precinct swarms with such criminals as the burglar whose story we have indicated; but bad as matters still remain in this human sink, it is confidently believed that such settled relations of business between thieves and policemen have been broken up and exist no longer.

That the Russians, Poles and Slavs are going to remain with us is perfectly plain; that their great numbers and their multiplying habits are going to continue as large factors in our City life needs no demonstration; and that they are a danger, a detriment, a drag to our City's progress, is self-evident. What is the outlook? Will these people improve? Can they be fused into the mass of American citizenship without debasing it? Can our institutions stand the strain of the process? These are vital questions. Our country is like a great smelting pot, into which is poured the dissimilar elements of the world's population, to be fused and refined into a common mass, that shall be homogeneous, and adapted to the high conditions of life and activity that are demanded by the genius of

American institutions. The important question in these days is: Will the pot stand the weight and the heat? It is severely tried in this part of New York. If any one doubts it, let him inquire of the school teachers, the ministers, the priests, and the other humanitarians who work there. I have made many inquiries on this line among intelligent Hebrews of the district, and uniformly they recognize the unpleasant traits of their people and the danger which they have brought to us; but they say that the conditions will improve, because immigration is falling off, because the children under the influence of education are distinctly an improvement on their parents, and because the campaign of 1894 opened a relation of sympathy and intercommunication between many of the Hebrews and Americans in other districts, who are seeking to elevate the whole City, and who have furnished inspiration and information to the Jews. The danger of giving these ignorant and illiterate people the ballot as we do is one that cannot be lightly considered. The rotten police administrators that have been given to New Israel have demoralized adults and children. Teachers have observed children playing "election" and going through the forms of covertly buying and selling votes. We have seen hideous women swarming on the streets, lolling out of windows, and sitting on stoops, making wanton exhibitions, inviting customers, and indulging in their peculiar methods of speech and action, in full view of hundreds of children, who romped about the streets, looking curiously at the women betimes, and noting well all of the degrading commerce. Some of the keepers of these brothels have publicly testified that they secured immunity from police interference by large and regular payments of money. The defiant publicity of their operations was a perfect corroboration of these stories. We have seen the business cards of a few of the famous houses that were running wide open and publicly exhibiting the charms of their brazen attractions in the "good old days," as they call them.

The "cafes" of Chrystie, Forsyth, Stanton, Rivington and Houston Streets, and such miserable places as "The Palm" on Chrystie Street, are the decrepit survivors of the old system, and they indicate some official inefficiency or complaisance. The children understood the whole disgusting business, and their play and their language with each other was full of its suggestions! That these conditions should have existed under the eyes of the police force of the City, and that they and a host of other officials and politicians should have fattened on these crimes, was a disgrace that can never be forgotten or wiped out. The long, arduous, emphatic and dangerous campaign of the Society for the Prevention of Crime in this district, leading, as it did, to the partial reorganization of the police force and the popular overthrow of the corrupt city government, has resulted not only in checking the advance of crime in the district, but more than that —in awakening a feeling of responsibility among the better elements of this dense population, in bringing these elements into sympathetic relation with the patriotic impulses that exist in other districts; and, most of all, in abolishing very much of the public exhibition of vice that was demoralizing the children. When the Lexow Committee turned its attention to the crimes of oppression perpetrated through the local police and the police courts, there was an awakening among the Hebrews, who felt that the time had come for their deliverance. They had bowed so humbly to the yoke of their oppressors that it seemed a hopeless task to fill them with any such controlling love of liberty as would work their deliverance and make them fit to enjoy the freedom designed by American institutions.

Here is an incident in the birth of the American spirit among the serfs of New Israel, and the important facts related may be found embodied in a legal proceeding before the governor of the State.

Philip Kievent and his wife were victims of the Essex Street despotism. They had refused to pay blackmail to the combination, and several of the hangers-on were selected to manufacture a case against them. Kievent and his wife were arrested on a charge of robbery. They were advised to pay if they wanted to regain their freedom, but they steadfastly refused, and, persisting in their independence, they were convicted on the testimony of the conspirators and were sent to prison. The story of their wrongs was well-known throughout the Tenth Ward, and was a matter of general conversation among the Jews, who trembled at the thought that any one of them might happen to be the next object of attack. While the Lexow investigation was in progress, and before it had made any serious impression on the defiant police force, several leading Hebrews determined to apply for the pardon of Philip Kievent, who was still in prison, he having received a longer sentence than his wife. They called a public meeting in order to secure a popular protest against the conviction and a popular demand for a pardon. It was arranged to take place very close to the station-house, and close to the haunts of the thugs who upheld the power of oppression with their brawn. There had not been in any other part of the City a public defiance to the police oppressors by any class that had suffered from them. Even the large body of respectable American fruit and produce merchants on the west side of the City, which had been harassed almost beyond endurance, remained cowardly to the end, and could hardly be persuaded to give the information that was necessary to break up the system of plunder that was in force. When the time for this Hebrew meeting arrived, the room was filled with Jewish men, who were thoroughly typical of the life of New Israel. Policemen were present, and representatives of the tyrants were there for the purpose of spotting and reporting all who assisted in the demonstration and who joined in supporting it. One after another men arose, and, either in Hebrew jargon or broken English, denounced the police and the Essex Street gang, and urged the passage of the resolutions. They shook their fists at the policemen in the doorway, and defied the Essex Street power. The meeting was a revelation of the possibility of bringing this groveling multitude of people up to a position where they might be worthy to have and to enjoy the privileges of citizenship. When I was called upon to make the closing address, I could not refrain from complimenting them upon their rare exhibition of bravery—a bravery which had not been equaled at that time in any part of the City. A speaker reminded them of the espionage to which they were at that moment being subjected, and of the personal danger to each man that participated in the meeting, and told them that it prophesied the political reconstruction of their district, and the overthrow of their tyrants. He said that many of them had fled from oppression in their native land, turning their faces with hope and confidence to free America, and that they had been cruelly disappointed, when, on settling here, they found the representatives of the government not only oppressors, but robbers, and that the boasted constitutional rights were, so far as they were concerned, "a delusion and a snare." They showed a quick and keen appreciation of this sentiment. He reminded them that in every case of oppression that had appeared the wicked act had been made possible by the perfidy of some of their own people. To this statement they nodded assent. He told them that, while we have the best Constitution and the most liberal government in the world, that no declaration of principles on paper had ever given freedom to a people that was not worthy of it, and that worthiness of liberty was evidenced by a passionate love for it which would lead its devotees to sacrifice property, home and life rather than to suffer slavery; and that if they had been made slaves in free America it was not the fault of the Constitution and the other institutions of the country, but rather it was their own fault; for they had bent their necks under the heel of their oppressors, had groaned and suffered in silence, and had made no effort to publish their wrongs, and to invoke the assistance of the masses of patriotic citizens, who would have rushed to their rescue had they known of their trouble. He told them that their action was brave, that it put them in line with the elements of progress in the City, that it would result in breaking the shackles of their slavery, and that they would understand better the genius of American freedom and the glory of the American Constitution. Those uncouth, long-bearded men, with unpronounceable names and alien manners, broke out into unmistakable American cheers for the flag, the country and the Constitution; and they left the gathering thrilled with the new idea of freedom and duty. That district, which had blindly rolled up immense majorities for its Tammany oppressors, routed them in the contest for local officers in 1894, and gave a splendid majority for the county ticket of the anti-Tammany forces.

This is a good place to mention a few typical instances of the persecution and oppression that characterized the control of the district by its horrible criminal and official combination. The most famous of these cases was that of the poor Russian widow Kaele Uchital. That case was so thoroughly proven, so completely shown to view, so full of pathos and tragic interest, and it so completely exhibited the methods of oppression, that it touched the hearts of the whole people, and more than anything else aroused the terrified Jews to self-defense.

In the early days of the Lexow investigation, my office was haunted by an impoverished, grief-stricken woman, who never could get beyond a flow of tears and a deluge of foreign words, always closing with, "Mine shildren! Mine shildren!" I could not understand her, and, supposing her to be one of the cranks that were so persistent at that time, tried to avoid her. One day she intercepted me, and after her usual outpour of words, bowed before me, seized my hand, kissed it passionately, and flooded it with her tears, while she cried in unmistakable anguish, "Mine shildren! Mine shildren!" That kiss on my hand would not rub out. It spoke to me through all the care and labor of the day. Then I hunted for an interpreter and got her story. It was too frightful to believe. When I was tempted to throw the translation away, the touch of those burning lips and the patter of the falling tears recalled the pleading sounds of the foreign tongue. I had no peace with it, and determined to have the story thoroughly investigated. The investigation showed the truth of her complaint. It was developed publicly in all of its hideousness, and was thoroughly proved, partly by the mouths of her oppressors, in the eyes of all the people. In 1891 she arrived in New York, a widow with four children. She was assisted by the Hebrew Charities Association. She started a boarding-house with its help, saved a little money and bought a cigar store at Number 28 Pitt Street for one hundred and twenty-five dollars. She lived with her children in one room in the rear of the store. One night a man bought some tobacco, mixed up his change and looked about the store. The next night another man called and told her that a detective had been to her store and would arrest her for having a disorderly house, and would take her children away from her, if she did not pay him fifty dollars. She answered that there was nothing wrong in her place, and if that detective called again she would chase him out with a broom. The detective did come. He was police officer Ambrose W. Hussey. He told her that she kept a disorderly house there, and had hundreds of dollars saved up, and he would arrest her if she did not pay him fifty dollars. She protested that she was innocent and had no money to pay, but in spite of the supplications of her children and herself, he dragged her from the store. It was then about midnight. Two blocks from the store they met Max Hochstim, who spoke to them, and to whom she appealed for protection; but he told her that she must pay the detective the fifty dollars, and must thereafter pay ten dollars a month, so that she would not be hindered. She insisted that she knew nothing about a dishonest business, but it was no use. She was led through the streets until two o'clock in the morning. The detective insisted that she had money in her stockings. Weary and tired out, hoping to convince the jackal that had her, and to be permitted to go back to her little brood of children, she sat down on the corner of Essex and Rivington Streets and removed her stockings, to show that she had no money in them. Still he persisted. He understood the financial instincts of the race. She had twenty-five dollars in her bosom, which finally she gave him, and he divided the money with Hochstim. They sent her home with a warning to prepare fifty dollars, and at seven o'clock the detective called for it. She said: "I cried again and begged him to let me go, that I am not able to give him any more money; but he didn't want to hear me any more, and I had to follow. By a signal a detective appeared and he handed me over with the remark not to let me go until I gave him fifty dollars." That man was one of the king's executioners; his name was Meyer. She went with Meyer to several men and tried to sell her store for fifty dollars, but failed. Then the detective said to Meyer: "That bad woman don't want to give the money. Take her to the court." She was committed for trial, and appeared at the Special Sessions before that eminent trio of justices, Hogan, Koch and Divver. There two miserable specimens of mankind, Joseph Tatako and Robert Matthias, mere lads, being produced by officer Hussey, testified to illicit relations with this woman, the mother of four children, and to the payment of fifty cents apiece therefor; and despite the protestations of the defendant, her appearance, testimony of good character, and testimony of one citizen that Matthias, the self-confessed scoundrel, had proposed to him to settle the case for fifty dollars, the Court, instead of rejecting the palpably false accusation of the vile witnesses for the police, convicted her and sent her to prison. Her little home was destroyed, her children were taken by the Gerry Society, her honest character was aspersed—who can sum up the unutterable misery of this woman and her children? Her fine was fifty dollars. Her brother succeeded in selling her store for sixty-five dollars and paying the fine. She was released from the Tombs; but, to use her own language, "I ran then, crazy for my children, for I did not know where they were." She met Hussey, who told her they had been taken by the Gerry Society, and then she learned that they had been sent to the Orphan Asylum at 151st Street and Tenth Avenue. There she went, all ignorant of legal form, and begged them to give back her children, but she said, "None would hear me. Grieved to the depths of my heart, seeing myself bereaved of my dear children, I fell sick, and laid six months in the Sixty-sixth Street Hospital, and had to undergo a great operation by Prof. Mondie." The following are the last words of the translated communication which she brought to me: "I went again to Twenty-third Street, begging them to release my children, and that was denied again. My heart craves to have my children with me. I have nothing else in the world, only them. I want to live and to die for them. I lay my supplication before you, honorable sir, father of a family, whose heart beats for your children, and feels what children are to a faithful mother. Help me to get my children; let me be a mother to them. Grant me my holy wish and I will always pray for your happiness, and will never forget your kind and benevolent act toward me." When her story was first made public there was some difficulty in identifying the officer. Our investigations convinced us that Hussey was the man, and when she came into court again and her translated statement was put into evidence, she was asked if she saw the man who took her children. She jumped to her feet, and with all the vehemence of her pent-up feelings, she pointed straight at Hussey, saying, "That is the man! That is the man! That is the man who took the children away from me! That is the man who took me away with Hochstim! He and Hochstim together took the twenty-five dollars," etc. The officer who was thus accused, in the language of a leading newspaper of the next day, was "a tall, lithe man, with a narrow face and long front teeth, which gleamed like those of a wolf in a never-fading smile." Before Mrs. Uchital took the stand Hussey had been allowed to testify in his own behalf, and with great self-confidence he had given his own version of the arrest, in which he made statements at variance with his testimony at the Special Sessions, and in which he made accusations designed to charge a brother officer with the

MAX HOCHSTIM.

blackmailing of the poor woman and calculated to exonerate himself. Hussey had one of the Essex Street professional witnesses to back him up; but, unfortunately for him, that witness made contradictory statements. These circumstances, and the frank statements of the newly accused police officer, left Hussey in a bad plight. His overthrow was complete when Mrs. Uchital pointed him out as her oppressor and the stealer of her children. In the excitement of the moment Hussey forgot himself and turned upon a young Hebrew who had assisted in getting the information together, and threatened to put a bullet through his head. For a moment there was a wild commotion in the back of the court-room. Hussey was promptly recalled to the stand and became completely unnerved. His teeth chattered, he trembled, and he called for water. He denied the threat which he had just made. Four witnesses were immediately called and they proved it. While Hussey sat in court he was compelled to listen to other stories of outrage in which he and Hochstim and others of "Silver Dollar" Smith's coterie had wrung the shekels out of their fellows. Elias Mandell and his wife told how they were despoiled of one hundred dollars, which were extorted by five days' imprisonment of the husband. Mrs. Mandell told how her little children sat on the doorsteps for hours and far into the night, while their father was locked up, because they were unwilling to sleep in bed while "poor papa was in prison." It was our good fortune to succeed in restoring Mrs. Uchital's children to her; and when the reunion took place there was not a dry eye in all the thronged court-room. The poor woman was worn out with her suffering, her grief, her anxiety, her labor. She worked hard to support her children. They lived very happily together a little less than a year, and then she succumbed to the effects of shock and strain, and left her children orphans indeed, so that they returned to the kind Hebrew Home which they had found before in their distress. The satisfaction of having restored the woman's good name, reunited the broken family, removed the stain from the lives of those little children, and of having smashed that infamous combination, is beyond the possibility of measurement. While sketching this case of Mrs. Uchital, my desk is covered with the statements of similar cases, some of which were fully developed in the investigation, and some of which have never been published. The Uchital case was only a sample of many. With the record of the operations of those unspeakable villains before me—a record of assaults, stabbings, extortions and oppressions, such as cannot be duplicated elsewhere in this land (let us hope)—we feel that there should be reserved chairs waiting for them in the land of fire and brimstone. After all these unparalleled revelations, some of these men are still admitted to positions of influence and power, and it requires the most strenuous exertion to make headway against them. When officer Hussey was tried before the new board of police commissioners, and when it was perfectly clear that he had publicly made the threat against the assistant of the Lexow Committee above-mentioned and had denied it under oath, one of the commissioners, a kind-hearted gentleman, who thinks it is his duty to stand by his men, voted to dismiss the complaint, saying that the threat was no serious matter.

While the great villains of New Israel are now pretty effectually shut out of the Essex Market Court, there are still some miserable practices there, and the jackals prowl about the door, trying to extort or wheedle money out of the unfortunate people who are drawn there by the stern hand of the law. The gambling table is in full operation within sight of the court-room door, and the lawyers and runners and pimps and blacklegs, who manage to extract some of the juices of life in this cesspool of crime and misery, are in turn plucked by greater and brainier villains, who know how to play loaded dice and to deal marked cards. "The young man who drifts into the seething current of Essex Street becomes a wreck or a crook in nine cases out of ten." This remark is the language of a victim.

A large proportion of the people in New Israel are addicted to vice, and very many of their women have no other occupation than prostitution. Under the most thorough police administration it is difficult to cope with this evil. Women of all nationalities have drifted into the district, and are unable to live out of it. There has grown up as an adjunct of this herd of female wretchedness a fraternity of fetid male vermin (nearly all of them being Russian or Polish Jews), who are unmatchable for impudence, and bestiality, and who reek with all unmanly and vicious humors. They are called "pimps." A number of them are in the roll, above shown, of the Max Hochstim Association.

They have a regular federation, and manage several clubs, which are influential in local politics, and which afford them the power to watch their poor woman victims, to secure their hard and ill-earned money, and to punish them when they are refractory. One of these associations meets at 123 Allen Street, and bears the name of one of Hochstim's members. The women work for these beasts, who secure all of their shameful wages, allow them a bare pittance for support, and use the lion's share of it for gambling, for spending on women in other parts of town, and for depositing in the savings banks. Why do the women pay? Well, they can't help it. They can't work at any other trade, and they can't operate in any other district, for there is nowhere else such a demand for them. A woman frequently entertains twenty or thirty visitors in a day and collects as many dollars. The pimps lay in wait for them, and seize them, and extort the money from them before it is cold. If necessary they search their pockets and stockings, and sometimes they beat them. They stand by each other, and by the aid of the powerful politicians of the ward and of professional witnesses, they send refractory women to the "Island." One man that we know of has three women working for him, and in the evenings he rides about on a bicycle, keeping his eye on them. A man, who is appropriately named Wolfman, has a poor woman working for him, who, when she becomes seriously ill, has to go to the hospital, because she has no money, yet she keeps him in luxury, feeds his expensive gambling propensity, and enables him to bank money. The physicians of the neighborhood, who have to treat the unfortunate women, are treasuries of this sort of knowledge. One of these men, of more than usual brutality, in the days when disorderly houses were many and wide open, made a large income by "breaking in" new girls. That man is now a prominent "cafe keeper." Physicians have urged the girls to leave their tormentors, and have been convinced of their inability to do it. Sometimes five or six of these scabby fellows will tackle one poor woman, who has stolen her "company's" pocketbook, and explore her clothing and her person until they find it. It was this miserable class of men that led the attack on the agents of the Society for the Prevention of Crime in 1893. Then the vicious resorts of the Eleventh Precinct were running full blast. Devery was captain. He and Inspector Williams, with impudent defiance, declared that the complaints of the society were lies, and that there was no open vice in the precinct. The society suddenly swooped down upon the precinct, with clear cases against open houses in sight of the station-house. The superintendent and detectives of the society attended at court with counsel to prove their cases—cases which were so strong that they resulted in convictions, even by the most reckless of Tammany's police justices. The street outside of the court-house was crowded with a choice collection of repulsive "pimps." In one of the cases, information came that a man in the court-room had warned a defendant, so that she evaded arrest. A good judge, Voorhis, was on the bench. I apprised him of the circumstances, and pointed out the man. He directed the officers of the court squad to bring him to the bench. They looked at him, their faces paled, and their feet refused to move. I turned to the officer in command and said, "Why don't you bring that man here?" His teeth chattered. I said, "If you don't bring him I will bring him myself." Still he seemed fastened to the floor. I stepped down, took the man by the arm, and said, "Come up here. The Judge wants to see you."—"What do yer say?" was the impudent answer. "Step up there," was my reply to him, as I gave him a push. He saw the Judge's eye upon him, and sullenly he mounted the bridge. The Judge said, "You are accused of having warned a defendant in this case that the officers were after her. What do you say to -that?" There was no reply. I reiterated my statements to the Judge, and pointed to the agents who had observed the act. The Judge said, "What is your name?" The answer came, "Max Hochstim." I had never met that important personage before, and at once understood the terror that had seized the court officers. Apparently Judge Voorhis did not know him. Certainly he did not realize the situation. He gave Hochstim a scathing lecture, and ordered him to keep out of the Court. Hochstim went immediately to the counsel for the defendants and asked him if he thought it would cost him over one hundred dollars to demolish my face. He then went out on the sidewalk and harangued his supporters. Presently our detectives left the court-room, and the defendants' attorney, being moved by compassion and good-will toward men, held me and my associate counsel in conversation for a few minutes. Our devoted little band of detectives, as soon as they turned into Broome Street, were hustled, threatened and repeatedly struck by the leading members of a crowd of at least five hundred, who chased them all the way to the Bowery. Policemen who were passed on post laughed as the rapid procession passed along. At the Bowery a concerted rush was made for the men, just as they were about to board a Fourth Avenue car, and some very hard blows were struck, which left their marks on the persons of several of the detectives. Our men acted with rare patience and discretion, and did not draw their firearms. In the nick of time, police from the precinct on the other side of the Bowery appeared, and drove the Essex Market crowd away from the car, so that our detectives made their escape. This was looked upon as a very serious occurrence, and convinced the City of the criminal attitude of the police of the Eleventh Precinct. Had our men been less discreet there would have been bloodshed. Prominent in the crowd that assailed them were Hyman Sugar, Issy Putter and Charles Kramer, whose names appear in the roll of the Max Hochstim Association above given, and each of whom was a disreputable purveyor of vice. There is a marked tendency among these Hebrews of criminal instincts to cover up their Jewish origin and to disguise their names; thus Rosenthal becomes McCarthy, Rosenberg becomes Rose, Solomon becomes Smith, and the traveler meets men of unmistakable Hebrew features, who bear such names as Cooper, Butler and Lent.

"Sarah Schneider, aged nineteen, was charged by her father, mother and brother, who live at 17 Chrystie Street, in the Center Street Police Court this morning with immoral conduct. Upon the father's complaint she was arrested in a house at 73 Mulberry Street. The girl said that her father forced her to lead a bad life and to give him her earnings. When she refused to do so longer he had her arrested. She said she would be glad to go to any place where her father could not beat her. Magistrate Simms committed her to an institution."—News item.

Among the people who lived in the Tenth Ward before the Jewish invasion were many Irish mechanics, some of whom, eschewing politics (which with whisky are the curse of the Irish), rose to positions of importance in the building and contracting trades, for which pursuits they have a natural aptitude. When the Jews began to press in upon this locality, the American and Irish, with a considerable number of Germans (who were interested largely in saloon, restaurant and clothing businesses), moved further north, and filled up the sparsely settled east side streets as far as Kip's Bay and Turtle Bay. The lowest elements of the Irish congregated in the tenements that were erected near the river, the wealthier people gravitated to the districts west of Third Avenue, and the thrifty middle class filled up Third Avenue, which became a thoroughfare. It is by a continuous northward migration that the upper districts of our City have been filled.

Thirty-fourth Street and Third Avenue was the center of a district which was of great importance in the building up of the middle part of the City and in the shaping of the political history of New York. There were builders of Irish origin, like George J. Hamilton, William, John and James Fettretch, Edward McPherson, John Glass and William and Joseph McCormack. They filled these streets, into which the multitudes were pouring, with new houses, and rapidly they became wealthy men; but when the panic of 1873 caught them, they were carrying such burdens of mortgages that, without an exception, they were forced to the wall and had to begin life all over again. There were on the sides of Murray Hill many eminent and wealthy gentlemen, prominent in the large business affairs of New York, but their wealth, eminence and respectability made little or no impression upon the district in which they lived; and that is still a common condition of affairs in New

York, which if remedied would change the complexion of many sections of our City. Along Third Avenue, and in the cross streets near to it, were many earnest, patriotic, old-fashioned Americans, of the common people, and many patriotic, naturalized people of foreign birth, whose qualities stood out strongly, because they were sharply contrasted against the large hostile mass of people to the east of them, and because their views and habits, touching this antagonistic class closely, frequently caused conflicts with them. In the local politics of the district, this little body of earnest Americans met the election day colonizers, repeaters and ballot-box stuffers face to face, and frequently in defending their rights they suffered severe punishment. In the agitations that preceded the war, and in the conflicts of that struggle, and particularly during the draft riots of 1863, the lines of division were sharply drawn. In the American party there were such men as Christopher Pullman, who was badly beaten several times while trying to protect ballot-boxes; Thomas and Samuel Cooper, whose grocery at Thirty-third Street and Third Avenue was a landmark; Eli F. Bruce, who kept a bakery at Thirty-fifth Street and Third Avenue; and William H. Wood, the principal of the public school in Thirty-seventh Street. The dominant political organization was directed, at first, by Jimmy O'Brien the Famous. For many years he was the dominating spirit there. Richard Croker came into prominence under the wing of O'Brien, who nursed him into power and was then overthrown by him. There was no more thoroughly organized gang of election repeaters than that which was managed in this district; they voted all over the City. I have among my acquaintances to-day a relic of this old organization, from whom I have heard many strange and wonderful tales of the doings in the days of old, when Jimmy O'Brien ran the district. The conflicts between these two forces, the Americans and the Irish Protestants, centered in the Rose Hill Methodist Church in Twenty-seventh Street, and the Kip's Bay Methodist Church in Thirty-seventh Street, which were the only important evangelical churches east of Third Avenue. The Kip's Bay Church was closer to the center of the district, and therefore was a more important point in the conflict that waged for a number of years. In this district of turmoil and excitement there were several spots of delicious quiet and serenity, and among these was the Episcopal Church of St. John the Baptist, which still stands at Thirty-fifth Street and Lexington Avenue. It is a most enchanting little bit of architecture, and it is so placed on the hill as to show its proportions to the very best advantage. Its rector, Dr. Duffie (called Marm Duffie by the street boys), was a descendant of the Kip family, and he owned the ground on which the church stood. His flock was small, but very select, and he performed his part of the services regardless of the size of his congregation, and always in the serenest manner, no matter what waves of commotion were sweeping over the streets below him. When the snow lies on the roofs, and the full moon shines out of the cold sky, let the lovers of the beautiful and romantic repair to Lexington Avenue and Thirty-fifth Street, and feast their eyes upon this delightful picture. The little rural building seems to have come out of the "Sketch Book." A number of the pioneer builders whom we have mentioned belonged to the Kip's Bay Church, and in the days of the war its congregation was large, wealthy and influential. There is little in the old church now to recall those days of power and of great deeds, except in the memorial windows and in the flag which is carefully preserved in an air-tight wall-case; but in the days that tried men's souls, and when a very large proportion of the district's population was in sympathy with rebellion and riot, that church and its membership stood firmly for the abolition of slavery and the perpetuity of the Union, and were a tower of strength for the National cause. The young men of the congregation and the neighborhood enlisted for the war under its flag. Its ministers preached emancipation and union at every service. Its women picked lint, made bandages and sent supplies to the Union army, and relieved the wounded and sick soldiers in the City hospitals. Its men went to the war or served the nation in important places at home. There was never any uncertain sound from the Kip's Bay Church. When Fort Sumter was fired on, the ladies made the flag and the men hoisted it upon the building, and there it flew continuously to the end of the war. The church was in the midst of the riotous demonstrations of 1863. A demand was made that the flag should be hauled down. Alarmed by a threat that the church and the parsonage would be burned, a timid trustee slipped into the building in the morning and lowered it. Another trustee, missing the inspiring sight of the Stars and Stripes flying over this rock of patriotism, ran in and raised it again. The grand old Daniel Curry, the fiery William H. Boole, and the sainted William McAllister, occupied the pulpit. Dr. Curry preached an abolition sermon one Sunday night, in which he seized a chair and brought it down on the platform so forcibly that he smashed it; then, throwing its wreck aside, he leaped down to the lower part of the platform, and swung his gaunt arms and shook his bony fists in the faces of the people as he denounced the crime of slavery. William H. Boole preached the doctrine so persistently that the negro haters of the neighborhood determined to stop him on a certain Sunday evening. Learning of their intention, he prepared himself and notified several of his leading official members. The church was crowded to the doors. People sat all over the altar rail and on the steps of the pulpit. A trusty band of friends was close to him. He announced his text, laid a pistol upon the desk, and said: "I have been threatened with violence, and that this church would be made the scene of serious trouble, if I should preach another anti-slavery sermon. I am going to do it, and if there is any one here that proposes to object, let him do it now. I am ready for him." His opponents were there, but they kept quiet, and they got a fine expression of his opinion of them and their conduct.

Mr. and Mrs. Bruce are still living. When the riot broke out, Mr. Bruce was at the war. His store and his people were special objects of hatred, for he was classed as a black Republican and a negro lover. A load of flour was delivered. The German bakers did not dare to show their faces on the street. Mrs. Bruce rolled the flour from the curb to the cellar. The police were shut up in their station-house in Thirty-fifth Street. They suffered with hunger. Mrs. Bruce's little boys smuggled bread to them from the bake-shop. She had a pistol in the house. She gave it to a policeman who had none. News came of the barbarous murder of Colonel O'Brien almost in sight of the house. The mob broke into the bake-shop, stole all the bread, cake and rolls, and beat a baker who didn't run away, and left him for dead. Then word came that the building would be fired at night. Mrs. Bruce says that Jimmy O'Brien called on her and promised that for ten dollars her house would not be burned. She gave him the money, he put his protection over her home, and it was saved. The next day a detachment of the Seventh Regiment camped on that corner. Salvation had come. The strain was over. The baker's little daughter strayed from the house. Her mother, overwrought with the tension of three days of anxiety, thought the child

CHURCH AT THIRTY-FIFTH STREET AND LEXINGTON AVENUE.

New York, Vol. Three, p. 244.

was lost; but she found her in the arms of a soldier in gray, feeding him with a biscuit, patting his face, and saying, "My papa is a soldier." Mrs. Bruce fed the soldiers while they remained there. Father Clowry of St. Gabriel's Church did heroic service in restraining the violence of his countrymen during those eventful days.

Among the historic churches of this City there is none which deserves more the recognition and the fond remembrance of good people than does this old Thirty-seventh Street Church. It was eminently a church of the people. Its tremendous revivals resulted in many hundreds, if not thousands, of conversions during those exciting periods. Its members were active, earnest, intelligent and loyal, and their voices were heard equally with that of the minister. There was a democratic simplicity, a blunt heartiness, and an absence of caste and social distinction, that gave it an ideal religious life. It is now a mission of the New York City Church Extension and Missionary Society, and with some help from that excellent organization, its faithful little band of members, some of whom are descendants of the heroes of 1860, are struggling against great odds, and with most inefficient means, to preserve the organization and make it effective. They deserve encouragement. The church should be endowed and made a permanent uplift for the teeming multitudes about it. It served the City, the State and the Nation in the great crisis of our history, and made an ineffaceable impress upon that whole section of New York. Its history should be written, and it should be started upon a new mission to the people, with means adequate to the end aimed at.

We have digressed more than we intended, but in considering the growth of our City, very few realize the heroic and effective work that has been done by the patriotic and religious common people, who have again and again held their ground and sustained the cause of truth against overwhelming odds, and whose labors and sacrifices and battles for the right have produced and preserved the fruits that we enjoy. It is not to be doubted that other churches and organizations in various parts of New York City have made their impress, and are still impressing themselves, on the times and the people, with as much courage, force and success as was manifested in the "war churches." Many a struggling enterprise that is to-day barely holding its own amid masses of ignorance and opposition is conserving interests that will not perish, and achieving results that will live to bless the greater City of New York in the years to come.

Again we say honor to the plain earnest American citizens that held the Stars and Stripes aloft in this important district during the struggle for the Union!

We may make our way through New Israel into Grand Street and strike the East River in the neighborhood of Corlears Hook, where the Indians were massacred. Our trip back to the old Fort may be made by way of the Belt Line cars. We will pass ferries over which multitudes of people travel between their Brooklyn homes and their various occupations in New York. We will pass ships lying in the slips with their bowsprits hanging over the street, and warehouses and piers overflowing with discharged cargoes. The streets may be almost blockaded with trucks filled with merchandise, either just unloaded from vessels that have arrived or destined for vessels that are about to depart. At many places the river laves the side of the street on which the cars run. If our trip be made in early evening in late fall or winter, we will see the hurrying throngs of ferry passengers, the lights on myriads of river craft and in many factories on the Brooklyn side. The bright lamps of the Brooklyn Bridge, and the illuminated cars moving rapidly across it, will help to give to the scene that element of extraordinary and mysterious activity that is characteristic of New York life. Soon after turning out of Grand Street our car passes over the grounds which Peter Stuyvesant's famous old trumpeter tilled, and on which important Revolutionary fortifications were erected, and which in later days became notable for the exploits of a violently criminal population. We have already spoken of the hard characters that so few years ago made it unsafe for respectable people to venture into that locality. We will see a few dry docks, and they will remind us of the important shipping interests that once swarmed in the neighborhood of Corlears Hook. At one time there were over thirty shipyards there. Christian Bergh, father of Henry Bergh, had his home and office at the corner of Scammel and Water Streets. Stephen Thorn and Jabez Williams were at the foot of Montgomery Street. At Clinton Street was the yard of Carpenter and Bishop, and near it was Ficket and Thom's yard. James Morgan & Son were at the foot of Rutgers Street, and Joseph Martin at Jefferson Street. Sneden and Lawrence were at Corlears Street, Samuel Harnard at Grand Street, Brown and Bell, Henry Eckford and Adam and Noah Brown, were near Stanton Street, and above them were Smith and Dimon, William H. Webb, Bishop and Simonson, James and George Steers, William H. Brown, and Thomas Colyer's yards. Fifty years ago all of these yards were filled with artisans and mechanics busily engaged in building ships, and as far back as there was any regular ship-building in New York, it was to be found in the neighborhood of Corlears Hook. Many famous clippers and war vessels were built at these yards. Mr. Bergh built the Greek frigate "Hellas" and the six-gun schooner "Antarctic," and he superintended the construction of the American frigate the "President" at the Brooklyn Navy Yard. Henry Eckford built several warships, and in 1812 he and Bergh built a number of vessels, several of which went into the command of Commodore Perry. The

Brown brothers built the privateers the "Yorktown," "Teaser," "Paul Jones," "Saratoga," and "General Armstrong"; and they also built the first steam war vessel, the "Fulton." A part of the Bergh estate consisted of the property where he had his office at the northeast corner of Scammel and Water Streets, and that piece fell to the share of Henry Bergh, the humanitarian. On it he built ten five-story tenement houses, which were the first tenement houses in New York that allowed a floor to each family. The first Sound steamboats were built in these East River yards. Among the famous ships built by the Webbs for the China trade were the "Superior" and the "Splendid." The "Independence," "Roscoe," "Rainbow," "Sea Witch" and "Mary Howland" were built by Smith and Dimon. Among the vessels built by Jacob A. Westervelt was the United States steam-frigate "Brooklyn." The yacht "America" was built in the yard of James R. and George Steers in 1851. At Mr. Webb's yard, at the foot of Sixth Street, were built the "General Admiral," a Russian warship, and the "Dunderberg," which was sold to France. A newspaper of 1852 said: "New York is one of the great shipyards of the world. Our clippers astonish distant nations with their neat and beautiful appearance, and our steamers have successfully competed with the swiftest going mail packets of Great Britain. In the furthest corners of the earth the Stars and Stripes wave over New-York-built vessels." These old ship-builders were a robust and noble lot of men, and they did a great deal for New York in contributing to its citizenship and to its resources. Their business has passed away, and we need to be reminded of their accomplishments or we shall forget them.

Passing through this foreign City, almost devoid of American life and feeling, we have been reminded of the intense Americanism that prevailed years ago by the names of many of the streets, and we have noticed the incongruous groupings of unpronounceable Russian, Polish and Slavonic names in streets that commemorate heroes in the struggle for liberty that never occurred, so far as any interest of these people is concerned.

There are Essex, Norfolk and Suffolk Streets, telling of old England; Clinton, Tompkins, Rivington, Delancey, Broome, Bayard, Jackson, Montgomery, Jefferson, Madison and Monroe Streets, all redolent of grand and sacred memories.

Six streets were named after heroes of the War of 1812: Chrystie Street for Lieutenant-colonel John Chrystie, who was killed on the Niagara frontier; Forsyth Street for Lieutenant Forsyth of the Rifles, killed in Canada; Eldridge Street for Lieutenant Eldridge, scalped and killed in Canada; Allen Street for Lieutenant William H. Allen, wounded in the action between the "Argus" and "Pelican." Ludlow Street for Lieutenant Ludlow, who was killed in the action between the "Chesapeake" and "Shannon," and was buried with Captain Lawrence;

SCENE ON SOUTH STREET.

New York, Vol. Three, p. 249.

and Pike Street for General Pike, who was killed in the attack on York (Toronto).

Now in place of Colonel Marinus Willett, who lived grandly on the block bounded by Columbia, Broome, Delancey and Lewis Streets, and who gave his name to Willett Street; and Colonel Rutgers, whose mansion was between Jefferson, Clinton, Monroe and Cherry Streets, and whose name is preserved in Rutgers Street; and Judge Ogilvie, the last New York slaveholder, who lived between Sheriff, Delancey, Columbia and Rivington Streets; instead of the ship-builders like Stephen Smith, who lived on East Broadway opposite Sheriff Street; Mr. Bergh, who lived on Scammel Street; John Dimon, who resided at the corner of Rivington and Columbia Streets; Jacob A. Westervelt, whose house was on East Broadway near Gouverneur Street; William H. Webb, who lived on Henry Street, and hosts of American business men, artisans and mechanics that made the Seventh and Tenth Wards an honor to the chief American City, there are Abrahamsohns, Sarasohns, Isaacsohns and Jacobsohns. Those names blaze like ancient stars in a galaxy of lesser lights like Mortnick, Duberstern, Shifrin and Rosov, Kuppenberg, Klinkowsten, Corotinsky and Bokshizky.

Even Ludlow Street Jail has yielded to the new racial forces of the Tenth Ward, as may be seen by this list of keepers: Rumpf, Behre, Finkelstumpf, Kayser, Bader, Feidler, Bengert, Freudenthal, Hartnagel, Buttner, Scherrman, Strassner, Haeckeling,

Schneider, Lux, Kullman, Kutscher, Von Deesten, Maier, Benckler and Stemme.

There is not an Irishman among them.

What these people do, what they think, how they live: these are mysteries, at least to Americans. Words, names, signs, faces, dresses,—they dazzle and mystify, and leave intelligence still grasping at the air. As an illustration, here is a bill of fare copied out of the window of Mrs. Grovman's eating-house on Chrystie Street:

Obed iz Sklenka Pivo . . . . 15c.

| | | | |
|---|---|---|---|
| Bif Styk . . . . . | 10c. | Goulasz . . . | 10c. |
| Riba . . . . . . . | 5c. | Peczonka . . . | 3c. |
| Kapusta iz Mencom . | 5c. | Borszczi . . . | 5c. |

Sup. . . . . 5c.

What intelligent idea can an American gain from this hotch-potch? Would he know any more if he ate the whole menu? Would he still possess ideas and the power of speech? The questions remain unanswered, for the martyr to science and discovery has not yet appeared. Maybe the foreign occupation is a judgment upon us, for this vast territory belonged to the tory Delancey, and was confiscated by the government and auctioned off in lots without any regard for poor Delancey or his family.

General Zebulon Montgomery Pike, for whom Pike Street was named, was a born soldier. His father was an army officer, and a descendant of Captain John Pike of New Jersey, a famous fighter in the Indian wars. He was trained from his cradle to the habits of military life, and he grew up into a hardy, chivalrous and noble manhood, which he enriched by the cultivation of his intellect and his spirit. He was one of the notable explorers of our Western wilderness, and divided honors with Lewis and Clarke. Pike's Peak was named in his honor. While in the field he wrote these beautiful words to his wife: "Should my country call for the sacrifice of that life which has been devoted to her since from early youth, most willingly shall she receive it. The sod which covers the brave shall be moistened by the tears of love and friendship; but if I fall far from my friends and from you, my Clara, remember that 'the choicest tears which are ever shed are those which bedew the unburied head of a soldier'; and when these lines shall meet the eyes of our young ——, let the pages of this little book ('Dodsley's Economy of Human Life') be impressed on his mind as the gift of a father who had nothing to bequeath but his honor, and let these maxims be ever present to his mind as he rises from youth to manhood:

"1. Preserve your honor free from blemish.

"2. Be always ready to die for your country.

"Z. M. PIKE."

The day before the fateful expedition against York he wrote to his father these prophetic lines:

"I embark to-morrow in the fleet at Sackett's Harbor at the head of a column of 1,500 choice troops on a secret expedition. If success attends my steps, honor and glory await my name: if defeat, still shall it be said that we died like brave men and conferred honor even in death on the American name. Should I be the happy mortal destined to turn the scale of war, will you not rejoice, oh, my father? May Heaven be propitious and smile on the cause of my country! But if we are destined to fall, may my fall be like Wolfe's—to sleep in the arms of victory." No braver charge was ever made than that which General Pike led against the British forces at York. Lieutenant Forsyth, whom we have mentioned, was with him. In every part of the field victory came to the Americans. The cause of his death was the explosion of a prepared magazine concealed in a road. The explosion hurled a heavy stone against his breast. As he sank to the ground he said: "I am mortally wounded—comfort my—" Just then, as the troops recovered from their momentary disorder, he said: "Push on, brave fellows, and avenge your general." While the surgeons were carrying him away he heard cheers, and tried to turn his head in the direction of the sound. A sergeant told him, "The British Jack is coming down, General—the Stars are going up." He smiled, but could not speak. The captured British standard was brought to him. It was placed under his head, and he died.

One who wrote while those events were fresh in mind said: "Gallant spirit! Thy country will not forget thee; thou shalt have a noble memory.

When a grateful nation confers upon the heroes of Niagara and Erie the laurels they have so nobly earned, she will bid them remember that those laurels were first gathered on the shores of York, and were watered by the blood of a hero; and hereafter, when our children and our children's children shall read the story of patriots and heroes who have fallen greatly in the arms of victory, when their eyes glisten and their young hearts throb wildly at the kindling theme, they will close the volume which tells of Epaminondas, of Sidney or of Wolfe, and will proudly exclaim: 'And we, too, had our Montgomery and our Pike.' "

Our car brings us quickly to Catherine Market, one of the most celebrated of our old markets. It was erected in 1786 by Henry Rutgers on almost the same spot where the present buildings stand. Mr. Devoe says, quaintly:

"The first introduction in this City of public 'negro dancing' no doubt took place at this market. The negroes who visited here were principally slaves from Long Island, who had leave of their masters for certain holidays, among which 'Pinkster' was the principal one; when, for 'pocket-money,' they would gather up everything that would bring a few pence or shillings, such as roots, berries, herbs, yellow or other birds, fish, clams, oysters, etc., and bring them with them in their skiffs to this market; then, as they had usually three days' holiday, they were ever ready, by their 'negro sayings or doings,' to make a few shillings more. So they would be hired by some joking butcher or individual to engage in a jig or break-down, as that was one of their pastimes at home on the barn-floor, or in a frolic, and those that could and would dance soon raised a collection; but some of them did more in 'turning around and shying off' from the designated spot than keeping to the regular 'shake-down,' which caused them all to be confined to a 'board' (or shingle, as they called it), and not allowed off it; on this they must show their skill; and, being several together in parties, each had his particular 'shingle,' brought with him as part of his stock in trade. This board was usually about five to six feet long, of large width, with its particular spring in it, and to keep it in its place while dancing on it, it was held down by one on each end. Their music or time was usually given by one of their party, which was done by beating their hands on the sides of their legs and the noise of the heel. The favorite dancing-place was a cleared spot on the east side of the fish market in front of Burnel Brown's Ship Chandlery. The large amount collected in this way after a time produced some excellent 'dancers'; in fact, it raised a sort of strife for the highest honors, *i.e.*, the most cheering and the most collected in the 'hat.' Among the most famous in their day was 'Ned' (Francis), a little wiry negro slave, belonging to Martin Ryerson; another named Bob Rowley, who called himself 'Bobolink Bob,' belonging to William

Bennett, and Jack, belonging to Frederick De Voo, all farmers on Long Island. Jack was a smart and faithful man, and when he was set free by the laws, he became, after a time, a loafer, and died at this market. He was brought up by Mr. De Voo, who thought a good deal of him, and on the day when he was made free he fitted him out in a new suit from 'top to toe,' and then said to him: 'Jack, if you go home with me, you shall never want; but if you leave me now, my home shall never more know you.' Jack could not be persuaded to return home by many of the butchers and others, but would stay in the City. It was not long before his former master was importuned by several persons to take him back, but his answer was: 'The laws set him free and he left me —now let the laws take care of him.' Many New Jersey negroes, mostly from Tappan, were after a time found among them, contending for the prize, and oftentimes successfully too; they were known by their suppleness and plaited forelocks tied up with tea-lead. The Long Islanders usually tied theirs up in a cue, with dried eel-skin; but sometimes they combed it about their heads and shoulders, in the form of a wig, then all the fashion. After the Jersey negroes had disposed of their masters' produce at the 'Bear Market,' which sometimes was early done, and then the advantage of a late tide, they would 'shin it' for the Catherine Market to enter the lists with the Long Islanders, and in the end, an equal division of the proceeds took place. The success which attended them brought our City negroes down there, who, after a time, even exceeded them both, and if money was not to be had 'they would dance for a bunch of eels or fish.' "

He says: "There was an old man engaged in the market about the year 1815 by the name of Sam Way, a great 'shark-catcher.' The dead fish thrown out from the many fish-cars and smacks no doubt attracted many shark in our then quiet waters around this slip; and when Sam heard the cry of 'shirk around the slip,' he would drop his broom, have his 'chain-hook' out and baited, and in a few minutes the cry was, 'Sam's got one hooked'; then, being a large, strong man, he would soon lay the 'shirk' on the dock; and he had been known to take seven in one day, some of them fourteen feet in length. One day he hooked 'a big one,' and he had got into a skiff which lay tied at the end of the slip; the shark took to pulling and broke loose the skiff with Sam in, and away he went down the river, at race-horse speed, nearly as far as Red Hook, before he tired out, or Sam could hold him up; he, however, mastered him and brought him back, and Sam after that concluded not to be run away with again. So he stuck to the raft or dock when he fished for 'shirk.' "

We go on, crossing Fulton and Wall Streets, past the site of the old Stadthuys; then we cross Broad Street, and ride over the old basin where the

Dutch vessels used to lie at anchor, and in a moment we have reached Whitehall Street, and we behold once more the block on which stood the old Fort, the germ point of New York's marvelous life.

### Back at the old Fort.

Have we been to a foreign land since we left this historic spot? Have we not mistaken our course and gone to the lands which are indicated on the State Street signs? Surely we have been among people, have seen sights, and have considered conditions that are foreign to any Dutch, English or American principles of ancestry, and that are no outgrowth of the germs that were planted here. The land that we have traversed, verily, it is ours, but it has been usurped. While we have slept an enemy has sowed tares, and the growth has been mighty. To what an extent is honesty and intelligence and patriotism overgrown by the rank, unwholesome tangle of the Fourth, Sixth and Tenth Wards, and other districts beyond them! These foul things that we have witnessed (and much that our superficial view has not discerned)—heathenism, barbarism, crime, illiteracy and bestiality—are close to our greatest business achievements, close to our newspaper offices, close to the courts, the judges, the professional men; close to the busiest haunts of the most active and brainy people of the land. The operations of New York's vast business army are conducted daily in the midst of and touching these danger spots. Our people pass by and through them daily. What is being done to neutralize and to overcome the tremendous anti-social forces that reside in these districts, and press out from them? To be sure, there are great districts in the City which are filled with the evidences of wealth and refinement. Opposed to the barracks and hovels of the slum districts are palaces and sumptuous hotels. Against the associations of low bar-rooms and the balls of "Soup Green" and similar associations, there are the receptions at Sherry's, the social dinners at Delmonico's, Charity Balls, and First Nights at Operas, with their gorgeous accompaniments of robes, diamonds and shirt bosoms. The gatherings of young thieves at Walhalla Hall and other such places, and the fellowships of jail and penitentiary, are antagonized by select schools and colleges, whose achievements in the gaining and imparting of knowledge are ever advancing. Opposed to the brothels and gambling-houses and dens of vice are ethical associations, Christian associations, Sunday-schools and churches. If there is an army of the ignorant and the vicious growing up on Manhattan Island, there is also an army of the cultivated, the enlightened, the good and the spiritual.

If the salvation of New York is to be worked out through a hostile campaign of the good against the bad, with the object of stamping out evil by throttling, confinement and punishment, then perhaps we are doing well to continue as we are, and to depend upon the criminal courts, the juries and the prosecuting attorneys to keep the degenerate and vicious classes of our population from overrunning the City and destroying our property and our peace. There are many who believe in this method of treating gross ignorance and crime. They have no patience with the illiterate and the vicious, and look with doubt and disfavor upon all efforts to remedy social evils. There are many others who give a sentimental and wordy indorsement to reform measures, but whose hearts are entirely cold, and whose brains are never stirred with the subject; and there are some who are steeped in luxurious vice and anti-social intolerance. There are a few others who are devoting their minds, their hearts and their means to works of philanthropy, some wisely directed and some not so wisely ordered; and there are a few who have really got their sympathies into the work of lifting up the poor, the fallen and the helpless, because of their belief in the fatherhood of God and the brotherhood of man. There are, indeed, important agencies for uplifting the people, working under the administration of the City government, and supported by the tax contributions of all the people. Police protection, street regulation and cleaning, health oversight, hospital assistance and public schooling, are all being carried on vigorously, as portions of our governmental system. A few churches, Sunday-schools and missions, sustained with great effort under a disheartening pressure of financial needs, are maintained here and there, like flickering tallow candles in a dark and stormy midnight. There are a college settlement, a Christian association, a Jewish association, and some industrial schools. All of these agencies fail to prevent the criminal education of the boys, and the vicious environing of the girls; they fail to provide rational and helpful recreation and amusements for the people; they give little of refuge or helping hand to the multitude who might be stimulated to rise above their surroundings and to conquer their besetments. They do comparatively little toward the removal of the many schools of crime and temptations to vice and dishonesty which beset the young people on every hand, and make it almost impossible for them to grow up without taint of sin. These places do not yield to the perfunctory administration of rough and careless criminal officials as they would, and as they always do, to an enlightened and earnest public opinion founded upon actual knowledge. When the Society for the Prevention of Crime cried out against the conditions in the Eleventh Precinct that were rapidly making thieves of the boys and abandoned women of the girls, the great mass of decent people in New York hardly knew which to believe, the society which alleged the conditions of the precinct or the police who denied them. The people themselves knew nothing about it, and very few of them cared enough to gain any personal knowledge.

Standing upon this germinal point of our great City, remembering the good and true upspringing of its life, remembering too the lofty patriotism, the deep religious feeling, and the sentiment of

GREENWICH STREET, LOOKING SOUTH FROM CHURCH STREET.

62 TO 66 GREENWICH STREET.

brotherhood, which bound our forefathers together, so that they sacrificed their comfort, their property and their lives for the achievement of liberty and beneficent government to all the people—and with the pictures of our trip through the Fourth, Sixth and Tenth Wards fresh in our minds—does it not seem to be the overwhelming duty of the good people of New York, regardless of politics, races, or creeds, to unite in an earnest, continuous, fraternal approach to the masses that are lying in darkness, which shall break down their evil environments, lift them up by contact with that which is better than their present surroundings and more intelligent than themselves, and create a bond of sympathy between the people of all the geographical sections of our City? We have quoted the register of the "Max Hochstim Association," which has swooped down upon the ignorant people of the Tenth Ward like a flock of cormorants, and we could easily cover it with the membership rolls of eminent societies. The list of burglars, thieves and pirates might be covered with a roll of eminent doctors, lawyers, ministers, merchants, financiers and philanthropists. Then we could argue that in making up a general judgment upon the condition of New York City, such mercenary organizations as Hochstim's, Van Lear's and Kramer's need not be remembered. But that would not wipe out these organizations, which are conducted, not many miles away from us, but right here on the shores of Manhattan Island. They have been a reproach to the elegant, the learned, the philanthropic and the powerful societies that have discoursed on the rights of man, tenement house problems and kindred subjects, without ever getting near enough to the ground and to the people to touch them or to understand them, or to help them to health, purity and true liberty. We are not pessimistic in these views, for we believe that New York is a better City than ever before, that her tendency is upward, and that the victory for right over wrong is sure to come; but we do believe—I may say we know—that the greatest results thus far have been achieved in the main, not by the rich, the learned, the powerful, not by the social leaders, but by devoted companies of the common people, possessing relatively small means and numbering few who are considered eminent, that have struggled, labored, spent their hearts, their brains and their substance, suffered the criticisms and the sneers of many of the good people, and then encountered the dangerous antagonisms of those whose vicious habits and whose slimy incomes were threatened by their proposed improvements.

The exhibition of the wretched scenes that we have observed will fail in its purpose if it excites only a morbid or curious interest, and does not arouse the patriotism and touch the sympathies of the people of New York.

John Gilmer Speed writes of the money spent annually in "The Most Luxurious City in the

Nos. 11 AND 12 WEST STREET.

New York, Vol. Three, p. 272.

World," in the "Ladies' Home Journal." He asserts in a prefatory way that New York is the most luxurious city in the world, and that expenditures are made on mere living with an elegance and ostentation unknown in any of the capitals of Europe. The total wealth of New York would, if equally divided, give to each man, woman and child of that City $3,756.82—an amount greater than any other city in the world. Mr. Speed states that $20,400,000 are paid annually to lawyers; $11,328,000 to physicians and surgeons; $3,000,000 to clergymen; $2,665,000 to architects; $1,600,000 to dentists; $13,020,000 to brokers. An aggregate of about $100,000,000 is spent annually for clothing; $10,000,000 for furs; $20,000,000 for diamonds and other jewels; $3,500,000 for cut flowers and growing plants; $20,000,000 on yachting (the boats representing an investment of $20,000,000), which is something more than is spent yearly on horses and carriages. The elevated railroads take in $12,000,000 for car fare, and the surface lines $15,000,000—a total of $27,000,000 for going about New York. Mr. Speed estimates that $31,837,000 is spent by New Yorkers each year in European travel, $3,537,500 of which go for steamship tickets, and that they spend $30,000,000 for beer, and $90,000,000 for wine and spirits about sixty-six and two-third dollars for each person per year. In their gifts to charities they are most liberal, $9,000,000 being the annual sum thus expended. More money is spent in supporting and furthering church work in New York than is paid to all theaters and playhouses of the City. The total spent for amusements is $5,900,000, while considerably more than $6,000,000 is contributed to the support of churches.

Oh that we might find the way to turn the great tides of New York's wealth of mind and money, heart and spirit, into the dark districts, and so redeem our City and save its many ignorant and unfortunate inhabitants!

---

# CHAPTER TEN

## *THE NINTH WARD: GREENWICH VILLAGE*

Our last Trip from the Fort—Up the West Side—Immigrants—Strange Faces and Tongues—Turks, Syrians and Arabians—Old Time Gangs—Produce Merchants—Washington Market—Restful, Healthful, Hopeful Greenwich Village—Sir Peter Warren—St. John's Church—Minetta-water—Colored Folks—State Prison—Bedford Street Church—Pictures of Quaint old New York—Zion's Golden Wedding—Unique Entombment—Richmond Hill, General Washington, Aaron Burr—An Excursion to upper New York, where the Greenwich People are going—Revolutionary Relics—Battle-ground—Forts—The Acropolis—Return by the North River—Shipping—The rise and growth of Ocean Transportation—Ocean Liners—Sights of West Street—The Beginning-spot once more—Reverie—Finis

WE will start out now for our last trip from the old Fort, and will go up on the west side, through Greenwich and Washington Streets, making our way toward the Ninth Ward, whence we will return by the North River. There are many strange and interesting people close to the Battery in Greenwich and Washington Streets. On Washington Street we will be especially interested in observing the Syrians, Turks and Arabs that have settled there. On Greenwich Street we will see immigrants' boarding-houses which will bring us in touch with every nation of Europe. As we pass up the two streets, moving from one to the other through the cross streets, pressing northward, we will skirt the western edge of the governor's gardens of the oldest

Dutch's days; and while we do not see any relics of that period, nor of the time when Greenwich Street was the water's edge, we will observe many quaint houses, such as those on Battery Place, those in the rear of the first Broadway block, and those on Albany Street. The roar of the traffic on Broadway and the hum of its business are easily heard at this distance, and on the other side are the many evidences of New York's commerce which are to be seen on the busy river front; but in these streets we seem to be thrown back into the past. It is as though time and progress, which have done so much to transform the appearance of lower New York, had forgotten these old streets and had left them behind. Through the side streets we catch glimpses of the towering buildings on Broadway, and at one place, through Trinity's open churchyard, we have a beautiful picture of white buildings which are in strong contrast with the grimy foreground of Greenwich Street. So retired is this spot that the Turks, the Syrians and the Arabs, though close to the business of lower Broadway, are no more noticed than if they were on their native soil, and, indeed, have no more existence in the knowledge of the busy thousands who travel Broadway daily than if they were on the other side of the earth.

Immigrant boarding-houses contribute much to the picturesqueness of this downtown region, and their motley patrons remind us of our own foreign origin. On State Street we noticed various charitable and religious houses, like the Lutheran Pilger Haus, and the interesting Catholic Mission of "Our Lady of the Rosary"; on antique Pearl Street, just off State Street, the first New York street, there are one or two boarding-houses; and on Battery Place, and Greenwich, Washington and West Streets, they are quite numerous. The antiquated front of Battery Place is devoted entirely to the entertainment of humble foreign visitors, and they may learn the biting power of New York's five-cent whiskey in the Philadelphia, the Castle Garden, and the Svenska Beer Houses. Number 4 Greenwich Street is the Scandinavian House. The sign on Number 6 is "Gasthaus zum Württenbürger Hof." Numbers 8 and 10 are fine old wide houses without signs. Number 12 is a ticket agency, with this sign, "Eisenbahn Billette Nach Allen Theisen der Fereinigten Staaten und Canada." "Deutsches Arbeiter Verein, Männer und Mädchen erhalten hier die Besten Stellen." Number 14 is the Hotel Bremen. Number 16 is Pat Halloran's Reunion Hotel. Number 18 is the Stuttgarter Hof. Number 20 is Walhalla(!). At Number 22 is the Svenska Agentur Affar. Number 24 is the Skandanivska Emigrant Hemmet. Number 26 is a store kept by Gus Kaliski and Lewensohn. Some of these old houses were the mansion residences of leaders of society and business in the New York of fifty years ago. Across the street are several old houses now used for storage by the elevated railroad. One of them bears a sign, the "Punta Rosa House." On West Street, in the little hovels that once sheltered the fiercest breeds of land-sharks, are such places as Tracy's (Number 12) and the Cornish Arms (Number 11). At Number 7 Washington Street is the Hotel Dania; at Number 9 the Polski Dom Emigracyiny; at Number 11 V. Rozak's house; at Number 12½ Finnerty's, and at Number 13 Doyle's.

We have mentioned the existence of antagonistic religious sects side by side, differing in religious principles as they do in their native lands, but living here in peace. The little Syrian colony is divided between the Roman and the Greek Catholic churches. Recently a church was formally established by Archbishop Corrigan of the Roman Catholic Church at Number 83 Washington Street, and was called St. Joseph's Maronite Church of New York. The priest is Father Karkemas. The congregation was discovered by factory inspector Mrs. Nagle, who was told that there was a sweat-shop in the attic of the building. On investigation she found about fifty Syrians working on coats and vests in a room on the top floor, at one end of which were a rough altar, a crucifix, and a picture of the Virgin. She found that the people worked in the room on week days and worshiped there on Sundays. She communicated the fact to the pastor of St. Peter's Church, who presented the matter to the archbishop. Their agents found the priest living at Number 8 Carlisle Street, and immediately made arrangements for establishing the congregation. Father Joseph Yazbek of Boston presided at the opening service, and was assisted by several prominent Catholics, ministers and laymen. The other church is located at Number 77 Washington Street. Its members are of the same faith as the Greeks and the Russians, who have their principal church at Number 340 West 53d Street, and whose principal minister is the Reverend Agathodorus Papageorgopoulous. These people follow the Nicene Creed, and they show their devotion to it by standing during prayer. The pastor at the Washington Street Church is the Reverend Raphael Hawaweeny, the deacon is Constantine Abi-Adal, and the choir of men is led by Abdon Lutfy. The services are exceedingly earnest and impressive. Recently this little congregation had great joy in receiving an embroidery of the Burial of Christ from the Czar of Russia. This year they had their first service in America for the welcoming of Easter Sunday. The Archimandrite (the Rev. Hawaweeny) stood before the figure of Christ at midnight and began the service with a chant which was taken up by the choir. He passed through swinging doors still singing, and then reappeared dressed in shining robes with a crown upon his head, emblematic of the Resurrection. At appropriate intervals of the observances the choir and the congregation took part. There are many stores here containing notions, which the Syrians industriously peddle upon the streets. There are also coffee and smoking rooms and restaurants, which are patronized by Turks and Arabs. Signs in Syrian, Turkish and Arabian characters may be seen, and frequently the anglicized names of the store-keepers may be read on the sign-boards and window-panes in our own language. Some of the people of this region are Mohammedans. There are in the City about six hundred of the "Faithful," and they are planning to erect a mosque.

The Eastern people are to be found mostly in Washington and Carlisle Streets. At Numbers 25 and 27 Washington Street are two filthy tenement houses that are crowded with them. The store-keepers in these buildings are Calil Abraham and Saraya, and P. Khouri. At two corners of Morris Street are the stores of Zabi Azar, and Manassa and Kishbany. Majeeb Malluk keeps store at Number 16, and Ganim and Sadallah at Number 19. S. Elias and T. Abdoo are at Number 31. At Number 57 is a "Turkish Coffee and Pool Room." Moshy and Saad are at Number 59, and D. J. Faour is at Number 63. At Number 69 is Salim Elias, and at Number 71 is L. Atta's "Turkish Coffee Room." A. G. Mussawir's place is at Number 73. At Number 77 are the Greek Church, and the establishment of a merchant named Anton Tadross, which extends to Number 79. The Maronite Church is at Number 83, in the same building with A. Sahadi's store. Joseph Ayoob, at Number 81, keeps the peace between the two churches. At Number 87 is a relic of "ould dacincy," Mrs. R. Duffy's livery stable. At Number 89 is Amin Merhige and M. D. Kaydonh. At Number 91 is T. Shishim's restaurant. At Number 95 is Habib As-say's restaurant. Around the corner of Rector Street are Charley Sing's laundry and the Hotel Copenhagen. On the next block is a mixture of the nations, which includes George Forzly's Armenian bank, Hen Lee's Chinese laundry, Slevin's Irish liquor saloon, and J. Yamin's Syrian notion store. Close to them is J. Mahoney's boarding-house. Carlisle Street is full of Syrians. There are Elias Moussi's, Taunis Basha's and Slyby Kouri's stores, and near them is the shop of a bright-hued Italian named Pietro Callabrese. O. Von Krog, an expressman, represents the Knickerbocker type, and H. Kruse, a modern *Deutsch* grocer, "holds the fort" on the corner.

In the southerly parts of Washington and Greenwich Streets, between the Battery and Washington Market, there are many squalid homes, many vile saloons, and there is much dirt and ignorance; but the lawless "gangs" which were prominent a few years ago have passed out of existence. It is a wonder that when property is so valuable along Broadway and east of it that land-owners are forced to build sky-scrapers, that this large section so close to the center of business life should be overlooked and neglected. One of the noted "gangs" of the City was the "Stable Gang," about fifty strong, with headquarters at Number 14 Washington Street, which devoted its attentions principally to immigrants. The "Silver Gang" was near by, and its members relied upon the more fashionable calling of burglary to make their way through the world. The

"Potashes" hung around the Babbitt Soap Factory in Washington Street near Rector Street. Its leader was "Red Shay Meehan." It was a collection of hard fighters, who terrorized the whole neighborhood and even dominated the other gangs. Further uptown was the "Boodle Gang," which was located principally in a nest of double tenement houses on the block bounded by Greenwich, Washington, Spring and Canal Streets. These buildings made up a perfect hive of thieves, and it numbered many expert garroters. It made forays upon the market-men of Central Market, and on the provision wagons which passed through their neighborhood. We could name twenty or more of these "gangs" which were in active operation as organized bodies of thieves, robbers, and burglars a dozen years ago. They have no longer any public existence.

At John Hughson's house on Greenwich Street, between Thames and Liberty Streets, the negro plot of 1741 originated. Near to Hughson's was Mr. Comfort's tea-water pump, which is still indicated by the old pump near the corner. This pump, and the great tea-water pump at Roosevelt and Chatham Streets, gave the only water that was fit to drink or to use in making tea, and the slaves of persons living in the lower part of the City resorted to Comfort's pump to draw water. Hughson sold liquor, and enjoyed the society of the slaves who resorted to his house. There they exchanged stories of oppression and cruelty, and warmed the fires of hatred which smoldered in their breasts. There

77 WASHINGTON STREET.

91 WASHINGTON STREET.

SIGN AT 63 WASHINGTON STREET.

SIGN AT 103 WASHINGTON STREET.

New York, Vol. Three, p. 275.

were Pedro and Albany, Jack, Braveboy, London, Tickle, Bastian, Cæsar, Guy, and many others. They formed into bands, such as the "Smith Fly Boys," the "Geneva Club," the "Long Bridge Boys" and the "Free Masons," and they had the oaths, the tests and the silly formulas which might be expected of such great ignorant boys as they were. Out of their mummery, and the very natural expressions of resentment for many wrongs that were heaped upon them, was built the gauzy fabric of testimony which courts, lawyers and juries used ruthlessly in criminal prosecutions to terrify and subdue the black men.

Most of the slaves of lower New York were buried in the negro cemetery at Chambers Street and Broadway.

At Vesey Street we find ourselves in the midst of the produce district. Washington Market is here, and many blocks above it are monopolized by merchants in fruits and vegetables. At the corner of Vesey and Greenwich Streets is an old building that is believed to be the foundation of a light-house that stood on the shore one hundred and fifty years ago. When St. Paul's Church was new, there was nothing but orchard and beach between it and the river, and it is said that from its porch the light of this harbor beacon could be seen. The roof of the original building was destroyed by fire, but the heavy walls seem indestructible. In the building now there is a boot and shoe store, and that business has been carried on there for over seventy-five years. The boot on the roof has done duty since 1832. It was built for advertising by John C. Graham of 77 Catherine Street, and was an exhibit in the Croton Water Parade of 1842. It is still in the Graham family. Washington Market is the successor of Bear Market, which was erected in 1771 on the west side of Greenwich Street, between Fulton and Vesey Streets. That name was applied to the market, because in the river close by a butcher named Jacob Finck killed a fine large bear that was trying to cross from New Jersey. During the Revolutionary War the market was deserted, except that a little hay was sold. It was used for a barracks and depot, and a troop of cavalry was stationed there. In 1798 a physician complained to the mayor concerning the market in these words:

"S[r] — Our Intention is to show you the True State of bear Markett. We are Buisy filling up below, in Order to Keep Clear of filth, & M. Morrison Pays his attention in Seeing it Sweept. Mr. Culbertson (*Clerk of the Market*) also Pays his attention in Plasing the Huxsters. But when his Back is Turn[d] they all Do as they think proper—they Make a Costom When the Butchers is Gon, to Move in the Markett with their Coffee and Frute, and by that Means Collect Numbers of Idol, Drunken, & Durty Men Seting and Lying on the Stalls, So that the Butchers with Difficulty Can Scarcely make them Even Look Deasent, as the Huxsters, more or less of them, Stays until 9 or 10 O'clock at night, & their Frute Draws Large Gangs of unruly Boys, Disturbing the Peasable Inhabitants; this, S^r, you may Relye on as being Facts. New York, August 15, 1798."

The Deputy Clerks received orders to remove "all venders of fruit and vegetables from the public market-places and streets adjoining at sunset every day, except venders of vegetables on Saturdays."

The large business done at the market induced many persons to open eating-houses, and a report upon these places was made by a committee of the Common Council in 1810 in this language:

"They say that they draw a crowd around them, such as to render business altogether impracticable. The houses in the neighborhood of these markets are occupied principally by victualers, who calculate on the custom to be derived from market people, and have been induced to give very extravagant rents. They are well provided with every description of viands, and can satisfactorily administer to the wants not only of the fatigued countryman, but even to the dainty appetite of the most squeamish. Everything appears inviting and nice, and the salutary beverage so much applauded for its vivifying efficacy here flows abundantly. The early stirring and often chilled marketman can here quaff his ambrosial coffee at as cheap a rate, and with infinitely more comfort. Four cents a pint for coffee, and two cents for a muffin, is the usual price taken at the stands in the markets. So, also, in these houses they sell this, as well as every nourishment, at the same reasonable ratio.''

The report was confirmed. In 1813 the old building was destroyed, and a market-house on the site of the present market was erected. Then, as now, a considerable part of the market was devoted to the sale of milk products. It was called the ''Buttermilk Market,'' and Dutch women from Jersey, ''dressed in linsey-woolsey short gowns and petticoats, came in great numbers with their butter, pot-cheese, curds and buttermilk.'' In four months of 1816 the business done amounted to 1,644 beeves, 1,973 sheep, 3,165 calves, and 867 hogs. This business was considerably smaller than that of the Fly Market at that time.

The trip up Greenwich Street carries us past many queer old houses which were built in the days when the street was a rural road.

Admiral Sir Peter Warren was the original owner of the principal part of the Ninth Ward settlement. He was a jolly, high-handed rover of the seas, who grew wealthy upon the booty which he captured from the rich merchant vessels of the King's enemies in the days of the privateers. In 1727 he received the command of the ''Grafton,'' a ship of the line; then he had the ''Solebay,'' a frigate; then the ''Leopard,'' a ship of fifty guns; then the ''Squirrel,'' a twenty-gun ship; then the ''Launceston'' of forty guns, and the ''Superbe'' of sixty guns. After that, in 1743, he had command of a squadron. The ship with which New Yorkers were most familiar was the "Launceston," which frequently bore the gallant admiral into port after his successful forays upon rich Spanish merchantmen. On those occasions the captured goods were publicly auctioned, and the people took holidays to attend the sales. As years increased upon him, he began to desire a permanent home on shore, and looking about the suburbs of New York, he fixed upon the tract which had been called by the Indians Sappokanikan, and which was Governor Wouter Van Twiller's tobacco farm. It contained about three hundred acres and overlooked the Hudson River. He built his mansion where Fourth and Perry Streets now intersect, and his house stood for a century. In the French and Indian War, Admiral Warren had command of the naval force which co-operated with Col. Pepperell's soldiers in reducing the French stronghold of Louisburg. Warren, for his part in the brilliant movement, was gazetted rear-admiral. Subsequently he was knighted. He married a sister of Chief-justice Delancey of New York, and entered into the politics of the early City, becoming a member of Governor Clinton's council. In the contest between Clinton and Delancey, Warren was talked of as the successor of Clinton in the governorship, and Clinton did not rest easy, even when Warren was in England, until he died (in 1752). It is recorded that in four months, while the commodore was stationed off

Martinique, he captured twenty-four prizes. They were all sent to New York, and Stephen Delancey & Co. auctioned the spoil. The "Post Boy" of August 27, 1744, says: "His Majesty's ship 'Launceston,' commanded by the brave Commodore Warren (whose absence old Oceanus seems to lament), being now sufficiently repaired, will sail in a few days, in order once more to pay some of his Majesty's enemies a visit.

"The sails are spread; see the bold warrior comes
To chase the French and interloping Dons!"

On this visit to New York, we know that the "Launceston" was repaired at the careening place on the East River near Grand Street, a picture of which we have previously shown. The admiral had three daughters. Charlotte married the Earl of Abingdon, Ann married the Baron of Southampton, and Susannah married a colonel named William Skinner. Three of the streets in Greenwich Village were named after these husbands: Skinner Road, now Christopher Street; Fitzroy Road near Eighth Avenue, from 14th to 42d Streets, and Abingdon Road (otherwise known as Love Lane), close to the line of 21st Street, from Broadway to the North River. Abingdon Square still remains.

There was a time when St. John's Church, south of Greenwich Village, was a picturesque feature of a quiet community. When built in 1807 its locality seemed undesirable, for the ground was swampy, and it was not thought likely that it could be supported by a resident population. The far-seeing Trinity Church people had faith in their project, and were rewarded by having some of the most influential families of old New York move into the neighborhood of the beautiful church and its grounds. There attended it such people as Dr. Hunter, General Dix, General Morton, John C. Hamilton, Alexander Hamilton's widow, the Clarksons, Cammanns, Crugers, Drakes, Lorillards, Schuylers and the Lawrences. St. John's Park in front of the church was one of the prettiest spots in the City. Now it is occupied by the great freight depot of the New York Central Railroad.

The graveyard of St. John's Church at Clarkson, Leroy and Varick Streets will soon be transformed into a public park. When one has wandered through the quaint streets of Greenwich Village, and then comes upon this neglected spot, he realizes that he has found the most antiquated district of the City. There is nothing in Greenwich Village to tell the traveler that he is in the heart of a metropolis. In many blocks the comfortable old houses of fifty and seventy-five years ago still remain, respectable and well kept, but with few of the modern improvements which elsewhere are common. Even the elevated railroad of Greenwich Street is a stunted affair, and its trains seem more like those which ran on Fourth Avenue fifty years ago than like the rushing, snorting little monsters that make life on the avenues unbearable. The corporation of Trinity Church, which owns the graveyard, fought hard to retain it, but the legal obstacles to the condemnation proceedings have been overcome, and soon the children of the Ninth Ward will romp over walks laid on top of dead men's bones, as children do now in Washington Square, Union Square, Madison Square, and Bryant Park, which were all constructed over "Potter's Fields." Opportunity has been given for the removal of the remains in St. John's burying-ground, and quite a number of bodies have been taken away; but those which remain are so far forgotten that no one is left to do that office for them. The tombstones tell mostly of the common folk who made up the plain, substantial life of Greenwich Village. Here are a few of them:

"In Christ
John Reid
Jesus mercy."
(Involuntarily we say: Amen!)

---

"Bridget Keane, wife of James Keane (deceased), a native of Galway, Ireland; died 28 March, 1823, aged 63 years.

"Farewell, farewell, my children dear.
If aught on earth could keep me here
It would be my love for you.
But Jesus calls my soul away;
Jesus forbids a longer stay.
I bid you all ADIEU."

---

"To the memory of Jeanne Renoit Lagrave, born in Bordeaux, March 15, 1762; died in New York after a residence of fifteen years, June 15, 1837, aged 75 years."

"John Black, bookseller in this City, who departed this life Oct. 5, 1803, a native of Scotland for thirty years. He was beloved by all who knew him."

There are English, Welsh, Dutch, and Spanish names on the stones. Mrs. Elizabeth Wenman "Died of the Epidemic" in 1803. Her epitaph reads:

"Fearless and calm she met the fatal blow,
And left without a sign these scenes below.
A band of cherubs joined her on the road
And safe conveyed her to the bright abode."

William Berford, a sea captain, died in 1810. This inscription is on his tombstone: "For many years he battled bravely with the sea." There is a monument over two firemen, Eugene Underhill and Frederick A. Ward, who were killed at a fire on July 1, 1834. Of Captain Peter Taylor, who died on April 7, 1839, it is recorded:

"Long has he braved the swelling sea, well-known for skill as a man of his profession; but at last he has cast his anchor in the broad bay of sweet repose."

Christopher P. Collis, the friend of Robert Fulton, is buried here. The grave of Mary Westerly is marked with an inscription which shows that she was "the fruitful instrument of numerous offspring." She was "cut off in the epidemick prevailing in New York in October, 1805." Further on the inscription says: "Gratitude, that motive which is of the highest obligation, demands this tribute to the memory of a most endearing wife by an infinitely obliged husband and her five surviving children. Two other children, daughters, were cut off on the same day as their mother."

The streets of Greenwich Village are well adapted to the mood of the reminiscent rambler, for they lead everywhere and nowhere, and wander about in the most irregular ways. It is somewhat disturbing to the ordinary business man, who happens to be called into this quiet section, to walk through Fourth Street and find himself crossing Tenth, Eleventh and Twelfth Streets and landing in Thirteenth Street. If he walks along Bleecker Street, expecting to reach the Hudson River, which ought to be its westerly termination, he will land in Abingdon Square, where Hudson and Bank and West 12th Streets and Eighth Avenue are all jumbled together. The traveler needs a guide to make haste through Greenwich Village.

The ponds and streams and the hills of the old settlement made it an enchanting spot. We have spoken of Burr's Pond. The Minetta water was a brook that turned and twisted as it made its way to the Hudson River. Its waters are still flowing underground, and they frequently give trouble to builders. It was famed for its trout, and skilled anglers resorted to it. Men are living in New York to-day, who caught fish in Greenwich Village, who angled from the stone bridge at Canal Street and Broadway, and who hunted on the Lispenard Meadows and shot snipe at Tompkins Square. One recently said that he hunted close to Tammany Hall. All that we have now to remind us of the lovely, purling, shaded brook with the Indian name is the sweet little thoroughfare, Minetta Lane, with its dilapidated cottages, that for many years has been the home of a depraved, quarrelsome and criminal colony of negroes. The time was when the bloodthirsty character of the Minetta negroes was so well established that the street was practically closed to travel. Such men as "No-Toe Charley," "Bloodthirsty," "Black Cat," and "Jube Tyler," made national reputations—at least among the colored people—for their dexterity in the sanguinary use of the razor. This colony holds close connection with the larger negro population of Thompson and Sullivan Streets, and joins with them in playing politics. Hank Anderson of Thompson Street, who was the body servant of "Boss" Tweed, is the Democratic leader; for there are colored Democrats in New York City. He is a man who must be seen by Democrats who covet the votes of colored men and are willing to use practical methods in getting them. There is a continual scramble for the honors of Republican leadership. Caleb Simms, the negro lawyer, now seems to hold the position by virtue of his surpassing gift of oratory, of which the following is a sample:

(This extract is merely the prelude to an oration.)

"Mr. Williams is a young man surcharged with the ambition that kills. He is unskilled and impractical even as a linguist, of which latter there is abundant evidence, if any one has interest enough in the subject to investigate; and, while I am in unison with every advancing hope of young colored men, I am not blind to the amenities controlling all advancement, and shall not subordinate my love of young men to my love of truth and right. When Mr. Williams has demonstrated his fitness to the extent of all requirements consequent upon the position which he may seek, I will vie with his best friend to do him honor. Mr. Williams is lacking in ability to do what is required of an election district chairman(!), and his rushing into print is full evidence that he is lacking in skill and executive ability(!). Mr. Richardson, of whom 'inability' is charged, has given more evidence of high ability than Mr. Williams will ever be capable of, from a political point of view."

Here are astuteness and eloquence fitly mingled. The observer of the present life of the Ninth Ward will miss much amusement if he neglects the colored population on its border, and if he fails to see the "darky parade" on Carmine Street and lower Sixth Avenue on Sunday afternoons.

The State Prison which stood in Christopher Street near the North River was opened in 1797. A portion of the original wall may be seen in the great brewery that now occupies its site. The prisoners in this institution were a turbulent lot, and there were many escapes and outbursts, one of

25 AND 27 WASHINGTON STREET.

New York, Vol. Three, p. 276.

which had to be quelled by military force. The prisoners were deemed to be a menace to the people and village of Greenwich, and Newgate, as it was called, was superseded by the prison erected at Sing Sing.

This picture of the State Prison was much admired in its day. In 1815 a magazine published this notice concerning it, under the heading—

"DOMESTIC LITERARY INTELLIGENCE.

"A view of the New York State Prison has just been published at New York, in an 8vo pamphlet of 90 pages. We regard the penitentiary establishments of the United States as among the most useful and noble experiments, or rather improvements, of this age. That at New York is one of the most important we have, and the account here given of it forms a valuable statistical document. We could not but observe the number of convicts discharged from this prison by pardon.

"This is certainly a defective part of the system. Mercy should not be excluded, but punishment, however lenient, ought, in all ordinary cases, to be certain. The pamphlet is adorned with a neatly engraved view of the prison; we perceive that one of Moreland's hogs is feeding quietly under the prison wall; as it is to be presumed he was borrowed for the occasion, according to the custom of the art, this is, at worst, nothing more than a breach of trust in the artist, and no felony."

The social life of Greenwich Village and the old Ninth Ward was well exemplified in the two old churches, St. Luke's on Hudson Street, and the Bedford Street Methodist Church at the corner of Bedford and Morton Streets. The Bedford Street Church was a hot furnace of religious activity; St. Luke's Church was exceedingly respectable and aristocratic. St. Luke's supporters rapidly departed as the charm of Greenwich Village passed away, and it is now a dependency of Trinity Church. Its graveyard was crowded with the bodies of old Greenwich citizens, but most of them have been removed, and all the tombstones have disappeared. The Bedford Street Church has been more fortunate. It has not now the numerical and financial power of older days, but it is still an effective and aggressive organization.

This institution, more than any other that remains, fairly showed the sturdy American life of Greenwich Village. The faces of its old members are excellent types of the middle classes of the old Ninth Ward. The reputed founder of the society was Joanna De Groot, in whose house in Spring Street, before the present century, the meetings were held which led to the organization of the first class-meeting in Greenwich Village, and the founding of the church. The first church building was erected in 1810, on the site of the present church. There still lives a faithful member, Caroline Cropsey of Number 3 Jones Street, who attended the "Shingle Church," as it was

MURDERERS ALLEY, WATTS AND SULLIVAN STREETS.

New York, Vol. Three, p. 380.

called. Philip Allaire, an aged member, writes this letter:

"My father, Edwin Allaire, in the year 1829, built the house on Arden Street, on the site of which is now Number 22 Morton. I was then seven years of age, and went to the Sabbath school in the old church fronting on Bedford Street; it was shingled on the two sides and back, as well as roof. It became too small for them, and in 1830 it was enlarged. This I saw done. They had meetings of great power. Many fell under the power of God while the minister was preaching. We had 'Four Days' Meetings,' held through the daytime. People brought their lunches with them. The altar was crowded with seeking souls.

"They built the old church in 1816. I remember the high back seats. They stood straight up. On the sanded floor they knelt in prayer. From our house, 22 Arden Street, was a row of poplar trees down Arden Street. The basement of the old church was underground. It was reached on either side by stone steps. Here I went to Sabbath-school. The first superintendent in my days was Bro. William Hughson. He had but one eye. He was a precious man of God. Next came Bro. Caleb Leverich. While he was superintendent I was converted, under the preaching of Rev. John C. Green, in 1834, being twelve years of age, at the altar now in the basement of your present church. Hundreds have been converted while kneeling round it. One of the gates—for there were two gates—is at Red Bank, N. J. It was held for years by Bro. Earle. He was converted at this gate and took it with him when the church was torn down in 1839 and the present one was built.

"Rev. Noah Levings was the first minister I remember. I was then five years of age, and joined the infant class of the old class taught by Miss Febette Totten, who, with her sister and David Demarest, led the choir in the old and new churches."

In 1840 the present church was erected. At that time there were many famous people living in the Ninth Ward. On one block in Bleecker Street (between Thompson and Sullivan Streets) lived Dr. Valentine Mott, Alexander T. Stewart, Mayor Pelatiah Perit, the bankers Ward and Nathan, and the Livingstons. The neighborhood does not look like it now. A golden wedding was celebrated in 1890, and then many reminiscences of the old church and of Greenwich Village came to light. Mrs. Rachel Smith, daughter of the founder Mrs. De Groot, and her neighbor Charity Cokelet, David Demarest, Richard Horton, and a few other survivors of the good old days, received special honors.

The people here mentioned not only represent the Bedford Street Church, but they are thoroughly typical of Greenwich Village in the days that now interest us. George Lansing Taylor composed an ode on the church's golden jubilee, which contains

ALLEY OF HOUSE CORNER WATTS AND SULLIVAN STREETS.

New York, Vol. Three, p. 281.

so much information about old times that we will reproduce it here:

### Zion's Golden Wedding.

BY GEORGE LANSING TAYLOR, L.H.D.

Ring the bells! A golden wedding! Let them sound a joyful peal!
Echoing, with tumultuous gladness, shouting brass and clanging steel!
Let the singers lift their voices! Let the flutes and cornets blow!
Let the organ's diapason, like a river, swell and flow!
Let the preachers tell the story! Let the white-haired elders praise
Him whose cloud and fire have led them like His flock in ancient days!
Let the bard in cheerful numbers voice the rapture of the time!
Let the swift trochaic measures leap and throb in rapid rhyme,
Like the pulsing feet of dancers bounding o'er the fragrant sod,
When the poet-king to Zion brought the Ark of Israel's God!
Let the people, all the people, lift their hearts in glad accord,
Lift their grateful songs and anthems in thanksgiving to the Lord!
Glory! Honor! Adoration! to Immanuel, King of kings,

Him whose majesty and mercy every soaring seraph sings!
Him whose hand has led this people, soothed their sorrows, calmed their fears,
Filled this temple with His presence half a hundred wondrous years!
Ah, how long the length'ning vista! Thrice a generation's span,
Since the humble Methodist founders here their toils and prayers began!
In those days fair Greenwich Village slept by Hudson's rural shore,
Two miles out from New York City, with its bustle, rush and roar!
Then great Gotham's "eighty thousand" filled the New World with amaze,
And the City Hall was building, "out of town," in those "fast" days!
Then Canal Street was a tide creek, famed for piscatory charms,
And Broadway a country turnpike winding northward through the farms.
Then the stage from Greenwich prison drove to Wall Street twice a day—
Now the somber "Black Maria" oftener drives the other way!
Then great Fulton's wondrous steamboat first woke Neptune from his nap,
Shook the trident from his grasp like a sub-aqueous thunder clap!
Then the traitor and assassin, Burr, still reigned on "Richmond Hill,"

With its lordly park and mansion 'neath its great oaks, calm and still;
Those were the days when Methodist preachers, with their souls for Christ aflame,
With their songs, their zeal, their unction, first to Greenwich Village came.
Calm and peaceful lay the village, with its rural, restful air,
With its roadways arched by shade-trees, and its dooryard flower-beds fair;
With its trim and grassy sidewalks where the dandelions sprang,
Leading out to fields and orchards where the thrush and robin sang;
Leading on where lanes and footpaths led through grain and pasture land,
Or they climbed the wooded hillsides, or they wound along the strand.
Low peaked roof, and many-gabled, stood the houses each alone,
With its fruit-trees and its rose-bush bending o'er the doorstep stone;
With its well-kept kitchen garden, and its well-sweep arching high,
With its mossy, iron-bound bucket, hoisting nectar toward the sky.
Few were then the storied mansions—Lady Warren's charming seat
Brought the city wits and belles to its Arcadian retreat;
Grand George Clinton's country home received the humble or the great,

Where the neighbors called, or sages sought the mind
that ruled the State.
Oft the weary city merchants, lawyers, politicians,
fled
For a rural drive to Greenwich when the busy day had
sped.
Poor Tom Paine, debauched, penurious, here life's dregs
dishonored spent;
Too blasphemous to be civil, too besotted to repent;
Quakers, Methodists, Presbyterians, Churchmen, all with
oaths repulsed—
Damned while living! with the torments of the "sec-
ond death" convulsed.
Not a school then graced the village, and the boys and
girls in droves,
With their books and dinner-baskets rambled through
the fields and groves,
Gathering chestnuts in Burr's forest, picking berries
down Broadway,
Skating on Burr's pond in winter, fishing many a truant
day
From the "old stone bridge," where Broadway the Canal
Street tide-creek spanned;
Thus they sought the city schoolhouse, by the wise Dutch
dominies planned.
Then the old Dutch Church in Tenth Street, on the ham-
let's northern bound,
Stood, the sole suburban temple, 'mid the cornfields wav-
ing round;
And the villagers on Sundays to the city churches
walked,

Quaffed the famous spring at Morton's, and of Life's
blest fountain talked.
Such was life in Greenwich Village where the silvery
Hudson shone,
When the Methodist preachers found it, nigh a hundred
years agone;
When they came as "sons of thunder," arrows shot from
Wesley's bow,
Lightnings answering to Jehovah, "Here we are, to flash
and go!"
No cathedral hailed their coming, vaulted nave or tower-
ing spire,
But they preached in demonstration of the Holy Ghost
and fire!
Samuel Walgrove's humble house and wheelwright's
shop in Christopher Street,
Witnessed oft the dread Shekinah radiant o'er the Mercy
seat;
Good Joanna De Groot's plain parlor, where their mes-
sage first was given,
Oft became, like Jacob's Bethel, "God's own house, the
gate of Heaven."
Then the New York "circuit preachers," William Thatcher, Francis Ward,
Formed a "class" in Greenwich Village, six true souls to
serve the Lord—
Samuel Walgrove, the first member, good George Suck-
ley and his wife,
Sister Shultz, and William Tillou, Brother Elsworth led
the strife.

Such the lowly band first marshaled by the wheelwright's
dusty bench,
Few, but fired with heavenly ardor, zeal not earth nor
hell could quench!
Lo! "Old Bedford Street's" first temple, reared in eighteen hundred and ten,
Haloed o'er with hallowed memories, looms once more
on history's ken;
With its arched and fan-head windows, in a double row
all 'round,
And its frame of ax-hewed timbers, shingled o'er from
roof to ground;
Separate aisles for men and women—youths and maidens
far apart—
Yet young eyes across those galleries many a tell-tale
glance could dart!
Straight-backed pews, severe, uncushioned, shadeless
windows, sanded floor;
Towering pulpit, whence the preacher gazed the pews
and galleries o'er;
Antique sounding-board above it—though that, sure, was
scarcely missed
When one famous Boanerges split the book-board with
his fist!
Then came hundreds, thronging thousands, by the city's
growth unknown,
Changing miles of farms and gardens into miles of brick
and stone;
But the power on Zion resting with the worldly power
kept pace,

Miracles of outward progress matched the miracles of grace!
Soon the "shingled church" was crowded, the "Old Eel-pot" caught its fill;
Yet the human sea was swarming, shoals on shoals pressed onward still;
Till the village shrine twice widened, vanished from this sacred spot—
But its blessings, toils, and triumphs linger, ne'er to be forgot.
Then this massive Doric temple, pediment, pilaster, frieze,
Reared its cubic bulk toward heaven, the sunshine and the breeze;
Plain and strong, as were its builders and the earnest faith they taught,
Bold, clear-cut, uncompromising, pregnant symbol of their thought.
Not a flourish, not a gimcrack, naught of noble Art's abuse,
Strength, simplicity, proportion, dignity, repose and use;
Honest brick and honest mortar, no untempered daubing here,
Firm as Methodist experience, positive, assured and clear!
Then, like church, like congregation! Not the worldly, idle, vain,
Not pretentious snobs and upstarts, newly rich with ill-got gain;
Not their heirs of ancient lineage, haughty, arrogant and stiff;
Not "society's" dolls and monkeys, with their pert, ineffable sniff;

But the people, the plain people, the strong people, filled
these pews,
Men and women who earned good livings, worshiped God
and read the news!
Ah, then, how the good work prospered, pushed by many
a vigorous hand,
Preaching, Sunday-school, prayer-meeting, love-feast,
class-meeting, "band";
Methodism's whole armor burnished, all her weapons,
ardor, fire,
All that mortal zeal could render, all that faith and love
inspire!
Hark! the roll call of the preachers! There were giants
in those days,
Men of mighty faith and labors, men with minds and
souls ablaze!
Asbury, the apostolic; Garretson, the pioneer;
Saintly, eloquent M'Kendree, fragrant name to millions
dear!
George and Emory, Roberts, Hedding, Waugh and
Morris, Hamline, Soule—
Bishops by the Spirit's "succession," o'er all hierarch's
control!—
Scott and Baker, Ames the statesman, guiding men with
matchless ease,
Janes, th' unwearied master-builder; Simpson, our De-
mosthenes!
Pastors: Ward and Thatcher, founders; Rice and Hib-
bard, wits renowned;
Howe and Ross and Young and Prindle; Levings, able
and profound;

WEST STREET, FROM BRIDGE AT RECTOR STREET.

New York, Vol. Three, p. 283.

Ferguson, Greene, and Mead and Francis; Griffin, clerkly and austere;
Sage Van Deusen, hoary Nestor, whom to-day we honor here;
Cheney—fallen! Seys, like Stanley, who from Afric's shores returns!
Ammerman, Lee, and Marks and Nichols: Smith, whose zeal for Temperance burns;
Eloquent Newman, learned Poisal—soon to Dixie fled!
Cookman—wandering after "orders"! Hagany, Brown and Ferris—dead.
Gregory, Osbon, Reed, Van Alstyne, Darwood, Chadwick, names emblazed,
All D. D.'s like more before them! All too modest to be praised!
Ah, the "events" around these altars! baptisms, weddings, funerals sad;
Best of all, the great revivals, making earth and angels glad!
Glorious work, and glorious workmen! Glorious, too, the harvest reapt
From the good seed sown with weeping, while men woke, or while they slept.
Converts won by hundreds, thousands, members edified and blest;
Thousands toiling now for Zion, thousands "entered into rest";
Standard-bearers raised whose valor bore Immanuel's flag, unfurled,
On from conquering into conquest, half around the ransomed world.

Hail, Ann Wilkens! name remembered! Leader of our woman's host,
Now Christ's joyful Mary, running to each far-off heathen coast!
Thrice from Afric's fevers flying, thrice returning to the fight,
Twenty years on dark Liberia pouring Christian learning's light!
John M. Reid, revered though living! preacher, teacher, editor, scribe,
Sage in counsel, guide and pilot of our Missionary tribe;
Rogers, Knapp, M'Cutcheon, Chadwick, Merritt, Mundy —of Calvin's race!—
Turning all, from Fore-ordination to the glad news of Free Grace!
Ring the bells for Golden Wedding! Half a century of power
Since this temple's consecration ends with this triumphant hour!
Half a century, changing thousands into millions and renown!
Changing rural Greenwich Village to "Ninth Ward" ten miles downtown!
Changing seventeen to sixty millions 'twixt Columbia's shores,
While the tide of coming millions like an ocean swells and pours!
Threefold gain in half a century, spite secession, war and strife,
For our nation! But our Zion's travail teems with fourfold life!

Then six hundred thousand followers, now two millions
 and a half,
Spite "probation's" fanning-mill yearly blowing out the
 tares and chaff!
Lo! the third half-century ended since in Wesley's Lon-
 don room,
Sprang a century plant now crowning zones and nations
 with its bloom!
Now six millions in communion! Thirty millions in their
 train,
In all lands! and these redoubled ere the century rounds
 again!
One in doctrine, one in spirit, Wesley's sermons, Wes-
 ley's song;
Wesley's, Luther's, Paul's conversion; Wesley's system,
 clear and strong.
Let the cities, let the nations, double, treble, as they will,
Wesley's Church, baptized from heaven, yet shall double
 oftener still!
Toiling, praying, giving, loving, walking on in Truth's
 clear light,
True to Righteousness and Duty, girded with celestial
 might;
Humble, holy, fervent, faithful, Wesley's Church with
 him can sing:
"All the world is but my parish, and I'll take it for the
 King!"

The old-time Americans who remain in this neighborhood have watched its decadence as an American stronghold with many misgivings. The decline of American population and the growth of flat buildings are a constant subject of mournful converse. One of the veterans has paraphrased "Home, Sweet Home" in this way:

> "Flat, flat, dear, dear flat,
> Be it ever so humble, there's nothing so flat."

Between three and four thousand of the best and truest people of Greenwich Village were interred about the church building. As the changes of time went on and the demands for building space increased, and the needs of the church became harder to meet, it was decided to sell the burying-ground; but before any purchaser was allowed to take possession, an air-tight vault was constructed underneath the building, and the ground of the cemetery was carefully dug over by employees of the church, who gathered up every human relic and deposited it in the vault, which was then sealed up. Bedford Street Church stands to-day over the bones of several thousand of its former members and converts, which literally connect its present existence with its former days of glory. The church is their monument. Do their spirits still attend class-meetings and love feasts? What a shaking and what an upheaval there will be when Gabriel sounds his trumpet!

The house at Richmond Hill, Greenwich Village, in which Aaron Burr lived, was a notable resort for the learned and elegant people of New York. It was the same house which General Washington occupied for headquarters in 1776, and in which his life-guardsman, Hickey, tried to poison him; Lord Dorchester and Sir Guy Carleton lived in it during the English occupation, and it was the home of Vice-President Adams. Burr occupied it for a country residence when he became Vice-President. There he entertained Jerome Bonaparte, Talleyrand, Volney, Louis Philippe, and many other noble foreigners, as well as the leading members of New York's early aristocracy. His daughter, Theodosia, gave the charm of her unique and lovely personality to the open hospitality of the home. It was there that Burr laid his far-reaching political plans. Jefferson, Madison and Hamilton all visited and dined there. Mayor Edward Livingston, beloved of the people, was an especially favored guest. The mansion stood down on Charlton Street near Varick Street, and was built by Major Mortier about 1765. The gateway to the grounds stood about at the end of Macdougal Street, and north of the gate was a pond, generally called Burr's Pond. In later years the building was changed into a theater (1834).

When the lower City suffered from the scourges of fever, smallpox and cholera, the salubrious district of Greenwich was a place of refuge for the business people and for those citizens who could get away from the City, but could not go further. At those times the banks established branches here, and Bank Street is a reminder of the times when those branches were in operation.

With all of the changes that have occurred in Greenwich Village, and while its borders have been invaded by vicious and ignorant people, yet it continues to be a respectable district, and in the honesty, thrift and intelligence of a large proportion of its inhabitants it presents a barrier to the northward movement of the less desirable elements of our City life.

The limits of our work will not permit us to travel further in our observations of New York life. It would be interesting and profitable, even thrilling, to follow the great avenues of metropolitan progress, to investigate the shopping districts, the hotel and club centers, the residence districts of the wealthy, the varied and brilliant exhibits of life in schools, societies, theaters, colleges, and to explore the hives which contain the hundreds of thousands who compose the middle classes. Upper New York is as full of illustrations of the City's greatness, wealth and enterprise as the lower part, and there have been in it greater opportunities for picturesque development. We shall have to leave this rich field for the future, stopping, however, long enough to call attention to the important historical points in northern New York. In Greenwich, with its recollections of the Indians, of Governor Van Twiller, of Commodore Warren, of Aaron Burr and of General Washington, it is natural for our thoughts to pass to those interesting points in the northern portion of the City so easily reached by the elevated railroad, where the last stand was made by the patriots before Lord Howe succeeded in getting possession of New York City. At the Apthorpe Mansion, which stood at 91st Street and the Boulevard, Washington made his headquarters during the retreat in July, 1776. Howe's pursuit drove him on, and his next stop was made at the Jumel Mansion, which is still standing at 161st Street, east of Tenth Avenue, and which became his headquarters, while General Howe occupied the Apthorpe Mansion, which he had deserted. In the neighborhood of the Jumel Mansion were the earthworks thrown up by Alexander Hamilton which attracted the attention of Washington to his genius, and in later years Hamilton established his home near the spot, at 143d Street and Tenth Avenue. The Grange, with the thirteen trees which he preserved, still remains there. In the neighborhood of the old gateway of the Jumel grounds is a row of cypress trees which were planted by Stephen Jumel. They were sent by the Khedive of Egypt to France as a present to Napoleon Bonaparte, and while he was languishing at St. Helena, after the battle of Waterloo, and refusing to be carried off by Jumel, who had undertaken to deliver him from captivity, those trees were lying unpacked in Paris. Jumel obtained them, brought them to America on his own vessel, and set them out on his place. Those that have survived are at 159th Street and St. Nicholas Avenue, surrounded by rubbish and ash heaps.

The Battle of Harlem Heights happened on the high ground about Riverside Park, south of 125th Street, and in it the Americans that were engaged showed such courage and gained such an advantage over their enemies that the demoralization of the patriot army was checked. The remains of fortifications are still apparent in many places. The block-house on the high ground in Central Park at 110th Street near Sixth Avenue was one of a chain of little forts that were designed to protect the northern approach of the City. Further south in Central Park, on the McGowan Pass, and close to the historic McGowan Pass Tavern, were Forts Fish and Putnam, and north of the block-house were two forts, the remains of one of which are still visible in Morningside Park near 123d Street. Fort George, on the bluff around which Amsterdam Avenue turns, was a strong position. The place occupied by the fort is now a beer garden. All around it are relics of the English occupation. Near the gas tank over a thousand Hessian soldiers were buried. In the beer halls are many cannon balls, buttons and human bones, which have been unearthed. The cavern which was used by the British as a powder magazine is now a beer tunnel. Little King's Bridge, which still stands, was the connection between the island and the mainland over which the American and the English army passed and repassed. Buttons which were on the uniforms of the English 23d, 33d, 40th and 57th Foot Regiments, the 4th Brigade of Royal Artillery, the Royal Provincials, the 2d American Royal Regiment, the Queen's Rangers, the New York Royal Volunteers, and the Volunteers of Ireland, have been unearthed in the neighborhood. The Royal Provincial buttons were found near 200th Street and the Harlem River, where the British had a small fort. The 2d American buttons were found near 192d Street and Eleventh Avenue, and relics of the New York Volunteers were found at Inwood, near Prescott Avenue. Many skeletons and weapons, balls and bullets, have been dug up. Remains of Fort Washington may still be seen near the Fort Washington station of the Hudson River Railroad, in the neighborhood of 181st Street. Fort Washington was the center of the American earthworks. Washington's judgment was that it should be abandoned, but he allowed himself to be overruled by Congress, which was unwilling to give up the making of a decided effort to maintain possession of New York City. The garrison was nearly three thousand strong, and was commanded by Colonel Magaw. The adjutant's orderly, a traitor, furnished the English with a plan of the fort and with a scheme for attacking it. The attack was made in such a way as to deceive the Americans and to draw them away from the point where the invasion was intended. The English thus got possession of the fort while the garrison was practically outside of it, and when, being hotly pressed by the Hessian mercenaries, it retreated into the fort it was caught in a trap. The three thousand men thus captured were confined in the prisons which we have described, and suffered the extremes of the barbarous treatment that was meted out to the American prisoners. Many of them died of starvation and exposure. One of the most heroic incidents of the Revolutionary War occurred at this place. Margaret Corbin was the wife of a Pennsylvania gunner in Colonel Cadwalader's Philadelphia command, who had charge of a cannon in the outlying earthworks on which Baron Knyphausen charged. When the Americans began to retreat, Corbin stuck to his gun, his wife helping him to load and fire it. A bullet passed through the brave gunner and he fell dead at his post. Margaret Corbin did not falter. With her husband lying dead beside her, she continued to fire the cannon until she fell by her husband's body, severely wounded by a fragment of shell which struck her breast. She was permanently disabled by her wounds, and, being obliged to ask help from the government, her story was entered in the pension records. Looking across the river we see the site of Fort Lee, which also fell into the hands of the English.

This memorable region, the sightliest in our City, has been the most inaccessible to the masses of population, and it has been preserved from the evils of slums and tenement houses. Now the foundations of noble buildings are rising, and splendid institutions are being grouped upon the "Acropolis." The tomb of Grant, the Columbia University buildings, St. Luke's Hospital, and the Cathedral of St.

OLD HOUSE, CORNER BANK AND BLEECKER STREETS, USED AS A PRISON BY THE ENGLISH.

New York, Vol. Three, p. 285.

John the Divine, are rising to crown the noblest City hill on our continent south of Quebec. If we cross King's Bridge, and visit Van Cortlandt Park, we will find more relics of the struggle for independence. There is the old mansion which was occupied alternately by American and English commanders, and there is the little lake on the shores of which the camp-fires of the soldiers burned. There is, too, the burial lot which contains the remains of Indians who served as scouts for some of the American leaders. If we strike out to the east through the Parkway we will reach Bronx Park, a famous old Indian camping-ground. On the banks of the enchanting river, and close by the great chasm through which it dashes, are the ruins of the Delancey buildings of Colonial days. This is the river up which it was intended by the war office in England the English ships should sail to attack the village of White Plains in the rear. We may go still further to the east and reach Pelham Bay Park, where Anne Hutchinson lived, and where she was murdered by the Indians, and where many years afterward the patriots resisted the invasion of English troops that were landed on the shores of the Sound. In this park there were several brilliant little engagements, in which the advance of the English was effectively hampered and retarded. A rock in the park is still remembered, behind which fifty American sharpshooters ambushed themselves, and from which they fired on an advancing English column and drove it back.

The population of the Ninth Ward has been "moving up" into these historic neighborhoods. The enterprising and substantial life of West Harlem contains a great deal of that old American element. The descendants of the Ninth Ward may be found well represented in the large and thriving churches of that section.

Our return to the old Fort, by the North River front, brings us to the most striking evidences of the rapid progress of New York's commerce. West Street is blocked with merchandise landed from vessels, and with trucks carrying produce from or to the steamboat docks. The Belt-line cars make slow progress. Sailors and 'longshoremen lounge about the corners, and travelers hurry along the walks, and scurry across the streets. Leviathan steamships lie in the slips, and palatial steamers make ready to start out on their river and sound pilgrimages.

The absence of adequate means of transit, and the filthiness of the streets on wet days, amaze the stranger, who does not expect to see such lack of enterprise as is here shown, along with such stupendous business and far-reaching thrift.

Americans are fond of criticising our pile docks, by comparing them with the magnificent stone docks of Liverpool; but Englishmen manifest both surprise and pleasure when they see our piers, and enjoy the luxury of walking directly from the ships to the City streets—a luxury which is impossible of enjoyment in England, either at Liverpool or Lon-

GREENWICH VILLAGE, BLEECKER AND CARMINE STREETS.

New York, Vol. Three, p. 287.

don. It is indeed a marvel that such a vessel as the "Lucania" can be towed right into her slip, where she may lie and be unloaded and loaded again, with her stern almost touching West Street.

New York has done her share in the application of steam to ocean sailing, in the inventing and improving of ships and machinery, and in the sustaining of inter-ocean traffic.

The first steamboat, the "Clermont," sailed up the Hudson River from New York.

The first Hudson River Steamboat Company was started in 1817, with two boats, the "Robert R. Livingston" and the "Robert Fulton." There were two round trips to Albany each week, and the fare was six dollars each way. The company had a fight with Robert L. Stevens, who tried to run a rival boat, the "Phœnix," and it beat Mr. Stevens and maintained a monopoly for a number of years. The monopoly was broken in 1825 by the running of the "Constitution" and the "Constellation," and in the same year the "United States" and the "Linnæus" began to run to New Haven.

These pioneer steamboats started only seventy years ago. They were smaller than the "Brooklyn annex boats."

Tho first steamship, the "Savannah," was built by Henry Eckford at Corlears Hook in 1817.

The first American steamship to traverse the ocean in a regular mail and passenger service was the "Washington," which began its trips in 1847.

As late as 1846 (fifty years ago) a steamship of three thousand tons was called a "Monster of the Ocean."

The Cunard Company was the pioneer steamship company. It began its transatlantic business in 1840, and its first vessel was the "Britannia."

New York was not interested in the company's operations until 1847, and the "Hibernia" was the first "Cunarder" to come to New York.

One of the liveliest features of the active life of the North River is the dashing about of the powerful little tug-boats, which are peculiar to New York.

The first towing steamer was the "Henry Eckford," the engines of which were built by James P. Allaire at the largest steam-engine factory in the United States in 1825, located on Cherry and Monroe Streets, between Walnut (Jackson) and Corlears Streets. These were the first compound engines applied to marine purposes. Up to 1831 there were only three towing boats; now the "tugs" number over six hundred.

The following is an exact transcript of a poster nearly sixty years old, issued by a line to which the steamboat above pictured belonged:

## HUDSON RIVER STEAMBOAT LINE.

### DAILY.

These new and splendid boats will be despatched, daily, for New York and Albany during the sum-

ST. LUKE'S CHURCH, HUDSON STREET, THREE HUNDRED YEARS OLD.

**Built of bricks imported from Holland.** **New York, Vol. Three, p. 289.**

mer months, commencing the regular trips on Monday, the 5th of June, leaving the wharf at Cortlandt street, New York, at ten A.M., and the wharf near the steamboat office, South Market street, Albany, at nine. These boats are of the first class, and for extensive and airy accommodations, speed and quiet motion of their engines, and skilful management, are not surpassed by any boat navigating; and the proprietors assure the public that the most assiduous attention will be paid to the safety of passengers.

Agents,

A. N. HOFFMAN, No. 71 Dey street, New York.

A. BARTHOLOMEW, South Market street, Albany.

Freight of light articles, one shilling per cubic foot.

May 23, 1826.

The steamers have not driven sailing ships out of the foreign business, and there is a multitude of them that make regular trips to domestic ports.

The wheezy little tubs that labored about the harbor, and made perilous trips up the Hudson River a little more than fifty years ago, have been succeeded by a majestic fleet of steamboats, which (especially in the summer season) give to New York Harbor a beauty that is nowhere else to be seen. The little steamships that fifty years ago and less pushed their adventurous prows into the uncertainties of transatlantic voyages have been succeeded by a fleet of majestic steamships that have converted the perilous voyage into a large ferry service. The little provincial City that was filled with excitement at the appearance of an organ-grinder on the street, and torn with social convulsions at the wearing of mustaches, was filled with pride when the Cunard Company began its New York business with the old "Britannia." The City's amazing half-century leap is evidenced by the noble steamships, which, with imposing numbers and impressive size, arrive and depart on their regular trips without exciting any comment; being now an established and ordinary feature of our daily life.

### Ocean Steamers Sailing from the Port of New York.

Hamburg-American Line
Holland-American Line
Merchants' Line
West Coast Line
Red Star Line
Phœnix Line
Atlas Line
Royal Dutch West India Line
Insular Navigation Co.
Lamport & Holt Line
Quebec Steamship Line
Demerara Steamship Line
Booth Steamship Line
N. Y. & Baranquilla Line
N. Y. & Central America Steamship Line
Bordeaux S. N. Co.
Mediterranean & N. Y. Line
Allan-State Line
Trinidad Line
N. Y. & Nicaragua Line
Union Line
Compagnie Generale Transatlantique Line
Wilson Line
Royal Dutch Line
K Line
Portuguese Steamship Co.
Cunard Line
Wilson & Furness-Leyland Line
Atlantic Transport Line
National Line
Fabre Line

FOUNTAIN IN CENTRAL PARK.

New York, Vol. Three, p. 308.

Norddeutscher Lloyd Steamship Co.
Roland Line
Bristol City Line
Manhasset Line
Mallory Line
Norton Line
Merchants' Line
N. Y. & Cuba Mail Steamship Co.
White Star Line
Clyde's West India Line
French Line
American & African Line
Union-Clan Line
Munson Steamship Line
Compania Transatlantica Line
Espanola Line
Red Cross Line
Clyde Line
Thingvalla Line
Panama Railroad Steamship Line
Red D. Line
Arrow Line
New York & Eastern Steamship Co.
Anchor Line
Atlantic Line
N. Y. & Porto Rica Line
N. Y. & Hayti Packet Line
Prince Line
Bahamas Steamship Co.
Southern Pacific Co.
Cromwell Steamship Co.
Old Dominion Steamship Co.
Sicilian Steamship Co.
Transoceanic Line
Commonwealth Transportation Co.
Maine Steamship Co.
Sloman's Line
N. Y. & Eastern Steamship Co.
Netherland American Steam-Navigation Co.
American Line
Scandia Line
Ocean Steamship Co.

Besides special Steamers run by such firms as
Edward Perry & Co.
Carter Macy & Co.
Barber & Co.
Waydell & Co.
C. H. Mallory & Co.
W. P. Clyde & Co.

Among the ports that are thus in direct communication with New York are:

Aden & Algro Bay
Algiers & Alexandria
Amsterdam
Antigua
Antofogasta & Arica
Antwerp (Belgium)
Aux Cayes (Hayti)
Azores Islands
Bahia (Brazil)
Barbadoes
Baranquilla (U. S. of Colombia)
Belize (Br. Honduras)
Bermuda
Bordeaux
Boulogne
Bremen
Bristol (England)
Buenos Ayres
Callao
Campeche (Mexico)
Cape Hayti
Cape Town (Africa)
Cardenas & Caibarien
Carthagena
Carupano (Venezuela)
Catania & Catacola
Ceara (Brazil)
Hull (England)
Jacmel (Hayti)
Jaffa
Jeremie
Kingston
Cherbourg (France)
Christiania
Cienfuegos
Colon
Copenhagen
Curacoa
Delagoa Bay
Demerara (Br. Guiana)
Dominica
Dundee
Dunkirk (France)
Durban (Africa)
Genoa
Gibraltar
Glasgow
Gonaives (Hayti)
Grenada
Greytown (Nicaragua)
Guadaloupe
Guantanamo (Cuba)
Guayaquil
Halifax
Hamburg
Havana
Havre

OLD HOUSES AT FOOT OF CHRISTOPHER STREET.

New York, Vol. Three, p. 310.

Hodeidah (Arabia)
Hong Kong & Hiogo
La Guayra
Leghorn (Italy)
Leith (Scotland)
Lisbon
Liverpool
Livingston & Port Barrios
London
Londonderry
Macoris (San Domingo)
Madeira
Malaga
Malta
Manaos
Manchester
Manzanillo
Maracaibo
Maraham
Marseilles
Martinique
Matanzas
Mayaguez
Messina
Mollendo
Montovideo
Montserrat
Mossel Bay (S. Africa)
Naples
Nassau
Newcastle
Nuevitas
Palermo
Para
Paramaribo
Pernambuco
Petit Goave
Plymouth (England)
Port au Prince
Port Elizabeth
Port Natal
Progresso (Mexico)
Puerto Cabello
Puerto Plata
Pinita Arenas
Queenstown (Ireland)
Rio de Janeiro
Rosario (Argentine Rep.)
Rotterdam
Sagua La Grande
San Domingo City
Sanita Martha
Santiago de Cuba
Santos (Brazil)
Savonilla
Shanghai
Singapore
Southampton (England)
St. Croix
St. John (N. B.)
St. Marc

| | |
|---|---|
| St. Thomas | Turk's Island |
| Stettin | Tuxpan |
| Swansea (Wales) | Valparaiso |
| Talcahuano | Venice |
| Tampico | Vera Cruz |
| Trieste | Windward Islands |
| Trinidad | Yokohama |

These are some of the majestic "liners" that ply between New York and Europe in the regular passenger service:

AMERICAN LINE.

| Name. | Gross ton. | H. power. | Length. | Breadth. | Depth. |
|---|---|---|---|---|---|
| St. Louis . . . | 11,629 | 20,000 | 554ft. | 63ft. | 50ft. |
| St. Paul . . . . | 11,600 | 20,000 | 554ft. | 63ft. | 50ft. |
| Paris . . . . . | 10,795 | 20,000 | 560ft. | 63ft. | 57ft. |
| New York . . . | 10,803 | 20,000 | 560ft. | 63ft. | 57ft. |

ANCHOR LINE.

| | | | | | |
|---|---|---|---|---|---|
| City of Rome . . | 8,144 | —— | 561ft. | 53ft. | 37ft. |

(And five others of 4,000 to 5,000 gross tonnage, Anchoria, Bolivia, Circassia, Ethiopia, Furnessia.)

CUNARD LINE.

| | | | | | |
|---|---|---|---|---|---|
| Campania . . . | 12,950 | 30,000 | 620ft. | 65ft. | 43ft. |
| Lucania . . . . | 12,950 | 30,000 | 620ft. | 65ft. | 43ft. |
| Etruria . . . . | 7,718 | 14,500 | 501ft. | 57ft. | 38ft. |
| Umbria . . . . | 7,718 | 14,500 | 501ft. | 57ft. | 38ft. |
| Servia . . . . | 7,391 | 10,000 | 515ft. | 52ft. | 37ft. |
| Aurania . . . . | 7,268 | 8,500 | 470ft. | 57ft. | 37ft. |

(And the Gallia and Bothnia of over 4,000 gross tonnage.)

THE LIBRARY OF COLUMBIA UNIVERSITY.

New York, Vol. Three, p. 311.

FRENCH LINE.

| Name. | Gross ton. | H. power. | Length. | Breadth. | Depth. |
|---|---|---|---|---|---|
| La Touraine . . | 9,778 | 12,000 | 536ft. | 55ft. | 38ft. |
| La Gascogne . . | 7,416 | 9,000 | 508ft. | 52ft. | 38ft. |
| La Bourgogne . | 7,400 | 9,000 | 508ft. | 52ft. | 38ft. |
| La Champagne . | 7,110 | 9,000 | 508ft. | 51ft. | 38ft. |
| La Bretagne . . | 7,010 | 9,000 | 508ft. | 51ft. | 38ft. |
| La Normandie . | 6,112 | 6,000 | 459ft. | 50ft. | 34ft. |

HAMBURG–AMERICAN LINE.

| Name. | Gross ton. | H. power. | Length. | Breadth. | Depth. |
|---|---|---|---|---|---|
| Fuerst Bismarck . | 12,000 | 16,400 | 520ft. | 58ft. | 40ft. |
| Normannia . . . | 12,000 | 16,000 | 520ft. | 57ft. | 40ft. |
| Augusta Victoria . | 12,000 | —— | 520ft. | 56ft. | 38ft. |
| Columbia . . . | 10,000 | 12,500 | 460ft. | 56ft. | 38ft. |
| Pennsylvania . . | 23,500 | 6,000 | 560ft. | 62ft. | 42ft. |
| Palatia . . . . | 8,000 | 5,500 | 460ft. | 52ft. | 32ft. |
| Patria . . . . | 8,000 | 5,500 | 460ft. | 52ft. | 32ft. |
| Phœnicia . . . | 8,000 | 5,500 | 460ft. | 52ft. | 32ft. |
| Prussia . . . . | 7,000 | 5,000 | 446ft. | 51ft. | 30ft. |
| Persia . . . . | 7,000 | 5,000 | 446ft. | 51ft. | 30ft. |
| Armenia . . . | 7,000 | 3,000 | 400ft. | 50ft. | 30ft. |
| Arcadia . . . . | 7,000 | 3,000 | 400ft. | 49ft. | 30ft. |
| Arabia . . . . | 7,000 | 3,000 | 400ft. | 49ft. | 30ft. |
| Asturia . . . . | 7,000 | 3,000 | 390ft. | 53ft. | 29ft. |
| Andalusia . . . | 7,000 | 3,000 | 400ft. | 50ft. | 30ft. |
| Adria . . . . | 7,000 | 3,000 | 400ft. | 50ft. | 30ft. |

HOLLAND–AMERICAN LINE.

| Name. | Gross ton. | H. power. | Length. | Breadth. | Depth. |
|---|---|---|---|---|---|
| Rotterdam . . . | 8,000 | 5,000 | 470ft. | 53ft. | 34ft. |

(And seven others with gross tonnage from 3,329 to 4,539, the Spaarndam, Maasdam, Veendam, Werkendam, Amsterdam, Obdam and Edam—when they can find more dams, they will build more ships.)

NORTH GERMAN LLOYD.

| Name. | Gross ton. | H. power. | Length. | Breadth. | Depth. |
|---|---|---|---|---|---|
| Kaiser Wilhelm d'Grosse . . . | 13,800 | 27,000 | 649ft. | 66ft. | 39ft. |
| Kaiser Friedrich . | 12,800 | 25,000 | 600ft. | 62ft. | 38ft. |
| Friedrich d'Grosse | 10,500 | 7,000 | 540ft. | 60ft. | 34ft. |
| Königen Luise . | 10,500 | 7,000 | 540ft. | 60ft. | 34ft. |
| Barbarossa . . | 10,500 | 7,000 | 540ft. | 60ft. | 34ft. |
| Bremen . . . . | 10,500 | 8,000 | 540ft. | 60ft. | 34ft. |
| Spree . . . . | 6,963 | 13,000 | 462ft. | 49ft. | 34ft. |
| Havel . . . . | 6,963 | 13,000 | 462ft. | 49ft. | 34ft. |
| Lahn . . . . . | 5,581 | 8,800 | 448ft. | 49ft. | 34ft. |
| Saale . . . . . | 5,381 | 7,500 | 439ft. | 48ft. | 34ft. |
| Trave . . . . | 5,831 | 7,500 | 438ft. | 48ft. | 34ft. |
| Aller . . . . . | 5,381 | 7,500 | 438ft. | 48ft. | 34ft. |
| Ems . . . . . | 5,192 | 7,000 | 429ft. | 47ft. | 34ft. |
| H. H. Meier . . | 5,306 | 3,800 | 421ft. | 48ft. | 29ft. |
| Fulda . . . . | 4,814 | 6,300 | 435ft. | 46ft. | 36ft. |
| Werra . . . . | 4,815 | 6,300 | 435ft. | 46ft. | 36ft. |
| Kaiser Wilhelm II | 6,990 | 6,500 | 450ft. | 49ft. | 27ft. |

(The vessels of this line start from Hoboken.)

RED STAR LINE.

| Name | Gross ton. | H. power. | Length. | Breadth. | Depth. |
|---|---|---|---|---|---|
| Friesland . . . | 7,116 | ——— | 455ft. | 47ft. | 35ft. |
| Westernland . . | 5,736 | ——— | 419ft. | 47ft. | 35ft. |
| Norrdland . . . | 5,812 | ——— | 494ft. | 57ft. | 37ft. |
| Southwark . . . | 8,607 | ——— | 494ft. | 57ft. | 37ft. |
| Kensington . . . | 8,669 | ——— | 494ft. | 57ft. | 37ft. |

THINGVALLA LINE.

(There are five ships of 2,524 to 3,867 gross tonnage —the Amerika, Hekla, Island, Norge, Thingvalla—starting from Hoboken.)

WHITE STAR LINE.

| Name. | Gross ton. | H. power. | Length. | Breadth. | Depth. |
|---|---|---|---|---|---|
| Teutonic . . . | 9,984 | 16,000 | 565ft. | 57ft. | 39ft. |
| Majestic. . . . | 9,965 | 16,000 | 565ft. | 57ft. | 39ft. |
| Britannic . . . | 5,004 | 4,590 | 455ft. | 45ft. | 33ft. |
| Germanic . . . | 5,065 | 4,500 | 455ft. | 45ft. | 33ft. |
| Adriatic . . . | 3,887 | 3,500 | 437ft. | 40ft. | 31ft. |

This line will soon run the Oceanic, a steamship longer than the Great Eastern.

The Allan-State line runs the State of Nebraska, 4,000 gross tonnage.

The Wilson-Hill line runs the Ontario, Tower Hill and Ludgate Hill from Brooklyn, gross tonnage 3,920 to 4,063.

The Wilson line runs the Buffalo, Ohio, Colorado, Martello, Francisco and Hindoo from Brooklyn, gross tonnage 3,709 to 4,604.

(A City block on the avenues is a trifle more than 200 feet long. An ordinary avenue house is 20 feet wide; an ordinary avenue tenement house of five stories is 55 feet high.)

The first steam vessel that crossed the Atlantic Ocean was the "Savannah," which started from New York March 28, 1819, under the command of Captain Moses Rogers.

The vessel was built at Corlears Hook, and was launched in 1818 as a sailing packet ship to ply between New York and New Orleans. It was only three hundred tons burden.

Captain Rogers, who had commanded one of Robert Fulton's steamboats, saw the ship and induced Scarborough & Isaacs of Savannah to buy her. A ninety horse power engine was put into her, and she was fitted with paddlewheels that could be unshipped and stowed on deck in stormy weather. She depended mainly on sail power, for she started with only seventy-five tons of coal. This illustration from "Le Yacht" and the "Sun" shows the comparative sizes of the "Savannah" and the great new freighter the "Pennsylvania."

Learned men of England discussed the question whether vessels propelled entirely by steam power could ever cross the ocean, and they determined that it was impossible for a ship to carry coal enough for a trip. The log of the "Savannah" shows that she started from New York for Savannah on March 28, 1819, and depended entirely on the wind until April 2d, and then began to use steam power, and arrived at Savannah on April 6th. She left on April 14th for Charleston, and made the trip in one day, using steam. She returned to Savannah under steam, and on May 22d left that port for England. On June 18th her coal was all burned. She had then been using steam for ten days. She arrived at Liverpool on June 20th. On July 16th she took in a supply of coal and started for St.

SCENE ON WEST STREET ON THE ARRIVAL OF AN ATLANTIC LINER.

New York, Vol. Three, p. 316.

Petersburg, Russia. She stopped at Elsineure on August 9th, having used steam six days. After being detained in quarantine she resumed her trip and stopped at Stockholm, having steamed six days out of eight. The King of Sweden and the American and foreign Ministers visited her. She left Stockholm September 5th, and arrived at Cronstadt September 9th. There the Czar of Russia and the American and foreign ministers went on board. At St. Petersburg the vessel was exhibited in the harbor, and was visited by representatives of the Russian government. She returned to America, reaching Chesapeake Bay on December 14th. In the whole voyage from Savannah to St. Petersburg steam was used twenty-six days.

The London "Times" published this announcement on May 11th, 1819:

"GREAT EXPERIMENT!

"A new steam vessel of three hundred tons has been built at New York, for the express purpose of carrying passengers across the Atlantic. She is to come to Liverpool direct."

That she did arrive we have seen. The passage from Savannah to Liverpool took twenty-six days.

Nothing remarkable was accomplished by this trip, for the splendid American sailing ships made wonderful time. There is a record of two members of a commercial firm starting from New York—one for Bristol and one for Albany—and of their reaching their destinations on the same day. When the "Savannah" returned to America her engines were removed and she became a sailing packet again. At last she was wrecked on Long Island.

In 1838 the first great world's sensation in steam ocean traffic occurred. In that year there were thirty-nine steamboats located at the port of New York, sailing to points not further than Albany, and there were less than five hundred in the British Empire. The adverse calculations of the British scientists had discouraged the hopes of the people for the building of any steam vessel that could carry coal enough to make a transatlantic voyage, and little more was expected from the new propelling force than the improvement of local traffic facilities.

On April 23, 1838, the steamships "Great Western" and "Sirius" arrived at New York, the "Sirius" having made the passage from England in nineteen days and the "Great Western" in fifteen days. An English account of the occasion says:

"Even the Americans, with all their reputation as a self-possessed and considering people, have displayed unwonted raptures and antics on occasion of the first arrival of the 'Sirius' and 'Great Western' at New York, quite as much so as our Bristol neighbors on their return; and we are not sure that either party is to be blamed for it. We are not sure that the former are out of their 'reckoning' " (note the fine English humor) "when they speak of this as a new epoch in the history of the world. We can enter into the feelings of the myriads who crowded the wharfs at New York when the English boats were hourly expected, when, finally, after days of almost breathless watching, at length, on the morning of St. George's day, the doubts, the fears, the scorn, were removed from every living creature—even Dr. Lardner—*For now appears a long dim train of distant smoke*—it rises and lowers presently like a genius of the Arabian Nights, portending something prodigious; by-and-by, the black prow of a *huge steamboat* dashes around the point of a green island in that beautiful harbor against the wind, against the tide, steadying with upright keel."

A passenger on the 'Great Western' wrote in his diary:

"We passed the Narrows, sails all furled and engines at their topmost speed. The City reposed in the distance, scarcely discernible. As we proceeded, an exciting scene awaited us; coming abreast of Bradlaw (Bedloe's) Island we were saluted by the Fort (the same old fort whose walls surround the Statue of Liberty), with twenty-six guns—the number of States. The health of the British Queen had just been proposed, the toast drunk, and amid the cheers that followed the arm was just raised to consummate the naming, when the Fort opened its fire. The effect was electrical: down came the colors and a burst of exultation arose, in the midst of which the President's health was proposed. The

City now grew distinct: masts, buildings, spires, trees, streets, were discerned; the wharfs appeared black with myriads of population hurrying down to every point of view. Now we reach the 'Sirius' (which had preceded her to port). We passed around her, giving and receiving three hearty cheers; then turned toward the Battery. Flags were flying, guns firing, and bells ringing. The vast multitude set up a shout, a long and enthusiastic cheer echoed from point to point, and from boat to boat, until it would seem that they would never have done."

The City newspapers were not behind in ecstasy. One announced:

"*Side by side with the Old World at last*"; another:

"*Now for the Coronation; only fifteen days from Bristol, and sixteen from London.*"

The successful trip of these ships marked the decline of the beautiful American packet-ships, in the building of which New York led the world.

The "Great Western" carried twenty thousand letters back to England. On her trip, when three days out, she overhauled a brave old "Liner" "tearing" through the water under topgallant sails. A passenger wrote: "This new comer of ours is none of your old sort. See how she comes vaporing up, flapping her huge wheels like an eagle's wings; and snorting, as it were, with the thoughts of victory and the sight of game. She comes on apace. All her colors are strung out. The ship is almost caught, but leaps ahead and escapes for a moment. The steamer with a dignified air of conscious supremacy wheels around windward and passes the Liner on the other side with three hearty cheers. Then dashing ahead, as if satisfied, she hauls in her toggery and presses her helm hard a-starboard, and the Liner, brave old Liner, is seen no more. By-and-by, her owners will scarce know her. When she reaches port at last, she will bring no news, no letters, no specie: nobody will watch for her, nor speak of her. Alas! her day is going by. Who can think of her without a sigh!"

In the next month the English chroniclers said:

"The great experiment of traversing the vast Atlantic by the aid of steam has been triumphantly successful, the 'Sirius' and the 'Great Western' once again ride proudly in British ports. The generous and enthusiastic welcome with which the officers of the ship were received in New York does honor to the American people; they were welcomed as brothers by men who saw in the event the revolution which had been effected in the commercial and social relations of the two countries, an event which will form an epoch in the history of civilization itself, which tends to unite in the bonds of enduring fellowship the greatest nations of the Earth, allied by language, by literature, by interest and by blood; and offers to both a guarantee a thousand times more binding than treaties, for the preservation of the honorable peace which now gladdens and enriches them."—From the "Athenæum."

This was less than twenty-five years after the bitter struggle of our second war with England. Commerce overcame Hatred and War.

We have passed the freight depot of the New York Central Railroad, and on the other side of this noble river are other great railroads. These systems of transportation and communication, all focusing on Manhattan Island, bringing to it the products and the people of every State, and drawing life from the vast Metropolitan resources—they speak even more eloquently than do the steamships of the rapid and miraculous expansion of the City's life, and of her queenly position in this great nation.

The Erie Railroad commenced to run its trains from Piermont to Goshen in 1841. The long pier is still to be seen. That was made the New York terminus of the railroad, because any point below would have required tunneling, which would have bankrupted the road. Passengers were brought to New York from Piermont on steamers. The entire line, from Piermont to Lake Erie, was completed in 1851, and the great event brought President Fillmore and Secretary of State Webster to give official dignity to the ceremony of running the first train. The second trunk line from New York to the West, the New York Central & Hudson

DE WITT CLINTON TRAIN.

New York, Vol. Three, p. 331.

River Railroad, was not organized until 1869. The Pennsylvania Railroad completed its connections and established itself as the third trunk road from New York in 1871. The stupendous growth of railroads is familiar to all the people, and is part of the history of the country. We have no right to spend time on it here, further than to call attention to New York's vital relation to the railroad systems of the nation. From every direction the trains come, and New York is their destination. In a short time tunnels under the rivers will bring the train service direct to Manhattan Island.

The luxurious and practical appurtenances of railroad travel on these roads are the wonder of the world. They have come from the constant requirements of New York travel, which demands and supports the best that can be given.

What a change from the primitive conditions of forty years ago! The evolution of the bell cord is a simple illustration of the advance. Forty years ago, a conductor ran a cord through his train and tied it to a log of the wood fuel on the locomotive. He ordered the engineer to stop when he pulled the log once, and to go ahead when he pulled it twice. The engineer rebelled, and refused to take orders from the conductor. They fought: the conductor whipped the engineer and compelled him to obey. The dispute came to the attention of the officers of the company, who, seeing the utility of the device, established it on the train service with slight improvements. Now we have air-brakes, which are within reach of the passengers, and which work automatically in cases of accident.

In slow old Greenwich Village our senses were enthralled by the soporific fumes of Wouter Van Twiller's antique tobacco, which have grown only a little more intangible and seductive as the years have passed. On the river front we were bewildered, pleased and amused by the conspicuous contrasts of life and achievements at the foot of Christopher Street, where the monster steamships look benignly across West Street at the little shanties that have stood more than a century, and at the serio-comic hotels designed for the accommodation of "European tourists."

Our observations and speculations concerning the growth of transportation facilities were conducted from crowded sidewalks and muddy cross streets, and through a tangle of cars, wagons, vapors, odors and people such as no other civilized city dare show to an amazed world; and now at last we have reached the end of the meandering in which we have tried to follow the current of New York's progress—we are back at the old Fort.

Our journeys of the previous chapters pass in review through our minds. A while ago we started out with all the anticipation of great sights to be seen, and marvelous progress to be observed. Now, wearied by traveling and tired with considering, we have returned to the spring from which flowed the

RIVERSIDE DRIVE, SHOWING GRANT'S TOMB.

New York, Vol. Three, p. 332.

tide of life, and the point where New York's greatness had its beginning.

At the time we have selected for this last visit the bustle of day has ceased, the hives of business are deserted. Occasional pedestrians make clatter of footsteps as they hurry along Broadway, but the old Dutch Streets are entirely clear of mortal presence, except as *we* peer curiously into them. Through the day, the sidewalks have echoed the patter of a hundred thousand restless feet, carrying those whose thoughts and acts were felt through the City, the nation, and the world. In the darkness the deserted buildings on the narrow streets reach upward, we cannot see how far; and their solid blocks and the close, substantial pavements between them rest heavily upon the earth beneath, as though, like some of our upstart families, they would crowd down and repress the memories and traditions of early simplicity and poverty that are mixed and mementoed in this ground that was trodden by honest feet before the days of opulence had dawned.

Do the founders—who built better than they knew—ever revisit the City which they planted or helped to sustain? Do they know how their humble planting has grown? Are they concerned with the future of that which they founded?

Voices of other days seem to sound in our ears, and our eyes are strained to detect the phantom forms that must be about us.

The buildings that were so substantial in daylight now seem vague, and other lines show through them with spectral phosphorescence. The Broadway car, that makes the scene luminous for an instant, seems to dash into a rampart of earth, which offers no resistance and doesn't dim its light. The night deepens, and *we* become the specters, as conceptions that have long lain dormant in our acquired memories take shape, and throng the region of their birth, making *us* seem uncouth and singular interlopers.

How the ancient men and women swarm about the old Fort, and circulate through these old streets! They are not of one mold either, and in appearances they do not altogether harmonize with each other; but they fit the place and its surroundings perfectly, and are at home in *it*, if not with each other. We see the counterparts of governors, some English, some Dutch, all bearing their royal honors with becoming dignity. One carries a mountain of physical pomp; another is minus a leg, but plus all the indications of an iron will; another wears the dress of a woman and smirks with counterfeit grace. Some of them are lazy, careless, luxurious and licentious in manner; others are apparently consumed with official cares and responsibilities. Soldiers there are in great numbers, some wearing red, and some yellow. At the faint tolling of a bell, a procession of rotund dignitaries, preceded by official insignia, pass into the Fort, and the tones of far-off, but stentorian, preaching come to us. Some there are who move rapidly through the throng, dressed more soberly and deeply agitated, and these give way to red coats, who, in turn, vanish. If these were not together we would think that we recognized fat Van Twiller, and testy Stuyvesant, and effeminate Cornbury; Sloughter, Lovelace and Fletcher; Nicoll, Dongan and Bellomont; Liberty Boys, Tryon's troopers, and Washington's patriots. But how could they all be here at once? Oh, Fancy! What prank is this that has filled the place with ghosts who should have been at rest generations ago! Are they here at the place of their earth-labors to protest against the materialism, the selfishness, and the forgetfulness, that have crowded them out of the memories of men, and repudiated that debt which is owed by every people to those whose achievements they have inherited?

A figure comes dashing down Broadway as though flying from an avenging hand; it disappears in the Fort. Others follow—men, women and children. A fiery cloud shines out in the north. Then in the track of those who ran in terror there comes an army of painted savages, brandishing weapons and shaking gory scalps. Men who did not reach the shelter of the Fort are felled by tomahawks, and lie motionless before their doors. The invaders almost reach the gate, when out of it rush a band of men who valiantly drive the Indians to their canoes. Shrieks of distress are heard from the direction of Nutten (or Governor's) Island, and the distant shores of Staten Island are ablaze.

Now and then little processions of sad-faced people make the short journey to the corner of Morris

Street, carrying with them precious burdens, which they leave there. The great building that we saw in the daytime is not present to the diggers of graves and to those who mourn.

These visions, which have come unbidden and unconjured, agree in details with the dull lessons we have learned from our histories; but how dead those lessons were, how alive these figures seem, how real their acts! The past has revealed itself to us, because we have put ourselves in sympathy with it; and we begin to feel less like interlopers. We discover that, notwithstanding many apparent differences, we are kin to all these people, and are ourselves concerned with the life and the development of that to which they gave themselves. The vision, if it be a vision, is most delightful in this, that we are not bothered with those nuisances of historic lore—days and dates—and we enjoy the proximity at one time of a Montgomerie, who framed a charter for our City's liberties, and a Montgomery who gave his life for national liberty, though they never met in their bodies. They and all these were concerned with the life of the City in which they lived, and in which we have interested ourselves.

We quietly walk through the side streets into Broad Street, and hear the water plash against the board sides of the ditch, and we hear the women snore, and the frogs croak most melodiously. Curious cottages and simple storehouses are the most solid encumbrances of the ground. Here and there

DEPARTURE OF AN ATLANTIC LINER.

New York, Vol. Three, p. 317.

quaint and stiff entertainments are being given. On Wall Street luckless wights are in the stocks and on the pillory, and negro slaves are being sold at auction. Further up the street a steeple rises, but not so high as our Trinity, and the bells that ring are not so loud nor deep as those we are wont to hear. Up and down this street pass throngs of people, and we recognize the features of the greatest men of the nation in the Colonial, Revolutionary and National periods. Nowhere else in this nocturnal ramble can we see such a gathering of those whose names are known and honored throughout the world. Looking over the churchyard we see dimly the spots where repose the earthly remains of some of the great ones who walked these streets. Space shortens, and we may not recount the forms and the faces that pass before us. Others may make this journey as we have done, and forgetting in night's darkness the glorious but hard realities of New York's daily life, slip back into the days of yore, and touch shoulders with those of the older City, whom they may choose to see, and, perchance, may even touch hearts with those whom they desire to know.

Looking and musing, we drift up the "Pye Woman's Street," and—our vision is gone. Printing House Square, with "Sun," "World" and "Journal," "Times," "Press" and "Tribune"—they are all against visions and senseless dreamings. We must needs be awake, and wide awake, for here are substantial specters of the night, who will forcibly convince us of their mortal condition if we be not watchful. But no; we will not yet relinquish this delight of looking away from the prosaic and drudging present. If we may no longer look backward, perhaps we may look forward. Here is the bridge, and its roadway leads alluringly into the clouds and the night. Then out on to the span, until we are as near the sky and as far from both cities as may be. The current flows beneath us, just as it did when the timid explorers of Communipaw made their famous visit to Hell Gate, and saw the devil cooking porpoises on the Frying-Pan rocks, while their own vessel was drawn into the fearful eddies and cast upon the shore.

Almost beneath our feet is the mysterious, murky district which was the stronghold of the fierce river pirates, and is now the great hot-bed of crime. To and beyond the bend of Corlears Hook, and as far as we can distinguish the outlines of houses, is the domain of ignorance and the training-school of vice. The City of Homes lies on our right, and nearly a million virtuous beds are honestly and healthfully occupied. Far beyond us to the northward are the streets and avenues of the Metropolis, some still pulsating with business that knows no night, some throbbing with wild and reckless life, and others becomingly silent and dark. Prayers have arisen from many homes, and sweet dreams are bringing happy smiles to those of good conscience. All over the City sleep and rest are restoring tired nature;

but moans and curses may be heard too, if your ears are acute enough; misery and anguish may be discerned if your heart be quick; and crime may be seen if your vision is sharp. In some places, benevolence, munificence, intelligence, culture, religion, are bearing rich fruitage; in others there is none to stay the hand of cruelty and oppression, there is no light to brighten mental darkness, there is no sympathy to lighten the ills of life; no message of love to give peace to the dying. Civilization still shows itself inconsistent and imperfect, and achievement is still earth-bound; for luxury and squalor are yet close neighbors, and poverty and wealth are yet largely accidental; great masses of the people still grovel upon the earth, looking for their best treasure in her caves and her muck-heaps.

What shall be done for humanity in this great concentration of population, wealth and opportunities?

The sun of the morrow will flood these streets and illuminate these buildings, and will bathe these people in an immeasurable sea of energy. A divine light and power, of which this is a faint figure, is pouring itself into the hearts of men, and is arousing many to higher aspirations and to nobler conceptions of duty. To hope for a Greater New York, which shall have a truer heart, a broader charity, a deeper sympathy, a higher purpose, may be "Utopian"; but the duty of every true New Yorker to work for such a greatness is perfectly plain. Then let us bind past and present together in intelligent sympathy, and try to link them to a noble future, which shall make New York the greatest and grandest City of the world.

While we have mused, the dawn has come, the visions have gone, the first rays of the morning have tinted the white top of the Bowling Green building, the waters of the glorious bay are glinting with the sun's fresh shafts. Day is here, our ramble is ended, and work begins.

www.ingramcontent.com/pod-product-compliance
Lightning Source LLC
LaVergne TN
LVHW020602110826
845149LV00002B/351